CHINESE AMERICAN NAMES

CHINESE AMERICAN NAMES

Tradition and Transition

by EMMA WOO LOUIE

with a foreword by HIM MARK LAI

McFarland & Company, Inc., Publishers
Jefferson, North Carolina, and London

139327

British Library Cataloguing-in-Publication data are available

Library of Congress Cataloguing-in-Publication Data

Louie, Emma Woo, 1926–
    Chinese American names : tradition and transition / by Emma Woo
Louie ; with a foreword by Him Mark Lai.
        p.   cm.
    Includes bibliographical references and index.
    ISBN 0-7864-0418-3 (library binding : 50# alkaline paper)
    1. Names, Personal—Chinese.   2. Names, Personal—United States.
3. Chinese Americans.   I. Title.
CS2990.L68   1998
929.4'0951—dc21   97-41692
                                                                              CIP

Manufactured in the United States of America

McFarland & Company, Inc., Publishers
    Box 611, Jefferson, North Carolina 28640

TABLE OF CONTENTS

TABLE OF CONTENTS

FOREWORD

"What's in a name? That which we call a rose by any other name would smell as sweet."

William Shakespeare

Large-scale Chinese immigration to the United States began during the mid-nineteenth century and has continued, with ups and downs, to the present. For almost a century, up to World War II, arrivals consisted mostly of merchants and laborers from Guangdong's Pearl River Delta. After the war, following the change in government on the China mainland in 1949, about 5,000 students who had come originally from all parts of China to study also decided to make America their home. They were soon joined by refugees formerly associated with the collapsed Chinese Nationalist regime. Immediately afterwards began a continuous stream of students from Taiwan and Hong Kong, most of whom eventually stayed in America. To these were added thousands of ethnic Chinese from troubled parts of the world such as Cuba, Latin America, Burma, Philippines, Vietnam, Cambodia, Laos, Malaysia, and Singapore. Beginning in the 1980s, relaxation of emigration controls in China allowed many more from mainland China to land on American shores. At the same time, continued political uncertainties propelled other thousands in Hong Kong and Taiwan to seek what they perceived as havens abroad. These successive waves of new arrivals have led to tremendous growth in the Chinese population in America, both in numbers and in diversity.

When the Chinese arrived in America, they brought their language along as cultural baggage as well as mores and customs that had evolved in one of the world's great civilizations. Once they stepped ashore, however, the Chinese encountered American culture, itself part of another great tradition, Western civilization. It soon became obvious that although there are similarities there are also many differences between the two. Chinese immigrants were a minority settling amidst a majority host society with a different culture. Thus even though their culture and traditions were deeply rooted, the pressure exerted by the

1

dominant host society led to numerous modifications and changes in Chinese culture in America, eventually transforming it into a Chinese American culture, influenced by both Chinese and western traditions.

Some Chinese cultural elements transplanted to the New World survived with little or no change from their practice in the land of origin. Many traits, however, underwent some transformations to adapt to conditions in the host society. Due to various motivations the Chinese in America also adopted elements from the host culture, often in modified form, or evolved new practices to accommodate to needs imposed by the new environment.

Even as basic an area as given names and family names became subject to these influences. Applications of all the above principles are evident in the way Chinese personal naming has changed under the influence of western culture in America. The changes constitute an absorbing study of how different cultures affect one another. Up to now, however, few scholars have devoted their attention to the phenomenon of Chinese American naming. Emma Woo Louie, author of the present work, is one of the few researchers of the subject and has pursued her research over a number of years, searching out, compiling and analyzing Chinese American names all over the United States. The fruit of her determined research is this fascinating story of the metamorphosis of Chinese names into Chinese American names in the American environment. Not only is it a useful reference tool for Chinese Americans researching their genealogy and family trees; it should also be highly informative to scholars studying the effects of cultural interaction and interchange.

Him Mark Lai, Historian
24 January 1997

Him Mark Lai is the acknowledged "dean" of Chinese American studies, noted for his scholarship and for sharing his vast knowledge and research on the Chinese American historical experience. In addition to writing numerous articles and books, Mr. Lai, an engineer by vocation, has taught at San Francisco State University and the University of California at Berkeley, and serves as a consultant in his field both here in the United States and in Asia. The cultural program In Search of Roots, *which he cofounded in 1991, is popular among young Chinese Americans wishing to research family history and to visit their ancestral villages.*

ACKNOWLEDGMENTS

I have many people to thank for making it possible to write a book about Chinese American names. The late Elsdon C. Smith, a founder of the American Name Society and author of several books on American names, was the first to encourage me in my research and writing about this subject. His books enabled me to see that the story of Chinese American names had parallels to other name stories, and at the same time, to realize that parts of the Chinese American story are unique.

I thank the following individuals for responding so graciously to my questions about Chinese name traditions: Dr. Yuen Ren Chao, the renowned linguist; Dr. Du Ruofu, of the Institute of Genetics in Beijing; Dr. Wu Tehyao, of the Institute of East Asian Philosophies in Singapore; Consul Ning Wen of the People's Republic of China; Bruce J.D. Linghu, of the Republic of China's Coordination Council of North American Affairs; and Victor Chuan, a direct descendant of a Manchurian Bannerman. Ben Tucker, of the Library of Congress, clarified certain points about usage of the Pinyin and the Wade-Giles romanization systems. It was wonderful to have such excellent firsthand information. The reader is advised that any errors in explanations are of my own making.

I especially want to thank Dr. Ruby Ling Louie, one of the founders of the Chinatown Branch Library in Los Angeles, for her counsel and friendship during the years of researching and writing this book. She comforted me in my struggles to write; appraised my writing with honesty, tact and gentleness; and inspired me to do my best in articulating my thoughts. I am eternally grateful to have such a true friend.

Words of gratitude go to the following who reviewed earlier drafts of this book: Dr. Alexander Saxton, author of *The Indispensable Enemy*; Phil Choy, historian and writer; Greg Dobie, an editor who suggested the format for this book; and my sisters Barbara Radke and Nina W. Matheson.

I thank the following for the publications of my articles: Russell Leong of *Amerasia Journal*; Kelsie Harder, Ed Callary, and Thomas J. Gasque, all of the

3

American Name Society; Ella Quan of the Chinese Historical Society of Southern California; and Him Mark Lai of the Chinese Historical Society of America.

Thanks go to Rosemarie Hanisch and Henriette Fremont for translating Dr. Wolfgang Bauer's German-language monograph on Chinese names; to Sullen Cheng, Ginger Chiu, and Ann Lau for translating Chinese-language materials; to Aurelia Chang for providing some pithy Chinese sayings; and to Mr. P.Y. Lau and Rebecca Voo for informing me of the Chungshan and Hakka dialect sounds for some of the common surnames. I thank Peg Marshall and the board of the Wing Luke Museum in Seattle, who gave permission to review the Chinese immigration documents in their holdings.

The late Willard Jue of Seattle was the first to send me a list of new patronyms and other accidental surnames for Chinese Americans. I am deeply grateful to him, and to Helen Chin Eng, Him Mark Lai, and the late Rev. Edwar Lee for telling me about other unusual Chinese American names.

The following individuals gave me assistance in different ways; many shared stories about their own names or someone else's name: Andy Ahn, Norman Bock, Ed Carpenter, Paul Chace, David R. Chan, Michael Chan, Ernest Chann, Henry Chann, Mrs. Tin-Yuke Char, Mrs. Grace Chow, Lambert "Buddy" Choy, Sarah Choy, Sue Fawn Chung, Lorraine Dong, Eleanor Hing Fay, Marion Fong, Pauline Fong, Henry Gaw, Elaine Gernstein, Edward Goo-Sun, Katherine Gould-Martin, Joseph Jein, James Ken Kin, Joe Kim, Lily Chow Kwock, Edwin Kwoh, Munson Kwok, Edwin D. Lawson, Ching Ming Lee, Dawes Lee, Moon L. Lee, Steve Way Leong, Joelle E. Louie, Lillian Dong Louie, Stella Chandler Louis, W. Young Louis, Charlie Lum, Ruth Sing Lung, Richard Lym, Toni Tung Chow Mark, Thomas McDannold, Herbert Moe, Eugene Wong Moy, Stanley Mu, Simon Ong, Charmaine Parkes, Rosebud Lai Mye Quong, Mitzi Sisson, Frank Tain, Edward Tankhim, William Tann, Ed Tanng, Henry Tiee, Brian Ten, David Wing, Ella Wing, Lilac Wing, Dolores Wong, Gage Wong, Jr., Gerrye Wong, Frank Woo, Wilbur Woo, Edward Yaplee, Howard Yuen, and Victor Sen Yung. I thank them all and apologize for missing anyone by name.

I also want to pay tribute to all the librarians who helped me. We are very fortunate in the United States to have free access to books and research materials in our public and university libraries. Thanks go to the staffs of the Regional Archives of the National Archives System located in San Bruno, Seattle, and Laguna Niguel for their courtesy and help.

I thank my sons, Steve, David, and Alan, and my daughter, Lisa, for their whole-hearted and unstinting support and encouragement. Thanks to my stepfather, Allen, for his homey comments on Chinese name traditions—they are priceless; as worthy as any observation made by onomasticians or name experts.

Last, but not least, I thank my husband, Paul, for years of patience and for accompanying me to cemeteries, libraries, and universities during our vacations. He shares my hope that in learning the story of Chinese American names, readers will discover parallels to their own stories.

INTRODUCTION

"The most important anchorage to our self-identity throughout life remains our own name."
Gordon Allport, *Pattern and Growth in Personality*

The traditional Chinese way of asking a stranger his name is *Gui xing?* which means, "What is your name?" The literal meaning, however, is "What is your precious family name?" The word *gui* means "precious" or "esteemed," and *xing* means "family name" or "surname." Your surname is indeed precious; it gives a sense of belonging, and as long as it is handed on from generation to generation, it holds your family in perpetuity. Since your given name is expected to be included in the answer to this question, it is equally worthy in identifying you as an individual.

Many people believe that the names we possess exemplify or have an effect on our personalities. Certainly, when we are absent, our names can evoke images of ourselves in the minds of those who know us or who might not know us. Many people also believe that the right name can bring success to one's life or career.

Our names are such a part of us that if they are misspelled or mispronounced, we may become irritated. I know that I have bristled when told that my surname, Louie, should be spelled *Lui* or *Lei* because these are dictionary spellings for Cantonese and Mandarin, respectively. I feel that I'm being told I don't know how to spell my own name. Actually, according to Elsdon Smith, the author of several books on American names, the correct spelling and pronunciation of a person's name should be based on the wishes of its owner who is, after all, the best authority in this matter.

In America, each different spelling for a family name is a name in its own right because there are no laws requiring Americans to have certain surnames. Nor are there any laws compelling the use of particular given names, although most Americans tend to select these from the pool of given names that accompanies the English language. Each spelling variant is recognized as an

7

independent name; even some nicknames, such as *Ned* for Edward, stand on their own.

Family identity is emphasized in a name in some countries, such as Hungary and China, where the surname comes first. Here in America, surnames are used as clues to ethnic group identity. Ethnic background can be blurred, however, by interracial and interethnic marriages, or hidden by the respelling of a family name upon arrival in the United States. Many family names that were brought to America have been Americanized because, as name experts have pointed out, names are a special part of a nation's language and culture.

Your name can tell you many things about yourself. Information such as family traditions, religion, education, gender, lineage, as well as the social values and attitudes of the name giver, are encoded in names. Your surname can tell you some things about the history — perhaps the early landscape — of the country from which it originated. American surnames are about migration patterns, and each can tell you something about the history of the ethnic group to which it belongs.

The connection between names and a nation's language and culture is wonderfully demonstrated in Chinese American names. Even though many Chinese Americans possess an American or Western given name, they are likely also to have a Chinese given name. And you can be sure that when the latter is stated or written in Chinese, the family name will come first, according to Chinese custom. Spelling for the surname is based on dialect sound, as in other American family names. However, wide differences in spelling the same family name can occur because of disparities in Chinese dialect pronunciation, such as the differences between Mandarin and Cantonese sounds.

But the surname character or ideograph will not vary for the family name, regardless of how it is spelled, because there is only one Chinese written language. (A simplified form is used in the People's Republic of China.) Chinese name traditions are similarly observed, regardless of dialect background, although there are regional and local variations; China is a very large country.

At the heart of Chinese name traditions are centuries-old precepts in regarding names as symbols of family ties. Given names must not be repeated from one generation to the next. However, a part of the given name can be repeated in the names of family members belonging to the same generation, so as to indicate their relationship. Usually it is one of the characters in a two-character given name — referred to as a "generation name" — that is repeated. Traditionally, brothers and sisters would have a different generation name.

Such name traditions have been brought to the United States since Chinese immigration began in the mid–nineteenth century, shortly after the 1848 California gold rush. In fact, Chinese name traditions are well-documented in American official records, such as federal censuses and the special immigration files that were kept on the early immigrants who came when the Chinese exclusion laws were in effect from 1882 to 1943. (During those decades, Chinese laborers could not come to this country although merchants and students, among others, were admitted.) Such records enable us to see the changes that have since taken place in Chinese American naming practices.

American name traditions have also had a strong influence on Chinese American names. But the Americanization of names and the transitions in naming practices are seen more clearly prior to World War II — particularly around 1940, when there were fewer than 80,000 persons of Chinese descent on the United States mainland and when more than half of these were native-born. This early group of Chinese Americans could all have fitted into one small-sized American city. Instead they were scattered across the nation, with concentrations on the West and East coasts and in Hawaii. Nonetheless, their experiences with the Americanization of their names were similar.

Most of the early surnames reflect the sounds of the Cantonese dialects brought from southern China. Due to Americanization, many look like other Euro-American names: *Chew, Dear, Gee, Lee, Louie, Lowe, Mark,* and *Young.* American given names also prevailed among the native-born. As I recall, some of my peers were named by Anglo-American schoolteachers. One day especially stands out in my mind: My second grade teacher suddenly stood up and pointed to a classmate, saying, "From now on, you're Jimmy!" To another boy, "You're Tommy!"

New surnames arose for the native-born Chinese American because many parents kept the tradition of placing the family name first. Illegal immigrants who came in spite of the exclusion laws adopted new names, called "paper names," and handed on the "paper" surnames to their children. Only the Chinese ideograph reveals the actual family name to the owner of a new surname.

Before the exclusion laws were repealed in 1943, and before the Chinese could become naturalized citizens, relatively few Americans of Chinese ancestry possessed names that reflected Mandarin and other dialect sounds. But a greater variety of dialect sounds was heard in the names of foreign-born students and scholars who came from different parts of China.

In comparison, almost all the major Chinese dialects are represented in Chinese American names today, with nearly two million persons of Chinese descent now living in the United States. (The 1990 census counted over 1.6

million, of whom 69 percent were foreign-born; the native-born ceased to predominate after the early 1970s.) This tremendous growth in population was largely fueled by (1) the settlement of several thousand foreign-born students and refugees after communism was established in the People's Republic of China in late 1949; (2) the removal of restrictions against immigration from Asia by the 1965 general immigration law; and (3) the huge inflow of ethnic Chinese refugees after the Vietnam War ended in 1975. (Another wave of new immigrants is expected since Hong Kong has reverted to being part of China.)

The new Chinese immigrants have added a rich variety of surname variants, echoing the sounds of the different dialects they speak. As a result, the number of surnames has greatly increased for Chinese Americans. We can see evidence of this phenomenon in the pages of telephone directories for every metropolitan area and in the enrollment lists of colleges and universities across America.

Surnames are thus real bonds of ethnicity for Chinese Americans who themselves form a diverse ethnic group. Some are only part Chinese in ancestry. Many do not speak or write Chinese. Chinese speakers usually cannot understand one another when speaking different Chinese dialects. As a group, they do not have the same views on being Chinese American, being Chinese, or being American. Nor do they share the same memories of Chinese American history because the vast majority came after the repeal of restrictive and discriminatory laws.

What Chinese Americans have in common as a group is their Chinese ancestry and family names that connect them to a legacy of name traditions, cultural habits, and, importantly, a common written language.

Everybody has a story to tell about his or her particular name. The purpose of this book is to relate the Chinese American experience with names. However, the name traditions of China will be presented first so as to lay the foundation for explaining Chinese American names. This book can be regarded as a historical snapshot of these names, because already the surnames that were forged in the first century of Chinese immigration are being overshadowed by the names brought in recent decades.

The book, however, is not a dictionary that gives explanations for all individual surnames. Neither can it fully explain the surnames brought by the new Chinese immigrants from different countries. It is my belief that the stories of their names belong to the countries where they resided before coming to America.

All examples of names in the book are names of real people. Some came from firsthand knowledge, others from stories told by family members and friends. Some names were found in federal census records, telephone directories,

English-language Chinese American newspapers and books about Chinese Americans. Names also came from bilingual materials, such as business directories, church and club membership lists, Chinese student listings and Chinese New Year souvenir booklets. The holdings of the Regional Archives System of the National Archives and Records Administration yielded many examples of names written in English and Chinese. My favorite source, however, is gravestones, especially those inscribed with both Chinese and English text.

Since some chapters are sprinkled with terminology that may be unfamiliar to the reader, a few explanations are in order. The term *Chinese American* is not hyphenated (the reason is given in Part II). The terms *American surnames of Chinese origin* and *surnames of Chinese origin* are used interchangeably because these are American family names. Both *American given name* and *Western given name* are used because sometimes an immigrant selects a Western given name prior to coming to America.

Most Americans refer to the family name or surname as the "last name" and to the given name as "first name" because they occur in this order in an American name. But these particular terms would be confusing in this book because the order of a Chinese name is just the opposite. Hence the terms *given name*, *family name*, and *surname* are used. As George Stewart explained in his book *American Given Names*, "The people of the United States — like other peoples generally — 'give' names to their children. These 'given' names stand in contrast to the 'family names,' which are inherited."

All examples of spelling variants for surnames are listed in alphabetic order, as in Der, Hsieh, Tse, Xie, and Zia. Chinese surname characters are in the traditional script rather than the simplified version because this is how most Chinese Americans write their names in Chinese. The officially recognized Pinyin system for spelling Mandarin is used only for the names of historical figures, dynasties, and provinces — as in *Guangdong* — but the names *Hong Kong* and *Canton* are used.

When the exact spelling for the name of an early immigrant could not be located, the name has been spelled according to standard Cantonese and placed within brackets. Cantonese spelling was chosen in these cases because the early immigrants were predominantly Cantonese and to spell their names in Mandarin could skew Chinese American history.

This book is written from the Chinese American point of view, with an emphasis on how Americanization has worked in particular ways for Chinese Americans. It is written out of the conviction that the overall story of Chinese Americans and their names should be shared. Americans of different ethnicities

11

may find that certain vignettes or stories of names resonate with their own experiences because the purpose of surnames is similar regardless of ethnic background. I hope the book will help readers realize why Chinese Americans have the names they do, and that Americans are somehow connected by the American way with names.

PART I

CHINESE NAME TRADITIONS

"Is it true that the Chinese first name is inherited?" an Anglo-American friend asked. My immediate reaction was "No, of course not." Then, as I switched my thinking from English to Chinese: "Yes, it is true," I answered, visualizing the family name as the first ideograph in a Chinese name. I thought again. No, the answer has to be that it isn't true, because "first name" in English refers to a given name.

Nor can it be true that the Chinese have a "middle name" when a name consists of three ideographs. In American terminology, the middle name comes between the given name and the surname. In Chinese names that consist of three ideographs, the first ideograph usually represents a family name and the remaining two, a disyllabic or two-character given name. Sometimes the first two ideographs constitute a two-character family name. Terms for names and names themselves reflect the culture and thought of the society from which they arise. American name traditions and those of China seem to be diametrically opposed, as we shall soon discover.

The Chinese are considered the first people to have hereditary or family names. For centuries, they have referred to their family names as "clan names" because of the interrelatedness of family and clan — a clan being a group of related families having the same surname, which they trace to a common ancestor. The family even served as a model for the government: The emperor was called "Father-Mother of the people," and all of China was regarded as his land — in theory, at least. The emphasis on family identity extends as well to the given name. For centuries, an elaborate naming system was honed and perfected to indicate family ties within the family and clan.

Names also reflect the changes that take place in society. Many societies

13

tend to lumber along in their development, set back at times by wars and other social upheavals. But even as social values and attitudes change, some old habits and ways of thinking never disappear entirely. Thus, in the continuum of name traditions, the myths and legends of ancient China can meet up with the historical facts of modern China in today's Chinese names.

The Chinese name traditions observed by Chinese Americans therefore run the gamut from centuries-old name customs to present-day practices being brought by new immigrants. However, the basic concept of names as symbols of family identity remains unchanged: The surname still comes first, as it has for nearly 4,000 years, and the given name is still a means of indicating family relationship.

1. HISTORY, MYTHS
AND FAMILY NAMES

"A man's life proceeds from his name, in the way a river proceeds from its source."

N. Scott Momaday, *The Names*

Tradition says that the Han Chinese people had family names in prehistoric times, during the glorious age of the *San Huang Wu Di*, or the Three Kings and Five Emperors, who ruled from 3,000 to 2,200 B.C. It is said that Fu Xi, the second of the Three Kings, regulated marriages and made surnames necessary. He is also credited as discovering the art of cooking and the system of writing in pictographs, and inventing the Eight Trigrams which is used in the *I Ching* or *Book of Changes*, a manual of divination.

Tradition also says that the first listing of surnames belonged to some of the sons of Huang Di, the first of the Five Emperors, who began his rule about 2800 B.C. As legend goes, Huang Di — or the Yellow Emperor — had four wives, twenty concubines and twenty-five sons. Only 14 sons received surnames because only they had merit and thus deserved surnames. A total of 12 different surnames were bestowed because two sons received the same name and two other sons received Huang Di's surname which was Ji (姬 — Chi). This may well be the world's first hereditary name although it is rarely seen today.

Later rulers also bestowed surnames on men who were deemed worthy and virtuous which indicates that, in the beginning, surnames were not hereditary names for family members but were honorary names for individuals.

Although historians regard the entire period of the *San Huang Wu Di* as a mythological age, the Chinese to this day consider Huang Di and Yan Di, the third of the Five Emperors, as their progenitors or founding ancestors. As an acquaintance who lived in the People's Republic of China wrote several years ago: "Even though we are oceans apart and even though we cannot communicate in each other's language, yet we are descendants of Yan and Huang." The Chinese, in addition, refer to themselves as "sons and daughters of the Yellow Emperor."

Nevertheless, historic records, which began with the *Sandai*, or the Three Dynasties (2,200 to 221 B.C.), composed of the Hsia, Shang and Zhou dynasties, indicate that there were fixed family names between 1,000 to 400 B.C. These belonged to the aristocracy of the feudal Zhou dynasty (ca. 1122–221 B.C.) — the common people did not have surnames. It was not until the onset of the Qin dynasty (221–207 B.C.), when feudalism was destroyed, that all Chinese were required to have surnames or *xing*.*

In comparison, hereditary names in Europe — which also appeared first in the aristocracy — began with the Italians around the tenth century A.D. The English acquired surnames by the end of the fourteenth century; the French had done so earlier and the Germans a bit later. In Japan, hereditary names were decreed by law in 1875 but these already existed among court nobles and the military class at an earlier date. Some countries did not begin using surnames until this century, such as Iran in 1926.

Exogamy and Marriage Taboos

Tradition furthermore says that Fu Xi forbade persons of the same patrilineage to intermarry and this rule was strictly followed by the Zhou aristocracy. The nobles were organized into clans and they paid great attention to lineage and blood relations. They practiced exogamy, which means that the men obtained wives from outside their own clan. Later on, this taboo against same-surname marriages was applied even to unrelated persons having the same surname because they are still considered to be descendants of the same common ancestor.

During the latter part of Zhou, when the *Liji* or the Record of Ceremonies and Proper Conduct was written, men were instructed that they could not marry a woman of the same surname — "not even after a hundred generations." The *Liji* was one of the Confucian Classics that was taught as part of a Chinese classical education until 1905.

This taboo, however, was not based on biological concerns because, from early on, first cousins were permitted to marry just as long as they did not have the same surname. A man could marry a cross-cousin, such as a daughter of his mother's brother. The offspring of sisters — called parallel cousins — likewise could intermarry. However, intergenerational marriages were forbidden, even

---

*Pronounced as "shing"— the sh is similar in sound to that of shield.

if the couple had different surnames. A man could not marry a niece because this not only smacks of incest, it muddies the generation order of men in the patriarchal genealogical records and upsets the observance of mourning rituals which are based on the hierarchical order of relatives. Family relationships must be clear in order to follow proper social etiquette and the correct mourning rituals.

These two taboos — which forbid the same-surname marriage and intergenerational marriage — were of extreme importance to the Chinese and form the basis of marriage laws for thousands of years.

Ancestor Worship and Adoption of Sons

Ancestor worship was observed by the aristocracy and this too reinforced the use of surnames. In this practice, the individual is regarded as a link in the chain of ancestors and descendants and is accountable to both for his actions. Sacrificial rituals must be performed for obtaining the good will of ancestors who, it is believed, have the power to either bestow blessings or to inflict harm on the living. Each generation therefore must keep the chain intact and continue the sacrificial rituals by producing sons. As the philosopher Mencius once said: "There are three things which are unfilial, and to have no posterity is the greatest of them."

Being a pragmatic people, the Chinese adopted sons to fulfill their filial duty when Nature did not oblige. Usually a brother's son was adopted. In any event, the oldest son and the youngest son were rarely given away because the oldest son is in the main line of descent and inherited the responsibility to continue the sacrificial rituals. (All sons in a family had equal inheritance rights; primogeniture ceased to exist in China after the feudal age.) It was permissible, though, for a son-in-law to be adopted by the wife's parents if her family had no sons.

Although it was against the law and against clan rules to adopt a boy of a different surname, in practice, nephews related through the maternal side of the family were often adopted. A recent study of adoption in imperial China by Ann Waltner shows that, by the nineteenth century, it was common practice to adopt a non-relative or stranger. This was because a stranger was less likely to abandon his adoptive parents by returning to his birth parents for reasons of filial piety.

Xing and Shi for Identity

Myths notwithstanding, we are definitely on firm ground with the Zhou dynasty on the early use of surnames. Yet the aristocracy who had family names did not use these in the same way as we do today. For example, we always include our family name or surname as part of one's personal name; this was not the case in the formative age of Chinese civilization. Proof lies in the two words *xing* (姓) and *shi* (氏)—pronounced as "shee." Both words mean family name, surname, or clan name. Nonetheless, *xing* indicates lineage—a meaning that does not apply to *shi*. The word *shi* refers to the maiden name or the original surname of a married woman—a meaning that does not apply to *xing*.

Therefore these two Chinese words meaning "family name" are not interchangeable words. Americans can use family name, surname and last name to mean the same thing but the Chinese cannot do this with *xing* and *shi*. In Chinese etiquette, one inquires about another person's name by asking "Gui xing?" One would never ask "Gui shi?" Today, though, *xing-shi* is often used as a compound word in reference to the family name.

It is important to mention these terms because almost all surnames of Chinese origin in common use today came from the *shi* or the clan names that arose during the feudal period. Only the women of the aristocracy used the *xing* after they married. Americans of Chinese ancestry may recall a mother or great-grandmother with a name such as *Leong Shee*. This means that she is of Leong lineage and the word *Shee* (a spelling variant) acts like the word *née* (e.g. Ruby Louie *née* Ling). In old Chinese tradition, a married woman was not identified by her given name; she was known by her maiden name or original surname. If the husband's family name were added, it would appear first, as in Louie Leong Shee or Mrs. Louie *née* Leong. This traditional way of a married woman retaining her own family name is traced back to the Zhou dynasty.

This does not mean that the Zhou noble women had equal status with men. Not at all. Women have always been in a subordinate role in a patriarchal society. The Chinese word for wife—婦 (Fu)—even underscores this point because it is composed of the words "woman" and "broom." It seems that the custom of the Chinese woman retaining her own surname arose because it provides proof that exogamy had indeed been practiced.

The Spring and Autumn period (722–481 B.C.) and the Warring States period (403–221 B.C.) are especially pertinent to the story of surnames in China. This was when writing flourished, when great philosophers lived—such as Confucius (551–479 B.C.), his major disciple Mencius (ca. 380–289 B.C.), and

Zhuangzi, the Daoist (369–286 B.C.?) — and when the noble clans wielded great power. Only twenty-two *xing* existed during the Spring and Autumn period and this evidently represented the total number of noble clans.

It is often pointed out that the *xing* may have once represented matrilineage. Certainly the character 姓 lends itself to such conjecture. Its left half is the "woman" radical (女) and the right half (生) — pronounced "sheng" — means life or birth. (Most Chinese words consist of a combination of a radical and a phonetic part — the radical represents the word's root meaning and the phonetic part holds a clue to pronunciation. This clue may no longer be relevant because of changes in the spoken language over the course of time.) To bolster this belief, it is usually mentioned that eight of the most ancient family names have a "woman" radical. Only two are commonly seen today: *Jiang* (姜) and *Yao* (姚).

Instead of being identified by their *xing*, men of the Zhou aristocracy were identified by a *shi* or clan name, which stood for their particular branch of the clan. It went without saying which *xing* a noble possessed. The *shi* was their badge of prestige. And all through the Spring and Autumn period, new *shi* arose because branches of clans multiplied as new generations came along.

The Spring and Autumn period also signaled the eventual demise of the noble clans and their *xing* and *shi* custom. About 170 feudal states and statelets existed at its onset except that constant skirmishes and battles among the feudal lords kept paring down this number. Finally only seven large powerful states remained when the Spring and Autumn segued into the aptly named Warring States period. Warfare thereafter turned more violent as each of the seven feudal lords sought to become the sole ruler of the Han Chinese. It was in the midst of this era, especially due to the changes in the art of war, that family names were no longer the prerogative of the privileged noble class.

Early in the Spring and Autumn, the nobles battled from horse-drawn war chariots, according to rules of chivalry. Their downfall began in the sixth century B.C. when battles involved armies of infantrymen and it was hastened by the invention of the deadly crossbow in the fifth century, which raised the stakes of battle higher. A century later, a new military tactic was added. In 307 B.C., the king of the Chao feudal state stopped using the clumsy war chariot and began deploying squadrons of mounted archers instead, a maneuver he borrowed from the horse-riding Mongolians whose steppes bordered his state.

Such large-scale undertakings for warfare naturally called for men with fighting, technical, managerial, and other skills, and this created a new class of men who rose from commoner status. Thus, claims to noble birth and the prestige of a clan name were rendered meaningless in those changing times.

19

The Qin (221–207 B.C.), the Watershed of Surnames

The Qin dynasty is the watershed of Chinese family names as used today. After conquering the other six feudal states, the First Emperor of Qin immediately abolished feudalism, established a centralized form of government, and made the nuclear family of parents and children the basic social unit. All Chinese thereafter acquired surnames. And the aristocratic *shi* became ordinary family names or *xing*.

Clans were anathema to this emperor. Evidently 120,000 families were rounded up and moved into new quarters in the capital to be kept under close surveillance. This massive forced relocation was to prevent organized opposition to the new regime, a tactic practiced by rulers before and after the Qin dynasty. In later centuries, clans would once again be strong, as in the Song dynasty (1127–1280), but never again would they rule separate kingdoms.

During his short-lived dynasty, the First Emperor of Qin revolutionized China by standardizing the written language and all measures and weights. He put together the sections of the Great Wall of China at a great cost of lives and taxation. He was much despised and is still thought of as an evil emperor who ordered the burning of all books. However, recent scholarship has discovered that many books were not burned as traditionally believed. Yet the imperial age he launched lasted two thousand years, until the 1911 revolution established the Republic of China.

Despite his efforts to destroy the noble clans, the First Emperor of Qin could not erase their social customs. Ancestor worship is still observed and married women can still retain their original surname. However, there were flip-flops in the use of the *shi*. In traditional society, this word was associated more often with a married woman's name. Now that the Chinese married woman has the dignity of using her full name, it is common to see a man referred to in Chinese newspaper articles by his surname only, followed by the word *shi*. Apparently *shi* has not lost its original sign of merit for a man after all.

Lingering Traditions

It should be pointed out that it was not simply tradition that led the Chinese to obey the taboo against same-surname marriages. The early warning against impropriety became law at some point in time and violators could be severely punished. For example, during the last dynasty — the Qing (1644–1911), an unrelated couple of the same surname and the person who introduced them could be badly beaten before the marriage was annulled. If a married couple were considered blood-related by authorities — no matter how tenuous the relationship — they could be beheaded or banished to some remote part of the empire.

Laws against same-surname marriages went out with the Qing dynasty yet many people still frown upon them, believing that such marriages go against tradition. As to cross-cousin and parallel cousin marriages, these still occur but are now strongly disapproved. In his book *Ancestors*, Frank Ching recalls the harsh criticism against the marriage of his parents which took place in 1933. They were distant relatives with the same surname but his father was much older than his mother and had grown children. Their marriage outraged and scandalized relatives on both sides: His mother's father publicly disowned her, her brother refused to see her again, and his father was publicly denounced by some members of his clan. This marriage would not have taken place in imperial China because it violated the two basic marriage laws of traditional society.

The Chinese traditional family and clan system no longer exists per se. It is often idealized in the literature as several generations living together under one roof, getting along by observing Confucian rules of proper conduct and carrying out duties and responsibilities as expected of them. This system lent stability to the agricultural society but apparently does not work as well in a modern industrial society.

As the Chinese strove to modernize their country and to bring her up to date with the rest of the industrial world, the social values and attitudes of the traditional society were systematically challenged and eroded. One of the aims of the People's Republic of China, when it was established in 1949, was to transfer the loyalty of the people from the family to the state. As the sinologist C.P. Fitzgerald commented: "It is most improbable that the traditional system will ever be revived."

Be that as it may, surnames of Chinese origin will always serve as reminders of the beginnings of Chinese civilization and culture to anyone who asks, "How did my surname originate?"

2. SOURCES
OF FAMILY NAMES

"One surname branched out into many clan-names, and one clan-name branched out again into many family names."
from the Chinese classic *Zuo Chuan*

Although the most common surnames of Chinese origin stemmed from the *shi* or clan names of the Zhou aristocracy, they originated from the same kind of sources that are cited for surnames of other countries. For example, many clan names were placenames and patronyms — the latter being a surname that is derived from the given name of a father or grandfather. Since clan names arose in the aristocracy, some were derived from titles, ranks, and official occupations of that feudal society. Some were created due to errors in writing or to deliberate deletions and additions to the original surname character. And some arose to commemorate an event in the life of an ancestor.

However, there can be more than one source for a surname. The same clan name could have been adopted in different feudal states at different times and for a variety of reasons. For example, the surname Wang (王) — meaning "king" — was adopted by many unrelated clans in the ancient world. The surname 駱 — Lo, Lock, Lok — was both a placename and patronym. As one story goes, when the eldest son of a feudal lord received his own kingdom, he renamed it *Lo* to honor his father whose name was *Da Lo* or "Great Lo." Later on, descendants took the placename for their surname.

The surname 趙 — Chao, Chew, Chiu, Jew, Zhao — and the surname 魏 — Wei — could have been names of districts before these developed into feudal states, and one or the other may be cited as a source by different authors of books on Chinese family names. This also occurs for the surname 黃 — Huang, Ng, Oei, Wong; the surname 謝 — Char, Der, Hsieh, Jay, Shieh, Tse, Xie, Zia; and the surname 彭 — Pang, Peng.

On the other hand, a few family names have come down through the centuries untampered by change. The surname 伍 — Eng, Ing, Ng, Wu — is consistently identified as an ancient clan name. The surname 郭 — Gok, Guo, Keh, Kuo, Kwak, Kwok — is mentioned as an example of "genealogical purity" by Chi Li, author of *The Formation of the Chinese People*. It arose out of the name "the two Kuo" which refers to the fiefs bestowed upon two brothers during the early part of the Zhou dynasty.

Sometimes the different sources cited for a surname seem totally unrelated. One explanation for the surname 雷— Lei, Loui, Louie, Lui — says it came from the title Lei Gung or Duke Lei that belonged to a son of the Yellow Emperor. Another explanation says Lei Gung was a minister to the Yellow Emperor. Still another explanation says that this surname came from the name Fang Lei Shi belonging to one of the wives of the Yellow Emperor. To make matters more confusing, this same name is also said to be the name of an ancient ruler from which the surname 方— Fang, Fong — arose.

Given the antiquity of Chinese family names, it is not surprising to find different explanations for a surname, liberally mixed with history, myth and folk lore.

Placenames

Placenames have been a common source for surnames in all countries because it is a most natural and easy way for a person to identify himself to a stranger. No doubt many a placename was adopted when surnames were required of all Chinese. Many new ones arose in later centuries, especially the Song dynasty (tenth to twelfth centuries) when men, according to Chi Li, replaced their family name with the name of their birthplace. The sinologist Herbert A. Giles listed the sources for 438 family names in his article *The Family Names*— called *Bai Jia Xing* (*Pai Chia Hsing*) in Chinese — and over 40 percent of these names were derived from placenames.

This includes names of large feudal states, city states, districts, residences, or just a place in the countryside. The Chinese word for a "state" is *guo*, which also means "country," "kingdom," and "nation." During the Zhou dynasty, a *guo* could be a feudal state of any size or even a walled city. The ancient Chinese were wall builders, and feudal lords, along with their descendants, lived and governed the affairs of their kingdom from behind the walls of their cities.

The following surnames belonging to Chinese Americans came from names of feudal states:

Selected surname spellings	Surname character
Cai, Choy, Toy, Tsoi, Tsai	蔡
Cao, Choe, Tow, Tsao	曹
Chan, Chen, Chin, Ching, Tan, Ting	陳
Chee, Hsu, Tuey, Xu, Zee	徐
Cheng, Jann, The, Trinh, Zheng	鄭
Chi, Qi	齊
Chiang, Gong, Jiang, Kong, Kiang	江
Chiang, Jiang	蔣
Co, Hee, Hsu, Huie, Shu, Xu	許
Dang, Deng, Tang, Teng	鄧
Eng, Go, Gouw, Ng, Ung, Wu	吳
Goo, Gu, Koo, Ku	顧
Hom, Hum, Tam, Tan, Tom	譚
Hsiao, Shew, Siaw, Siu, Su, Sue, Xiao	蕭
Hsueh, Seid, Sit, Xue	薛
Jen, Ren, Yam, Zen	任
Lai, Le, Li	黎
Law, Lo, Loh, Luo	羅
Leong, Leung, Liang, Luong	梁
Ruan, Yuen, Yuan	阮
Song, Soong, Sung	宋
Wan, Wen, Won, Woon	溫

The following were once names of districts or places in the countryside:

Selected surname spellings	Surname character
Auyang, Ouyang, Ow Yang, Owyoung	歐陽
Chi, Ji	冀
Chiang, Jiang, Keung	姜
Chau, Chou, Chow, Joe, Jue, Zhou	周
Chu, Qu, Wat	屈
Choy, Cui, Tsai, Tsui	崔
Doo, Du, To, Tu	杜
Duan, Tuan	段
Fan, Fann	范

Selected surname spellings	*Surname character*
Guan, Kuan, Kwan, Quan, Quon	關
Ip, Yap, Ye, Yeh, Yep, Yip	葉
Iu, Yao, Yeo, Yew, You	姚
Kuang	匡
Lam, Lem, Lim, Lin, Ling, Lum	林
Linghu	令狐
Loo, Lu	盧
Look, Lu, Luke	陸
Miao, Mu	苗
Pan, Pon, Poon, Pun	潘
So, Soo, Su, Sue	蘇
Yang, Yeo, Yeung, Young	楊
Yen	閻

Some surnames once had a topographical radical on the right side of the word—the radical for "city"—as seen in the surname Deng 鄧. For some reason, it was removed from the following names:

Bei, Pei	貝
Chang, Chong, Zhang	章
Chu, Gee, Jee, Zhu	朱
Don, Dong, Jung, Tseng, Zane, Zeng	曾
Feng, Fong, Foong, Fung	馮
Mac, Mark, Mo, Mock	莫

On the other hand, this topographical radical was tacked on to a few surnames. The surname 邵—Chiu, Shao, Shiu—originally consisted of only the left half of this character, a word that was part of the title *Shao Gung* or Duke Shao. As late as 1726, this radical was attached to the surname 邱—Chiu, Hu, Hugh, Khoo, Qiu because the original character 丘 happens to be the given name of Confucius—they both have the same sound. Social arbiters at that time decided it was disrespectful to have a surname that was the name of this great philosopher.

According to Chen Tse-ming, author of a book on the *Pai Chia Xing*, both surname characters have been in use since the founding of the Republic of China in 1911.

Emperors, Magistrates and Surnames

This forced change in the surname character undoubtedly came from the taboo that forbade an emperor's given name from appearing in the names of his subjects, as long as he was on the throne. Consequently, some family names were changed. The surname 嚴— Im, Yan, Yen, Yim — arose during the Han dynasty when the 莊— Chuang, Zhuang — clan changed their surname as a result of this taboo.

During the Five Dynasties period (A.D. 907 to 960), members of a 沈— Shen, Shum — clan in Fujian province changed their surname out of respect for their district ruler whose name included this character. The surname 尤— You, Yu — was created when the "water" radical on the left side of the original name was removed and a dot was added to the upper right corner.

Surnames were sometimes changed when an emperor rewarded a man with a new surname in recognition of his accomplishments or when he punished a man for his misdeeds by bestowing a surname with a contemptuous meaning. Emperors were known to grant their own family name to deserving men: it was the surname 劉— Lau, Lew, Liu — during the Han dynasty; the surname 李— Lee, Li — during the Tang dynasty, the surname 趙— Chao, Zhao — during the Song; and the surname 朱— Chu, Gee, Zhu — during the Ming dynasty.

However, the name of a dynasty itself is evidently a rare source for a surname. Only two dynasties — the Xia and Shang — existed before the Zhou and these gave rise to the surname 夏— Ha, Hsia, Xia — and the surname 殷— Yin, which is another name for the Shang. The surname 周— Chou, Chow, Joe, Jew, Zhou, the eponym of the Zhou dynasty, was originally the name of the state in which the founder of this dynasty resided.

Many villages in China consist of only one family name. This phenomenon occurs because women traditionally, after marriage, leave their home village to go and live in the husband's village. Such villages may trace their surname to an official who had been sent to rule over them centuries ago or to the son of an important local personage who had moved into the area. It is not unusual to hear a Chinese American state that his family name can be traced back to more than twenty generations in the village where his ancestors lived.

Patronyms

The next most common source for surnames of Chinese origin is patronyms and these account for more than 20 percent of the family names in the *Bai Jia*

Xing. The common surname 張— Chang, Cheung, Jeong, Zhang — is probably the best known example. Tradition says this was the name of the Yellow Emperor's fifth son who invented the bow and arrow. In fact, the radical 弓 on the left side of this character is the word for "a bow."

Chinese patronyms are almost always one-character names since it was customary for the ancients to adopt only part of an ancestor's name for a clan name. The common surname 劉— Lau, Lew, Liu, Low — is said to come from the name *Liu Lei* who was a descendant of the legendary Emperor Yao. The following surnames are patronyms of yore:

Selected surname spellings	*Surname character*
Chang	常
Chen, Gin, Jin, Zhen	甄
Cherk, Cho, Chock, Chuck, Zhuo	卓
Chi, Ji	季
Chi, Ji	吉
Gam, Gan, Gum, Kam, Kan	甘
Gao, Go, Kao, Ko	高
Goo, Ku	古
Hou	侯
Huang-fu	皇甫
Hung, Kong, Kung	孔
Kang	康
Leo, Liao	廖
Man, Wen	文
Man, Wan	萬
New, Niu	牛
Shek, Shi, Shih	石
Sin, Soon, Suen, Sun	孫
Yin	尹
Yuan, Yuen	袁

In any event, there are no Chinese surnames equivalent to such surnames as Johnson or O'Brien — which mean "son of John" and "descended from Brien," respectively. To be sure, the characters for "son" and "grandson" appear in a few ancient double surnames, such as *Kung-sun* (Duke's grandson) and *Zhongsun* (son of the second son). But these are not patronyms; these were titles or appellations

27

that arose during the Spring and Autumn period to identify the sons and grand-sons of nobles. For example, the prestigious surname 孟 — Meng — was derived from *Meng-sun*, a name that identified the descendants of the eldest son of the feudal lord who ruled the state of Lu. Confucius was born in this state, as was his disciple Mencius.

Ranks and Official Occupations

Some surnames came from titles that indicated the ancestor's rank of nobil-ity during the Zhou dynasty. There were five ranks and their English equiva-lents are, in the order of their importance: Duke, Marquis, Earl, Viscount, and Baron. Some feudal lords took the loftier title of Wang or King for themselves during the latter part of the Spring and Autumn when the Zhou royal house was in its decline. When descendants adopted their *shi* from an ancestor's title, they customarily omitted the rank itself and took only the name that accompa-nied the rank. An example, that was just mentioned, is the surname Shao that came from the title *Shao Gung*. Other examples are the surname 胡 — Hu, Woo, Wu — from the posthumous title *Duke Hu* (胡公); the surname 莊 — Chuang, Chwang, Zhuang — from the title *Zhuang Wang* or "King Zhuang" (莊王). A close corollary would be if the descendants of Arthur Wellesley (1769–1852), the Duke of Wellington, decided to replace their surname with the name *Wellington*.

The surname 侯 — Hou, How — can easily be mistaken for the rank of mar-quis except that its source is either the name of a feudal state or the name of the man who was the "inventor of writing."

The following surnames originated from the titles of feudal lords who were Dukes (gung) and Earls (Po); some were posthumous titles:

Selected spellings	*Surname character*	*From title*
Bai, Bock	白	Duke Bai — 白公
Chang, Cheng, Trinh	程	Earl Cheng — 程伯
Chung, Tsung, Zong	宗	Earl Tsung — 宗伯
Chien, Gan, Jian, Kan	簡	Earl Chien — 簡伯
Dai, Tai	戴	Duke Dai — 戴公
Ding, Ting	丁	Duke Ding — 丁公
Hsuan, Xuan	宣	Earl Xuan — 宣伯
Leo, Liao	廖	Earl Liao — 廖伯

28

Selected spellings	Surname character	From title
Li	厲	Duke Li—厲公
Mao, Mow	毛	Earl Mao—毛伯
Mei, Moy, Mui	梅	Earl Mei—梅伯
Mew, Miao	繆	Duke Miao—繆公
Yu	俞	Earl Yu—俞伯

Some surnames came from the title of an official occupation:

Selected spellings	Surname character	From title
Be, Ma, Mar	馬	Minister of War
Chi, Ji	籍	Registrar
Chuan, Quan	全	Chancellor of the Exchequer
Fu	符	Minister of Imperial tallies and seals
Ling	凌	Ice cutter
Pu	卜	Court Augur
Seto, Situ, Soo Hoo, SsuTu	司徒	Minister of Instruction
Tso, Zuo	左	Court Annalist
Voo, Wu	烏	Ranger of the Hills

The last surname mentioned means "crow" or "black bird." Tradition says it arose because the legendary ruler Shao Hao, who succeeded the Yellow Emperor, liked to call his officers by the names of birds. The surname Ling seems to represent a menial occupation but at least it was connected in some way to the royal house. It is unlikely that descendants of nobles would take their clan name from an occupation unless it were connected to royalty. As Elsdon Smith, the doyen of American onomasticians, once observed: "Occupations which were looked up to and respected were more likely to produce permanent family names than those which call attention to servile status…" Nonetheless, it is surprising that no surnames represent such occupations as carpenter, barber, cook, and winemaker; one would expect such occupations to be of great importance to the aristocracy.

Two surnames usually thought to be derived from occupations are 巫 — Moe, Mu, Wu — and 陶 — Tao, Tow. The first name means "magician" or "physician" and the second means "potter." However, these names were also placenames. Although the surname 屠 — Tu — is listed as meaning "butcher," it was the name of a feudal state that had its topographical radical removed.

Fear of Persecution

There is a Chinese proverb that says the Chinese do not change their surnames but they have changed their names, especially when it involved a matter of life or death. The most famous name-changing story is about the surname 李 — Lee, Li — the most common surname in China. As the story goes, a *Li Lizhen* fled for his life after incurring the wrath of his ruler during the Shang dynasty (ca. 1766–1122 B.C.). After finding nourishment and rest under a li or plum tree, he took the name of this fruit for his new name as an expression of gratitude. Fortuitously, it had the same sound as the name he discarded. Adopting a new surname that is closest in sound to the original name is commonplace in the history of surnames in all countries. Other descendants of this man took the patronym 利 — also pronounced *Li* — from the first character of his given name.

Another example is the surname 田 — Tian, Tien. It was adopted by a member of a Chen (陳) clan who fled the state of Qi after assassinating his prince. At that time, both surnames sounded almost alike and Chen is still pronounced Tan in the southern Fujian or Hokkien dialect. Ironically, Tian's grandson became the ruler of Qi but, after this state was annihilated at the end of the Warring States period, his descendants adopted Wang (王) for their family name.

During the eighteenth century, some clans with the family name 徐 — Choe, Hsu, Xu — discarded their surname by dropping the "double man" radical on the left side and the result was the surname 余 — Yee, Yu, already a well-established surname. Consequently, certain Xu and Yu clans could not intermarry. According to Giles, the change of name came about because they wanted to avoid the same fate as a distant relative and his immediate family who were put to death by order of the Manchu emperor Yong Zheng (1723–36). This incident arose over a rather innocuous poem the victim had written about the peony, the king of flowers to the Chinese. Someone, who sought his ruin, told authorities that the poem contained insults to the emperor.

Rewriting and Errors

Both the omission and addition of radicals and other elements in surname characters contributed to the rise of new surnames. This is no different from Americans dropping or adding letters to their surnames and thus creating new surname variants.

For example, the patronymic 洪— Hong, Hung — arose when descendants of a man named *Gong Gong* (共工) took the first character of his name for their clan name. They added the "water" radical on the left side and created a differently pronounced name. The surname 龔— Gong, Goong, Kung — was created by descendants of Gong Gong's son, *Ju Long* (句龍), when they combined parts of the names of their ancestors to make one name.

Two surnames arose from the double surname 歐陽 — Auyang, Ouyang, Owyang — which means "south of Ou hill." First, Auyang was shortened to 歐 — Au, Ou, Ow. Then the radical on the right side was deleted to create 區, another surname of the same sound.

An error in writing the surname 余 — Yee, Yu — produced the surname 佘 — Sai, She. Close scrutiny of the two characters may be necessary in order to see that the tiny vertical line connecting the two horizontal bars in the first character is missing in the second surname character.

Non-Chinese Sources

Common Chinese family names are also found in the minority groups of China. Like minorities in all countries, they adopted Chinese names either out of conformity to the language and culture or to avoid discrimination. In former decades, school children were taught that there were five main groups of Chinese: Han, Manchurian, Mongolian, Muslim, and Tibetan. Today, there are 55 different Chinese minority groups, although the vast majority is still the Han Chinese.

The surname 苗 — Miao, Mu — is easily thought to have come from the name of the large minority group residing in the southern half of China, down into Vietnam. However, this is an old Han Chinese name. The Miao people, like other minority groups in China, borrowed this character to phoneticize its sound into Chinese.

During the Early Han dynasty, the surname 金 — Chin, Jin, King — which means "gold" or "metal," was presented to the son of a Turkic chieftain who was

31

defeated in battle in earlier years. As the story goes, the son was carried away as a child to be brought up in the Chinese imperial court and after growing up into a splendid young man, the emperor honored him with this surname in memory of the "golden image" that had been taken away from his father. This surname happens to be the most common one in Korea where it is pronounced *Kim*.

Toba emperor Xiao-wen, who ruled North China during the Northern Wei dynasty (386–534), went so far as to issue an order, in the year 494, demanding his people adopt Chinese names, intermarry with the Chinese, and give up their language and names. (The Toba, who are of Turko-Mongol origin, are also called Xian-bei and Tungus.) To pave the way to his Sinicizing efforts, the emperor himself took Yuan 元 for his surname. (Centuries later, Khubilai Khan, grandson of Chinggis Khan, would take this same character for the name of his Yuan dynasty (1264–1368).) As a result, the Tobas discarded their 99 polysyllabic tribal names and took such common Chinese names as Chen, Hu, Li, Yang, and Zhang. However, Emperor Xiao-wen's decree did not last long. It was rescinded in the next Toba dynasty, the Western Wei (534–557), and many of the original tribal names were restored.

The Manchus of the Qing dynasty also kept their polysyllabic tribal names. But their famous Eight Banners do not represent surnames of Manchurian tribes as is sometimes believed. According to Victor Chuan, whose grandfather was expelled from the Forbidden City for becoming a Christian, the eight banners identify the descendants of the men who served under the Manchu leader Nuerhachih. Each banner is of a specific color or a combination of white and another color so that it could be identified from afar. (Interestingly, the color black is not used because it is not easily seen from a distance.)

Finally, among the family names that commemorate an event is the surname 車 — Che — it means "cart" or "carriage." It memorializes two events: the death of three brothers who were buried alive and the journey of a famous Han dynasty personage who arrived at the Imperial Court by cart. The surname 武 — Mo, Wu — arose because it was thought that the youngest son of a Zhou dynasty ruler had the lines of this character on the palm of his hand.

The written characters of family names of Chinese origin are all visual reminders of a society that existed in ancient China. These give an intimate glimpse of social life, habits, and thought; information dear to the heart of anthropologists and sociologists and information that is not always available in history books. As these examples show, there is a story behind each surname.

3. SOME CHARACTERISTICS OF FAMILY NAMES

"A tiger leaves a skin behind him, but a man leaves his name."
Old Chinese proverb

Most Chinese Americans can find their surname character listed in the *Bai Jia Xing* (百家姓 or *Pai Chia Hsing*) that was alluded to in the last chapter. The middle word in the title of this well-known compilation of family names means "family" but since the first word *bai* (also spelled *bo* and *po*) means "a hundred," the title is often translated as "The Hundred Family Names." However, *bai* also means "hundreds" and "many." Therefore the title can be translated simply as "The Family Names." This listing is easily obtainable because it can be found in the Chinese almanac which is sold in Chinese American bookstores at the onset of each lunar new year.

According to Giles, the *Bai Jia Xing* was compiled during the Song dynasty, in Hangzhou, which was the capital of the Southern Song dynasty (1127–1279). Certainly the author of this compilation left a few clues behind that indicate he was working on this list of names during that period of time.

The first family name honored is 趙 — Chao, Chew, Chiu, Jew, Zhao; the family name of the Song dynasty emperors. They ruled all of China from 960–1127 during the Northern Song dynasty and only the southern half of the country during the Southern Song. North China, meanwhile, was ruled under the *Jin* or "Golden" dynasty by a Tungusic Ruzhen tribe that originated from northern Manchuria.

The second family name 錢 — Chien, Qian — honors the Governor of Zhejiang province who was in office when the *Bai Jia Xing* was compiled — Hangzhou is located in this province. The third family name 孫 — Sun — belonged to Chien's favorite concubine, and the fourth surname 李 — Lee, Li — honors the Governor of Nanjing (Nanking), located in Jiangsu province, which is north of Zhejiang province. Both of these provinces lie south of the Yangzi River.

33

An additional note of interest about the *Bai Jia Xing* is that the family names are arranged in rhyming groups of eight. But this is not a poem. The rhyming was a mnemonic device and one of the requirements of the pre–1905 classical education included memorizing this long list of names.

This title, by the way, is similar to the terms *bai xing* and *lao bai xing*, which the Chinese often use in referring to themselves. These terms are often translated as "the people" or "people of a hundred surnames." Tradition says that the term *bai xing* arose when Yao, the fourth of the legendary Five Emperors, identified families according to surname. However, this does not mean there were 100 surnames during the prehistoric age; one interpretation is that this description referred to the aristocratic families. Nonetheless, the idea that the Chinese have only a hundred surnames still persists.

Number of Family Names

This brings up the question of how many Chinese family names exist. As mentioned earlier, there were only twenty-two *xing* during the Spring and Autumn period (eighth to fifth century B.C.). The *Bai Jia Xing* in Giles' article contains 438 family names — 408 one-character names and 30 two-character surnames. The Chinese call these "single surnames" and "double surnames," respectively. For some unknown reason, today's version has 486 names: 408 single surnames and 78 double surnames, a two-fold increase of the latter.

Many more family names may have existed during the Song dynasty because, according to the late anthropologist Chi Li, nearly 4,000 were in use when the Qing dynasty was founded in 1644. Mu Lien-sen, whose dictionary on Chinese family names was published in the mid–1970s, mentioned 6,000 names. This included 3,700 single surnames, 2,500 double surnames, 127 three-character names, 6 four-character names and 2 surnames consisting of five characters.

In 1988, Professors Du Ruofu and Yuan Yida of the Institute of Genetics in Beijing estimated there were over 10,000 surnames, a figure they derived from their research of the 1982 census of the People's Republic of China. Almost one billion people were counted then. (Since 1990, this population has gone over the one billion mark and their dictionary, published in 1996, lists over 11,000 names.) According to Chen Tse-ming's book, published in 1983, there are 1,700 family names for a population of about 21 million people in the Republic of China on Taiwan.

Koreans and Vietnamese also have a limited number of surnames — nearly 300 family names exist in Korea and about 200 in Vietnam. In contrast, Japan, with a population of 126 million people, has an abundance of surnames: a recent estimate is 130,000 surnames.

The United States has an even greater number of surnames. At least one million American family names occur in a population of less than 250 million people. Back in the early 1930s, when almost all American surnames originated in Europe, it was thought that this country had three times the number of surnames of any country. This may still be the case.

Actually, far fewer surnames are in common use in both the United States and China. A little over 2,000 surnames are found in one half the American population. In comparison, a mere *19 surnames* occur in over half of the Han Chinese population, according to Professors Du and Yuan. The Chinese call these their *da xing* or "great surnames." And only *100 surnames* are found in 87 percent of the Han Chinese people. It seems that the Chinese could be accurately described, after all, as the people of a hundred surnames!

Most Popular Surnames

Li (李) is the most popular Chinese surname. Wang (王) is next, followed by Zhang (張). (At present, the literature on names usually says that Zhang or Chang is the most common Chinese name.) According to the two professors, these three surnames are borne by over one percent of China's population, which means that ten million persons bear the surnames Li, Wang, or Zhang.

The remaining 16 "great surnames" are, in the order of their popularity: Liu (劉), Chen (陳), Yang (楊), Zhao (趙), Huang (黃), Zhou (周), Wu (吳), Xu (徐), Sun (孫), Hu (胡), Zhu (朱), Gao (高), Lin (林), He (何), Guo (郭), and Ma (馬). However, there is a difference in the most common surnames of northern and southern China. The great surnames in North China are *Li, Wang, Chang,* and *Liu.* In comparison, the great surnames in South China are *Chen, Zhao, Huang, Lin,* and *Wu.* Nevertheless, as Professor Du mentioned, the surname Li is the most common Chinese surname for all of China, including Taiwan.

Next two pages: The first 8 family names of the *Bai Jia Xing* are seen in the far right column on p. 36. Listed also are 40 other names. Above 24 double surnames on p. 37, in the upper left corner, Confucius' mother is depicted. (From a *Chinese Almanac.*)

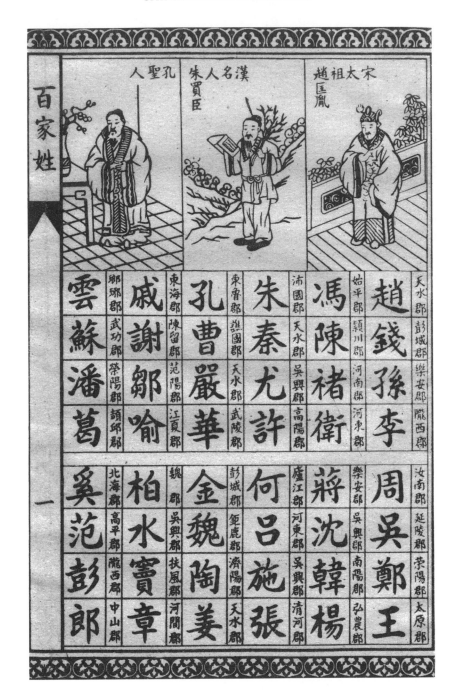

百家姓

一

人聖孔　人名漢　宋太祖
　　　　朱買臣　趙匡胤

天水郡	始平郡	沛國郡	東魯郡	東海郡
趙	馮	朱	孔	戚	雲
錢	陳	秦	曹	謝	蘇
孫	褚	尤	嚴	鄒	潘
李	衛	許	華	喻	葛
周	蔣	何	金	柏	奚
吳	沈	呂	魏	水	范
鄭	韓	施	陶	竇	彭
王	楊	張	姜	章	郎

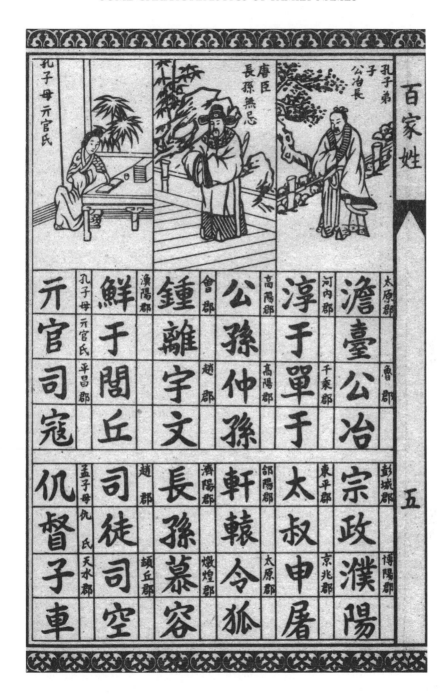

The 10 great surnames of Taiwan — found in 50 percent of the population — differ in the order of their importance from those mentioned above. Chen (陳) is the leading surname, according to a report by the Taiwan Archives and Document Center. It is followed by Lin (林), Huang (黃), Chang (張), Li (李), Wang (王), Wu (吳), Liu (劉), Tsai (蔡), and Yang (楊).

This recent finding that *Li* is the most common family name and *Chen* is the most popular one in southern China would not come as a surprise to many Cantonese speakers. An old Cantonese saying (my stepfather loved to recite it with relish in his dialect) states: "*Guangdong Chan, Tin Ha Lee.*" Translated, it means that Chans (or Chens) predominate in Guangdong province while Lis predominate in *tin ha* (*tian xia* in Mandarin) or the rest of China. Literally, *tian xia* is an ancient name for China that means "all under heaven." It seems that research has given support to what the southern Chinese have claimed, perhaps for centuries!

In addition to Chan, the next most common surnames in Guangdong province are: Lee (李), Cheung (張), Wong (黃), Ho (何), Chau (周), Au (區), Woo (胡), Ma (馬), and Mak (麥). (The spelling reflects standard Cantonese spelling.) The surname Mak originated in this province, according to the historian Him Mark Lai.

As a note of interest, the most common American surnames are Smith, Johnson, and Williams, according to the Social Security Administration records of 1984. In Japan, the most common surnames include Suzuki, Sato, Tanaka, and Nakamura. In Korea, nearly one-fourth of the people bear the surname Kim. And in Vietnam, Nguyen is the most popular surname — it is believed to be owned by nearly half the population.

Do Surnames Have Any Meaning?

Chinese Americans are often asked about the meaning of their surname, but many Chinese speakers do not believe that their surnames have any meaning even though almost all are ordinary words found in a dictionary. As the late Dr. Yuen Ren Chao, the internationally renowned linguist, explained: "Even if the character happens to be a common word with meaning, in the context in which it is used as a surname, one usually disregards the meaning except when intentionally making a pun of it."

Elsdon Smith made the same observation about the surnames of European origin. As he pointed out, the dictionary meaning today could be different from "the meaning of the word at the time and in the place where the family name came into existence."

Nonetheless, when a Chinese American is asked about the meaning of his or her surname, it seems easier to give the dictionary definition, as in the following surnames:

Selected spellings	Dictionary meaning	Surname character
Bai, Bock, Pai	the color white	白
Be, Ma, Mah, Mar	horse	馬
Cai, Choy, Tsai	weeds, herbs	蔡
Chiang, Gong, Jiang, Kiang	a large river	江
Chu, Gee, Jee, Zhu	red, vermilion color	朱
Hsiung, Hung, Xiong	a brown bear	熊
Huang, Hwang, Wong	brown or yellow color	黃
Lam, Lin, Ling	forest	林
Lan	the color blue	藍
Lei, Loui, Louie	thunder	雷
Mei, Moy, Mui	plum	梅
New, Niu	ox	牛
Ngan, Yan, Yen	color	顏
Shek, Shi, Shih	stone	石

Sometimes the dictionary meaning is puzzling as to why the following surnames were adopted:

Selected spellings	Dictionary meaning	Surname character
Hall, He, Ho, Hoh	what, how	何
Hu, Woo, Wu	I, me, myself, we	胡
Mac, Mo, Mock	not, if	莫
Yee, Yu	why, what, how	余
Yu	in, at, with	于

Sometimes the only dictionary definition is "a surname," as seen for the following names: Chai, Chak, Zhai (翟); Chia, Jia (賈); Hao (郝); and Nee, Ngai, Ni (聶).

Matrilineal Surnames

Chinese surnames, as a rule, are patriarchal names. Yet matrilineal ones have long existed in China although not to the extent that they occur in Japan. The Japanese people are far more accepting than other Asians of a man adopting his wife's surname officially so that her family name can continue to exist. Perhaps due to the Japanese occupation of Taiwan from 1895 to 1945, many Chinese matrilineal surnames arose among the Taiwanese. Parents either alternated in conferring their surnames to their children or they bestowed both surnames.

About 35 patrilineal/matrilineal surnames, such as *Chang-Chien* and *Fan-Chiang*, have been officially recognized according to Chen and Fried, authors of a study of names in Taiwan. Dr. Ed Tanng, a Presbyterian minister who emigrated from Taiwan, explained that matrilineal surnames arose because the Japanese required proof of property inheritance through the surname. This is why his surname is spelled in this particular way: *Tan* is his mother's surname and *Ng* is his father's.

After the People's Republic of China was established in 1949, parents on mainland China could give either the patrilineal or matrilineal surname to their children. But, according to one report, the one child-per-family policy in 1979 put a stop to this practice. Instead, more parents began to use the mother's surname as a given name for a child and it is predicted that there will be an increase of Chinese personal names consisting of two surnames.

Euro-Americans are generally familiar about using surnames as given names since it has long been an American name tradition to give the mother's original surname as a middle name for a child. We may not even remember that the following given names were once family names: *Beverly, Douglas, Jackson, Kimberly, Ryan, Scott,* and *Shirley.*

Surname Changing and New Surnames

Chen and Fried also noted a "massive name changing into Japanese surnames" in Taiwan during the Japanese occupation. However, the Chinese reverted to their original family names immediately after World War II ended in 1945. Even though they adopted Japanese surnames, the Chinese carefully took one that gave a clue to the actual Chinese family name. For example, the surname Lei (雷) is pronounced in Japanese as *Amada*. A person with the surname Chen (陳) might adopt *Egawa* because it is the Japanese pronunciation of the name *Ying Chuan*, the ancient territorial name of the Chen clans. (Clan territorial names are explained more fully in Part III.)

The Chinese in other Asian countries have also felt obliged to take on new names to conform to the language and culture of the host country. For example, *Chin* is the Chinese surname of the well-placed Sophonpanich family in Thailand and *Liem* is the original family name of the Salims of Indonesia who are descendants of Liem Sioe Liong who took the Indonesian name *Sudono Salim*. Many Chinese family names were Hispanicized in the Philippines, according to the writer Lynn Pan, and tend to end in "co"—as in *Cojuangco*. This stands for the Chinese word meaning "elder brother," which the early Hokkien emigrants used in addressing one another. Some of these surnames have been brought to America in recent decades.

An ethnic Chinese from Indonesia once mentioned that her surname *Agung* was adopted by her family because, beginning in the late 1960s, all citizens are encouraged by the government to have Indonesian names. A recent report on names and human rights, however, points out that the Indonesian government enacted laws that forbade public use of Chinese written characters and the existence of Chinese language schools. It believed that the Chinese would be more assimilable if they discarded their Chinese names and Chinese language. Thailand also has a name law which compels the Chinese there to adopt Thai names.

Several countries in Europe, such as France and Germany, have name laws as well that require citizens to have officially approved names. In comparison, the United States does not have legislation regarding names. Americans are free to select whatever name they wish for themselves and their children; they can even change their names as long as it is not for criminal purposes.

While the Chinese are generally free to choose their names, they have had some name taboos and rules which were primarily for the purpose of showing respect to authority. Otherwise the Chinese, as a people, have tended to follow certain name practices, honed over the centuries, which would place the individual firmly within the hierarchy of his family and clan, avoid the repetition of names among family members, and keep the family and clan's genealogical records precise and clear. Interestingly, the compelling reason for a Chinese to change his or her name is to avoid having the exact same name as another person.

4. ON CHINESE GIVEN NAMES

"We avoid the name, but do not avoid the surname. The surname is common; the name is peculiar." (In reference to speaking of the dead.)
Mencius (372–289 B.C.), Bk. 7, Pt. 2: 36

An oft-repeated observation about the Han Chinese is that they are a pragmatic people with a taste for "a balanced, symmetrical and hierarchical view of things." Certainly this "hierarchical view of things" is imbued in their name traditions. As a rule, names are not repeated from one generation to the next. Children are not named after fathers and grandfathers — a taboo once forbade them to state their names aloud. No Jr. or numbers, such as II and III, appear at the end of a Chinese name although Professor Wolfgang Bauer of Germany discovered, in his in-depth and extensive study of Chinese personal names, that sons have been named after their fathers.

Be that as it may, the prevailing custom is that children are not named after a close living relative — a taboo also observed by Ashkenazi Jews. Nor can they be named after dead relatives. As Margaret M.Y. Sung observed in her study of name customs in Taiwan, children are not named after parents, grandparents, uncles, aunts or any older family relative, including in-laws.

In traditional etiquette, children do not address their elders by their given name — you may only call or refer to a younger relative by name. Kinship terms are used instead. Hence there are no Aunt Barbaras or Uncle Peters. They would be called by such terms as "Aunt Number Four" or "Paternal Older Uncle Number One." Incidentally, the number after a kinship term is by gender order, not birth order. Although "Paternal Older Uncle Number One" may be the first son, he could be the fourth child. You would always know from the kinship term for a paternal uncle whether he is older or younger than your father because the Chinese are more specific on paternal rather than maternal relationships.

Some traditional families even name their children according to birth order — the word Seven can be a name. Close relatives of the same generation may even ask to speak to "Cousin Seven." Because of these name traditions, a person may not know the given names of older relatives.

Another name taboo forbade naming a child after a hero or too famous a person because this was considered presumptuous and disrespectful. The way to get around it, according to Professor Bauer, was to select just one of the characters in that famous person's name for a namesake. Like parents everywhere, Chinese parents may hope that by choosing such a name, some of the qualities that led to such fame or wealth will rub off on their child.

Despite these name taboos, the Chinese have been quite creative in their selection of given names. This is because they compose their given names, taking words from the common written language; words deemed suitable for names. Moreover, over the centuries, the popular practice of having two characters for a given name has enabled them to avoid the repetition of names among family members. Thus, in contrast to the limited number of Chinese family names, there is a seemingly limitless number of Chinese given names — this is in reference, of course, to the disyllabic or the two-character name.

Manufactured Names

Still, certain patterns occur in the selection of names. Manufactured names offer a wonderful opportunity for parents to choose a good name for a child, to express hope and aspiration for a good life, to wish the child good luck, health, prosperity, and knowledge. For example, the architect I.M. Pei's name, *Ieoh-Ming*, means "pen, engraving." A name like *Shao-sun* means "continue, faith." Patriotism may be voiced, such as *Guo En* which means "nation, favored." Politics of the times may be revealed. During the Cultural Revolution (ca. 1966–1971), the word *hong*, meaning "red," took on the meaning of "revolution." Therefore a name such as *Hong Hong* can mean either "red rainbow" or "revolution, rainbow."

A wide range of subject matter is seen in Chinese names. Some are animal names, such as Tiger or *hu*, Dragon or *long*, and Ox or *niu*, which are very popular for males. Names of flowers appear in women's names, such as Orchid or *lan*. Names of precious stones are commonly seen, such as Pearl or *zhu* and Jade or *yu*. You can even find directions for North, East, South and West in names. Words meaning "hill," "dew," and "brocade" are used for names. A current name fashion is to select a "lucky" name based on the number of strokes in a character.

Nonetheless, certain words appear more frequently in names, such as *wen* (*mun* in Cantonese), which means "wisdom"; *sheng*, "to conquer"; and *de*, "virtue." Because most given names consist of two characters, those who have *De* for a name are not just plain *Virtue*— they can be *Kind Virtue* or *Virtuous Rule*. Those who are named *Orchid*— a popular name for females — may be *Introduce Orchid*, *Moon Orchid*, or *Jade Orchid*. It is this combination of two characters for a given name that makes Chinese names so unique — there is certainly no drought of Chinese disyllabic names.

Moreover, this increases the mathematical odds against a name being repeated. If you were to walk into a room and met 60 Chinese men and women who all have the usual two-character given name, it is highly unlikely that you will find a single repeat of names. But if they all had monosyllabic or one-character given names, then several names are apt to be repeated due to the penchant that the Chinese have for certain names. Two persons may even have the same personal name — surname and given name — because of the paucity of surnames.

The repeat of one-character names is similar to finding repeats of names in a group of 60 American men and women. In all likelihood there will be two Pauls and two Johns for an older group of men and undoubtedly there will be two Mikes and two Joshuas in a group of younger men or children. Fewer repeats in names happen for women because parents tend to be less conservative when naming daughters.

Repeats in American given names occur because of name fashions and the custom of naming a child after a family member. For several decades, *Mary* was the most popular name for American women born before the 1950s; *Ashley* became popular after 1990. Even though Americans also have manufactured names, such as *Twenetta* and *Wonderful*, these form no more than 15 percent of American names, according to George Stewart, the author of *American Given Names*.

Meaning of Given Names

Even though Chinese given names may be composed of meaningful words, it is not unusual to be told by a Chinese speaker that the two-character name is not necessarily meaningful. For example, *Yutang*, the given name of the writer Lin Yutang (1895–1976), mean "language" and "hall," respectively. It does not mean "Hall of Language."

Coincidentally, this explanation applies as well to European dithemic names. As Elsdon Smith explains, *William* is a dithemic name composed of two elements: *vilja* or "resolution," and *helma* or "helmet." *William* means "resolution" plus "helmet," not "helmet of resolution."

Sometimes one can conjure up a picture of a name being bestowed. When a young Chinese American was asked for the meaning her Chinese name *Houming*, she immediately replied: "It doesn't have any." Then she admitted that *hou* means "empress" and *ming* means "cry." In thinking further about her name, she added, "My mother did tell me that I cried a lot as a baby." One can readily picture her mother sighing resignedly each time her bundle of joy wailed: "There goes the empress again!"

Unisex Names

"If names are not correct, language is not in accordance with the truth of things," Confucius commented.

Actually, the philosopher was referring to the need for a ruler to behave like a ruler, a father to behave like a father, and a son to behave like a son, because of the expectations that these terms can conjure up. According to Dr. Wu Tehyao of Singapore, who has lectured widely on Confucius, the Chinese believe that this comment extends to personal names. They strongly believe that there is a power to names and therefore a given name must be chosen with great care and aforethought.

Yet it is not always possible to distinguish a man's name from a woman's name or vice versa. *Jade* or *Yu*, for example, can be a name for a man. *Ping* or "Peace" and *Mei*, which means "beautiful" or "excellent," are two other popular unisex names. (*Mei* is an especially popular Chinese name for Chinese American women.) A Chinese language school teacher once expressed surprise that one of the girls in his class was named *Wah*, which is another term for the country of China. He thought it was more appropriate as a boy's name.

But, by and large, the Chinese have long accepted the custom of men and women having the same words in their names. In some countries, unisex names are not allowed by law. The reason stated by a government bureaucrat in Germany was "...if a name is on a list and nobody knows if it's a man or woman, then difficulties can arise."

"I-want-a-son" Names

However, there is a type of woman's name that would never be mistaken for a man's name. It expresses disappointment in the birth of a daughter — the obsession about having sons is so strong. It is not unusual for a woman to have a name like *Zhao-di*, meaning "Ask for a brother" or *Pan-di*—"Hope for a brother." A friend once said that her mother's name means "Don't want."

Yet sons can also receive terrible names at birth because of superstitious beliefs. Such names as *Dustpan*, *That Dog*, and *Flea* have been bestowed in the hope of fooling the gods into thinking that the baby was not worthy of attention and therefore will let him live. Boy babies have even been named *Girl*, revealing long-established social attitudes toward women. The parents of the late Bruce Lee, the actor known for his prowess in gungfu, named him *Girl* because their first-born son had died in childbirth. To further bolster this deception, they dressed him as a girl and even told friends that he was a girl.

Multiple Names in Name Traditions

A miserable name given a boy in infancy, however, was not usually used when he grew older. In traditional Chinese society, a man could have more than one given name — called a *ming*— to see him through the different stages of life. These include:

1. a milk name or *xiao ming* (meaning "small name") that was bestowed at birth;
2. a *da ming* (meaning "great name") or school name which could be bestowed a few months after birth or when the child entered school;
3. a *hao* (號), variously translated as an adult name, a marriage name, or style;
4. a *zi* (or tzu, tzyh — 字), also known as a style or a courtesy name;
5. a *bie hao*, a nom de plume or pen name.

The terms *hao* and *zi* can be quite confusing because in the literature on Chinese names, the *zi* is called an adult name and the *hao* a courtesy name. According to Dr. Yuen Ren Chao and Professor Bauer, the meanings of these two terms were switched around in modern usage.

Because of the high respect for teachers, they were often asked to bestow the *da ming* or school name and even the *hao*. Incidentally, a man's *da ming* and *hao* could be opposite in meaning or act in tandem. For example, if his *da ming* means *War*, then his adult name may mean *Peace*. An example of these names acting in tandem is seen in the names for the son of Confucius. He was named *Carp* because when he was born, the family received this fish as a present. Carp's adult name was *Bo Yu*, meaning "first-born fish."

Art experts rely on the *bie hao* of an artist for authenticating the provenance of a Chinese painting. Famous writers usually had several because this could create an illusion of wide support. For example, the scholar and diplomat Hu Shih had twenty-four *bie hao*.

One of the *bie hao* used by Sun Yat-sen, the Father of the Republic of China, is *Zhongshan*. After his death in 1925, and to honor their favorite son, this became the name of the former Xiangshan district (*Heung Shan* in Cantonese) where he was born in Guangdong province. Dr. Sun adopted this *bie hao* when he sought refuge in Japan before the overthrow of the Qing dynasty in 1911 — it is *Nakayama* in Japanese. To this day, the Cantonese call him *Dr. Sun Chung-shan*.

Regardless of how many names a Chinese person owned, none was ever discarded. Of course, friends would never call a person by his *milk name* if he had other names — it was reserved for family use. But not everyone in traditional China had several names. A working-class man most likely had only a *milk name*. Women had a *milk name* and a *marriage name* which consisted solely of their original surname, as in *Pang Shee*. Relatively few women would have had a *school name* since regular schooling for girls was not required until after the Republic of China was established.

One-Character vis-à-vis Two-Character Given Names

Historically, the one-character given name is the older form of name than the two-character name. It was not until the Ming dynasty (1368–1644) that the two-character given name stabilized in usage, but it was not until 1900 that it comprised 80 percent of all given names. According to Professor Bauer, one-character and two-character names see-sawed in popularity prior to the Ming, mainly in response to social conditions and politics of the day.

During the Early Han dynasty (202 B.C.–A.D. 9), one-character names formed 70 percent of all given names. Two-character names became even more scarce, dropping to a mere 2 percent of all names when Wang Mang (A.D. 9–23) usurped the Han throne. In his intense dislike of such names, he issued an edict to stamp them out. His law was not repealed until four hundred years later. This was during the fifth century, toward the end of the Sixteen Kingdoms period (A.D. 301–439), an era of social and political turmoil.

China was divided in North and South divisions: the North was ruled by non–Chinese tribes, such as the Toba Turks, and, as more non–Chinese poured into the country, the Han Chinese began moving south. Chinese government officials belonged to the elite *shi* or "scholar-bureaucrat" class but had to provide proof of their pedigree, preferably one that was traced back to an official of the Han dynasty. As a result, genealogy studies flourished and more Chinese began using the two-character given name. As we shall see in the next chapter, this provided an excellent means for establishing lineage.

Reunification of China occurred with the Sui dynasty (581–618) and during the mighty Tang dynasty (A.D. 618–907) that followed, two-character given names became so popular that they reached a peak of 60 percent of all names. This was the first time when disyllabic given names outnumbered monosyllabic names. But the one-character name took over again in the Five Dynasties era (907–960) that followed the Tang.

Two hundred years later, when the Southern Song dynasty (1127–1279) reigned, the two-character given names made a comeback and peaked anew at 60 percent. This was the era of Neo-Confucianism when the teachings of Confucius were reinterpreted, when clans were strong, and when the traditional family and clan system was in its glory.

Then when the Mongols ruled China during the Yuan dynasty (1264–1368), people went back to having a one-character name. When the Han Chinese ruled again during the Ming dynasty, the two-character given name made a solid recovery. And it was during the Qing, the last dynasty, that the two-character given name became the quintessential Chinese name because the Manchus admired and promoted Chinese culture.

The Vocative "Ah" in Names

One more ancient name custom should be mentioned because of its direct bearing on some surnames belonging to Americans of Chinese descent. It involves the vocative *Ah* for calling a person by name, as in "Ah Wei." This is a central and southern Chinese name custom. The use of *Ah* denotes familiarity when addressing a person by name, whether man, woman, or child, and seems to

The middle character of the Chinese name engraved on this gravestone is commonly used for the syllable "Ah" in names.

Also used for the syllable "Ah" is the third character down in the Chinese name found in the center column of this gravestone.

soften the abruptness of a monosyllabic name. Kinship terms are also prefixed by this syllable, as in *Ah Gung* or "Ah maternal grandfather" and *Ah Gu-gu* or "Ah father's sister."

Historic records indicate that about two thousand years before our common era, a Shang dynasty ruler called his trusted adviser "A-hang." James Legge, translator of the Chinese Classics, believed that this was his title. This may explain why some authors define *Ah* as an "honorific" or as a close equivalent to "Mr." Be that as it may, this vocative was definitely a prefix to a given name during the Han dynasty: "A Kiao" was the *milk name* of a consort to the Emperor Wu Ti and "A Man" was the *milk name* of the Emperor Xuan-zong of the Tang dynasty.

The Cantonese not only use *Ah* as a prefix to a name, they repeat it after the name when trying to catch a person's attention, as in "Ah Ngoon ah!" The Hokkien of southern Fujian province place *Ah* after a name, as in "Ying Ah." In North China, familiarity is indicated by the use of *lao* (meaning "venerable" or "old") as a prefix to the surname, as in *lao Wang* or "old Wang."

Perhaps this use of the vocative *Ah* and the word *lao* is due to the fact that neither the family name nor the monosyllabic given name can be stated by itself. As Dr. Y.R. Chao points out, it is only the two-character given name that can stand by itself. In addition to the vocative *Ah*, the monosyllabic given name is usually mentioned with the surname. The surname by itself can be more formally stated with a title, such as Teacher Wang or Premier Li.

Chinese name traditions and etiquette in addressing relatives are the same all over China, albeit with local and regional variations. For thousands of years, names have been regarded as a means for pinpointing family relationships. And this concept is exquisitely expressed when one of the characters in a disyllabic given name is used as a *generation name*.

5. THE GENERATION NAME

"...Generations forever and ever glorifying their ancestors."
a line from a Woo clan generation name poem

Since early on in their civilization, the Chinese have placed the surname first in a name, which seems to emphasize that the family comes first in an individual's identity. Other Asians, such as the Japanese, Koreans, and Vietnamese, also place the surname first. In Europe, Hungarians and Rumanians follow this name order as well. But the Chinese went a step further: they developed a naming system in which the given name indicates relationships within a family and clan.

In traditional society, brothers usually have a two-character given name in which one of the characters is repeated in each name, and this character is also found in the names of their male first cousins who have the same family name. This constant element to their names is described as a *generation name* because it indicates that they belong to the same generation of the same family and clan. Traditionally, sisters have a different character repeated in their names and it would not appear in the names of their female first cousins. Although either the first or second character of a two-character given name can be used as a generation name, usually the first character is the constant element.

An analogy of a generation name for an American family would be if two brothers were named Alan and Alex and their sisters were named Lisa and Teresa. The "al" sound that is repeated in the boys' names and the "sa" sound that is heard in the girls' name represent their generation names. Today, many parents give the same generation name to both sons and daughters. Our hypothetical siblings could therefore be named Brian, Ryan, and Marion — names that end in the same syllable.

The Chinese call this naming custom *Pai-hang* (排行), which means "ranking in rows." It is uniquely Chinese. Its original purpose was to identify men according to generation in their family and clan so as to determine their relationship to one another. As such, it reveals both horizontal and vertical dimensions of a family and clan. As Professor Wolfgang Bauer explains, the

51

generation name in the names of siblings represents the horizontal *Pai-hang* and when all the generation names for a clan are listed together, this depicts the vertical *Pai-hang*. Each generation therefore must be distinguished by a different generation name. This naming system not only pinpoints the position of a man in the hierarchy of his family and clan, it facilitates the observance of proper etiquette and correct mourning rituals.

There were no laws requiring families to follow the *Pai-hang* naming system; yet, down through the centuries, most families have done so. This is similar to the fact that there is no law requiring Americans to have two given names—a name custom that originated with the early German immigrants—yet this is possessed by the vast majority of Americans. It seems safe to say that even though a Chinese American may not have two Western given names, he or she will have—that is, if there are siblings—a generation name in the Chinese name.

Because the *Pai-hang* naming system—also called *Zi-pai* and *Ban-pai*, among other local terms—reveals sibling and family connections, it is little wonder that in past centuries the Chinese turned to the one-character given name during times of political unrest and social turmoil. Still they returned to the *Pai-hang* time and again, perfecting it along the way over the course of centuries. The concept of names as a means of identifying family ties seems to exemplify the Chinese taste for a balanced, symmetrical, and hierarchical view of things.

Development of the Pai-hang System

The *Pai-hang* took almost a thousand years to develop; however, only the highlights of this complicated naming system can be discussed. According to Professor Bauer, it is divided into an "age *Pai-hang*" and a "generation *Pai-hang*," with the latter subdivided into "partial" and "full" *Pai-hang*.

The "age *Pai-hang*" came first. It began in the late Zhou dynasty— several hundred years before our common era—when the birth order of a son had to appear in his adult name (or *zi*), which was usually a two-character name. At that time, the adult name was an initiation name to signify that the son had come of age and was taking his place in the generation order of the clan.

Synonyms were commonly used instead of numbers to indicate that a son was the first, second, third, or fourth in gender order. Euphemisms were also applied, such as "a blade of grass" for the youngest son. By the Late Han dynasty (A.D. 25–220), gender order began to appear in the *da ming* that was given in

childhood. The status of being the youngest son, however, was not usually announced in this name since it was premature to be stated as fact.

Synonyms were already being used as names in the *da ming* of brothers to indicate their relationship, a naming practice that predates the generation *Pai-hang*. According to Professor Bauer, this occurred during the Early Han (202–A.D. 9). The "partial" generation *Pai-hang* refers to the radical of a word being used as the generation name. This naming practice arose as a result of Wang Mang's law forbidding the use of disyllabic names.

As mentioned earlier, the radical gives the root meaning of a word; and among the common radicals seen in Chinese names are those for gold or metal, man, water, wood, and fire. If, for example, the radical for gold were selected as the generation name, then this would appear in the one-character names for siblings. Certainly the "partial" *Pai-hang* provided a much wider range in name selection than synonyms do. An analogy would be if the names of brothers in an American family all begin with the same initial letter, as in Jamie, Jeffrey, and Jonathan.

In the "full" *Pai-hang*, the entire ideograph represents the generation name. This naming practice occurred as well in the Late Han except that it did not become firmly established until the end of the fifth century, when Wang Mang's law was repealed. As Professor Bauer points out, Koreans and Vietnamese adopted the *Pai-hang* naming system due to the influence of Chinese culture. The Japanese, in comparison, kept their own name customs.

Despite the importance of the generation name, it could be omitted legally when a man signed his name on official documents. For example, if *Chin Duk Soon*'s generation name were Duk, he could sign his name simply as *Chin Soon*. As we shall see later on, this may explain the unusually high number of monosyllabic given names among the early Chinese immigrants.

The Generation Name Poem

The last stage of development of the *Pai-hang* was reached when clans began to use a poem which predetermined the generation name in advance for each generation. According to Professor Bauer, this took place between the end of the Tang and the onset of the Song dynasty in the tenth century. A Liu clan in Guizhou province in western China is credited as being the first to use a generation name poem — called *pai-hang shi*, *zi pai*, among other terms. However, the use of poems did not generally take hold until the Ming dynasty.

The generation name poem gives a sense of meaning to the generation names used by the men of a clan, which otherwise would just constitute a long string of unrelated words when listed together. Most poems usually contain flowery praise for ancestors and hope for the longevity of the clan. For example, the poem for the Woo clan of Taishan district in Guangdong province is roughly translated as meaning:

> Beginning from Emperor Shun, illustrious descendants
> Merit patrimony with the cap of a horned dragon;
> Responsibility transmitted by each family,
> Generations forever and ever glorifying their ancestors.

No word is ever repeated in a generation name poem because each word represents one generation of men. And the number of generations that are represented depends on the length of the poem. When there are five words to a line, poems are either 10 or 20 words in length; the former covers ten generations and the latter, twenty generations. Poems having four words to a line are either 16 or 32 words long. When the last word is used, a clan may recycle the poem, add another line or compose a new poem.

Evidently only men used the poem. According to Chinese Americans who emigrated from southern China, the clan's generation name poem was used only when a man married and adopted a *hao*. For example, if a man of the Woo clan has the word *Responsibility* in his *hao*, this means that his father's generation had the word meaning "horned dragon" in their *hao*, and the word that means "to transmit" should appear in his son's *hao*. Therefore men in traditional China could have two different generation names: one for the *da ming* and one for the *hao*.

It is unusual, however, for a native-born Chinese American man to have more than one Chinese name. The early immigrants apparently did not insist on their native-born sons adopting a *hao* when they were married in this country. When my stepfather, who emigrated from China during the 1920s, was asked about this, he commented: "It's too much trouble to have two Chinese names. We're here in America."

Women and the Pai-hang

Women, again, were left out by these elaborate traditional naming customs. The generation name for sisters is described as a simple sister *Pai-hang* by

Professor Bauer. Nevertheless, in traditional Chinese society, the names of daughters were not included in their clan's genealogy records since they were considered temporary family members. A daughter left her family after marriage and joined the husband's family. She had no family inheritance rights either, family property was divided equally among brothers.

If a clan did list the daughters of a family, it was by number only, such as "Daughter Number Three." Her husband's family and clan were not interested either in recording her given name; only her family name was of importance because of the practice of exogamy. The woman was really an outsider to both family groups and some Chinese kinship terms even reinforce this point of view.

For example, the word *wai*, meaning "outside," always precedes kinship terms for female relatives as well as for male relatives on the maternal side. Maternal grandmother may be called "Poh Poh" colloquially but the polite term for her is *Wai Zu-mu* — the "Outside grandmother." A mother-in-law is the "Outside mother" and the children of a daughter are called the "Outside grandchildren." The practice of distinguishing between maternal and paternal relatives is seen as well in the two words that mean "cousin." *Tong* cousins are paternally related through the same surname because *tong* means "ancestral hall." The other word for "cousin" is *biao*— which means "outside"— and this tells you that these are relatives who are related maternally or through paternal aunts.

Some Modern Modifications

According to Professor Bauer, the *Pai-hang* began to weaken at the end of the Qing dynasty when the generation name was no longer required to be part of the names of male cousins. In the decades that followed the founding of the Republic of China in 1911, the traditional family and clan system was questioned by the Chinese whose thinking was influenced by Western thought, science, and technology. And name customs are usually affected when a society undergoes changes and when traditional ways are challenged.

Today's Chinese married women no longer identify themselves by the traditional marriage name. Men no longer are required to adopt a *hao* when they marry. Although Chinese families and clans tend to keep genealogy records, this activity apparently ceased for a while. From 1950 to 1955, shortly after the People's Republic of China was established, countless genealogies were sought out and destroyed along with numerous books of other subject matter. The late Dr. Hsiang-lin Lo, who lost his extensive collection of clan genealogies, attributed these destructive activities to the government's endeavor to eradicate "reactionary thought of bourgeois society and feudal ideology." No doubt this led to a decline in the use of the generation name poem.

Mr. Ning Wen, formerly a Consul of the People's Republic of China in Los Angeles, thought it unlikely that the generation name poem will ever be referred to again, especially by people in the big cities of China. Instead he sees a trend toward increased use of monosyllabic given names. For example, *Gong Li* is the name of a famous Chinese movie actress. Lu Zhongti, in his study of names in mainland China, traced the preference for a one-character name to the one-child-per-family government policy that was launched in 1979. Parents simply found it more convenient to choose a one-character name for their only child.

In contrast, the generation name is still being conferred to siblings in Taiwan. But the generation name poem is rarely used, according to Bruce Linghu, an Executive Secretary with the Republic of China's Coordination Council for North American Affairs in Los Angeles. Instead he sees two naming trends in Taiwan. One trend is for brothers and sisters to have the same generation name as a means of expressing family unity. (A booklet on Chinese methods for charting a family tree, published in 1987, may be encouraging this naming practice.) For example, the son and two daughters of Chang-Lin Tien, the Chancellor of the University of California at Berkeley, have the same generation name *Chih* in their Chinese names: *Norman Chihan, Phyllis Chihping* and *Kristine Chihyih*.

This modification of the *Pai-hang* naming system reflects present-day social attitudes regarding gender and equality. The traditional way is seen in the names of the famous Soong sisters (Madame Sun Yat-sen and her sisters) and their brothers. *Ling* is the generation name for sisters *E-ling, Ching-ling*, and *Mei-ling*, whereas *Tse* is the generation name for brothers *Tse-vung, Tse-liang*, and *Tse-an*.

The other trend in Taiwan is the use of a pithy phrase of four words as the source for the generation name. For example, the father of a friend selected the phrase *Jin Yu Man Tang* which means "Our house is filled with gold and jade." The first word *Jin* appears in her Chinese name as well as in the names of her brother and cousin.

Although ancient name customs and new naming trends are constantly being mixed together in today's Chinese personal names, the younger generation of Chinese Americans may not have heard of the generation name poem. Out of fifty Chinese Americans of assorted ages and different Chinese dialect background who were questioned not long ago about the name poem, only a handful knew of its existence. One was a native-born man in his fifties whose parents had selected a *hao* for him (though he could not recall it offhand). Another was a woman who emigrated from a country in southeast Asia — she stated that her family has been using a generation name poem for the names of sons and daughters for many years. The majority of the native-born had never heard of a generation name poem but a few of the young people who were born in China thought that one might have been the source for a grandfather's name.

Nonetheless, as we shall see in the next two sections, Chinese name traditions, language and culture must continually be referred to in any explanation of Chinese American names.

PART II

NAMES AS CLUES TO IDENTITY

We have seen how Chinese name traditions can reflect the development of Chinese society and the subsequent fall of the traditional family and clan system in the early part of the twentieth century. Chinese American names tell about the development and recent dramatic growth of an ethnic group whose history in America can be traced back to the mid-nineteenth century. The early immigrants brought centuries-old Chinese name traditions with them. The new immigrants who have come in recent decades brought name practices reflecting the social and political changes that have taken place in mainland China and Taiwan. They have also brought name customs observed in the Chinese communities of different countries.

Since emigration requires Chinese names to be rendered in a different writing system, spelling reveals the dialect divisions of the Chinese spoken language. Spelling variants disclose that various systems were devised to transcribe Mandarin — the Chinese national language — and other major dialects. But because of former restrictions on Chinese immigration, some of the major dialects were not represented in Chinese American names until recent decades.

Names are useful clues to identity in other ways. Name styles — the way names are stated or written — and the group names by which Chinese Americans refer to themselves can reveal how they perceive themselves as Chinese Americans, as being Chinese and as being American.

6. WHO ARE
CHINESE AMERICANS?

*"Let us speak plain: there is more force in names than most men dream
of..."*

James Russell Lowell, *A Glance Behind the Curtain*

Today all of the 100 common family names of China, along with an additional two hundred or more family names, are represented in Chinese American names. Ever since the Chinese began emigrating to this country in the
mid-nineteenth century, they have brought their family names and have tended
to retain them. Should these be referred to as Chinese surnames? Or can we recognize them as being native to this country? To Elsdon Smith, "All family names
in the United States can be and should be classified as 'American' names." Unfortunately, this perception of names being "American" has not been extended
unequivocally to Chinese Americans themselves or to other Asian Americans.

As late as 1989, John Kuo Wei Tchen, the featured speaker at the Martin
Luther King, Jr., Holiday Celebration sponsored by the Smithsonian Institution, pointed out: "Asians in the U.S. have been cast as perpetual foreigners, no
matter how many generations we have been here." Nor is it unusual for a native-
born Asian American to be told, "You speak English very well!"

"Where do you come from?" is a question that can be annoying because it
assumes that the native-born Asian American is a foreigner. As a respondent in
a *Dear Abby* column explained, no bias would be attached if white persons asked
this of one another. But, in his experience, people who ask this question invari-
ably "find it hard to believe that an Asian-looking person is actually a native,
true-blue, 100% American — and not a recently arrived immigrant from some
foreign country."

Our family was once jolted by this perception of being considered foreigners. After worshipping in a church in the small town where we lived in
Southern California during the early 1960s — a town that had perhaps three non-
white families at the time — a kindly white-haired lady approached our sons, who

were about twelve and ten years old. She asked: "Do you speak English?" We were all startled by this question since we were already conversing in English with some of the churchgoers. But the youngest son quickly recovered and blurted out, "I do, but he doesn't!"—whereupon they both ran off giggling.

Many people who lump all Asian Americans together as foreigners are undoubtedly not familiar with the history of Asian Americans; they are only aware that there are large numbers of new immigrants from Asia. Of the six largest Asian American groups—those of Chinese, Filipino, Japanese, Asian Indian, Korean, and Vietnamese descent—only Japanese Americans are predominantly native-born. Up until the 1970s, the majority of Chinese Americans were also native-born except that new immigration reversed the ratio: the 1980 federal census listed the foreign-born at 63 percent and their numbers increased to 69 percent in the 1990 census.

Prior to the 1970s, there were relatively few Asian Americans; their numbers dramatically increased after the general immigration act of 1965 removed all former restrictions on immigration from Asia. The end of the Vietnam War in 1975 contributed to a sudden influx of new immigrants from southeast Asian countries, many of whom are ethnic Chinese. Since 1980, immigration from Asia has surpassed that from Europe and Latin America and, it is estimated, by the year 2000, Asian Americans will comprise about 4 percent of the total U.S. population. In comparison, they made up only 1.5 percent of the total U.S. population in 1980.

Group Names

Asian American is a relatively new term; the old terms include *Oriental, Oriental American*, and *Asiatic*. Although the early Chinese immigrants who arrived during the mid–nineteenth century were called *Chinese*, they were more often referred to as *Chinaman, Chinawoman, Chinee* (without the letter "s"), *Mongolian, Celestial*, and *coolie*, a derogatory term. Evidently, *Chink* came into usage around 1900. While many Chinese Americans regard *Chinaman* as derogatory, they are quite united in regarding *Chink* as a most offensive term.

The term *Asian American* was coined during the Asian American Movement that was launched in the late 1960s, one of the last of the "ethnic-consciousness" movements of that turbulent decade. The young activists and their many supporters were inspired by African-Americans who had spoken out earlier against racism and economic oppression and they, too, wanted to change the future and have America live up to her promises. They wanted a better world for all peoples.

These young activists objected to the word *Oriental* because it tends to conjure up the image of an "exotic, mysterious, strange, and foreign" person. Moreover, this word gives the impression that Americans of Asian ancestry are "strangers" even though their families may have lived here for several generations.

When William Safire commented in his column in *The New York Times* that he intended to continue using the word Oriental, several respondents chastised him. One pointed out that this term is "Eurocentric." Another stated: "You have oriented the world from a Western standpoint ... and that's what's wrong with calling Asians 'Orientals.'" Interestingly, these comments were made by white males, judging from their surnames.

Asian Americans also did not want to be hyphenated Americans, either, because this implies being less than a first-class American citizen. As the fictional character Wittman Ah Sing, in *Tripmaster Monkey* by Maxine Hong Kingston, remarked: "'And Chinese-American' is inaccurate — as if we could have two countries. We need to take the hyphen out — 'Chinese American.' 'American,' the noun, and 'Chinese,' the adjective. From now on: 'Chinese Americans.'"

This relatively new term, *Chinese American*, seems fitting because Chinese Americans now seem to be a new group of people due to the influx of new immigrants. But not all Chinese Americans agree on this description. In 1988, the editors of *Amerasia Journal*, organ of the Asian American Studies Center at the University of California in Los Angeles, commented that Chinese Americans have yet to define themselves from their own perspective. They noticed that disputes exist over terminology for Chinese Americans, involving such matters as "political status, ethnic affiliation, residence and citizenship, and cultural and racial identification."

Before World War II, when the Chinese exclusion laws were in effect, it seems that both foreign-born and native-born Chinese Americans thought of themselves as being Chinese and that only white people were Americans. The terms *American-Chinese* and *Chinese-American* came into usage during the war because of a strong feeling of patriotism and a sense of solidarity in fighting a common enemy with other Americans.

I recall the time when my announcement that I consider myself an American brought on a choking reaction from my mother. "Go look in the mirror," she cried. "Do you think the *fan guei* will believe that?" (*Fan guei* and *guei lo* are commonly used by all classes of Chinese in reference to white people; terms that mean "foreign devil," "foreign ghost" or "barbarian"— in other words outsiders who don't count. Some Chinese Americans use the term *lo fan* meaning "old barbarian," which they believe is less offensive. Actually, a polite term for a white person is *xi ren* or "Westerner.")

Even a few decades ago, the idea of an American being a white person was still being assumed and it was not confined to the United States. When our third-generation daughter went to Greece in 1971 for a summer student program, her host family was extremely disappointed that they had not been assigned an "American" student. When our daughter visited Ecuador several years later, the natives there shook their heads in disbelief when she called herself an "American." Then when she lived in Taiwan for a college semester in the late 1970s, the Chinese she met laughed when she called herself a *meiguo ren*— which means an "American." "That's a white person!" they exclaimed.

It seems safe to say that the early Chinese immigrants did not think of themselves as being American; they were Chinese. They referred to themselves as *Gum sahn hahk*, *Tong yan*, and *Wah kiu*— terms that give a sense of locality. *Gum sahn hahk* means "gold mountain guest"; *Gum sahn* refers to California and, by extension, to the United States. (The better known term for America is *Mei Guo*, which means "Beautiful Country.") When the early immigrants returned to China, calling themselves *Gum sahn hahk*, everyone knew where they had been. And the Chinese were really "guests"— or unwanted intruders — since the 1882 Chinese exclusion law specifically denied them the privilege of naturalized citizenship.

The term *Tong yan* or "Tong people" is used by both the Cantonese and the Hokkien in the adjacent Fujian province to describe themselves. (The Chinese in other provinces use the term "Han people.") The word *Tong* recalls the glory and might of the Tang dynasty (618–907) when this area of China was heavily settled by people from other parts of China.

Wah kiu — or *Huaquiao* in Mandarin — means "overseas Chinese." According to one definition, it denotes a people who will always maintain, despite settling in another country, their distinctive Chinese culture. The Overseas Chinese Affairs office in Beijing defines this term as "those who still retain Chinese citizenship and who live permanently abroad...." Chinese nationals who become naturalized citizens of their adopted countries are called *Waiji huaren*.

Prior to World War II, both immigrants and their descendants were called *Wah kiu*. Old-timers might call themselves "old overseas Chinese." In comparison, new immigrants today might call themselves *Huaren* ("people of Chinese origin"), which indicates a "common ancestry and a shared cultural background."

Evidently the term *Zhongguoren* ("person of China") has more of a political overtone.

Because these terms are from the Chinese point of view, the historian Him Mark Lai believes that the term *Meiji Huaren*—*meiji* means "American citizen"—better represents the Chinese American point of view. However, there is an even more appropriate term that the native-born Chinese American can use and that is *Huayi* (or *Wah yeuih* in Cantonese) because it means "descendant of a Chinese person."

Incidentally, the terms *foreign stock* and *native stock* have been used by the U.S. Census Bureau in analyzing the nativity of the American population. The foreign stock category includes the foreign-born, the American who was born in another country, and the American who was born in this country of one or two foreign-born parents. Those in the native stock category are Americans who were born in this country and have two native-born parents.

Group Solidarity?

According to sociologists, the cohesiveness of an ethnic group can be measured by the acceptance of its name. If the 1994 issue of *Who's Who Among Asian Americans* is any indication, the term *Chinese American* is well accepted: over 72 percent of the 2,700 persons of Chinese descent listed described themselves as such. They were either born in the United States, mainland China, or Hong Kong. In comparison, those born in Taiwan tended to be described as "Taiwanese American." Birthplace was also mentioned in such descriptions as "Hong Kong American" and "Singaporean American." This variety of responses about ethnic origin was not found among Asian Americans of Japanese, Korean, Filipino, and Vietnamese descent.

"Conflict is implicit to a Chinese American identity," the writer Laurence Yep once observed. He attributed this to the emphasis on individualism in America and to the stress on interdependence in Chinese culture. Because of these opposing views, Chinese Americans—even those of part–Chinese ancestry—may have difficulty in defining themselves.

At one end of the scale of being Chinese American, some view themselves as being totally American. At the other end of the scale, the emphasis is on being Chinese. These perceptions may be linked to the number of generations in this country and to social, educational, and economic background. These perceptions undoubtedly have an influence on one's way of life. According to

Dr. L. Ling-chi Wang of the University of California at Berkeley, most of the educated Chinese who immigrated in recent decades adopt the "accommodation strategy" in adjusting to life in this country. That is, they become naturalized citizens and assume an American lifestyle in public without giving up their private Chinese lifestyle and Chinese cultural values.

The perception of being Chinese evidently involves other viewpoints. Recently a Taiwanese-American leader was quoted as saying: "Many people from Taiwan have trouble deciding whether they are Chinese or Taiwanese because the word *Chinese* does not provide a distinction between heritage and political identity."

Derogatory Names

Not surprisingly, Chinese Americans who do not speak Chinese may be told that they are "not really Chinese." This message is found in the term *ABC* which stands for "American-born Chinese." It implies that the native-born who cannot speak Chinese has either rejected or lost his Chinese heritage. Yet many native-born Chinese Americans cheerfully use this term in describing themselves.

ABC came into existence, I believe, during the 1970s at the same time as *FOB* — "Fresh off the boat" — a term that disparages the new immigrants. (The fact that they arrive at airports is irrelevant.) Apparently the term *ABC* distresses some parents who try to instill a Chinese identity in their children. As one woman wrote: "Many do not speak the Chinese language, but, in contrast to Chinese-American youths of the '60s and '70s, who tended to ignore their roots, the ABCs of the '80s are proud of their Asian heritage. My children speak the language..."

Prior to World War II, the belittling term for the native-born was *Jook sing*. It means "hollow of a bamboo." To the uninitiated, these may seem inoffensive words except that it is like calling someone *Airhead*. It implies that, due to the inability to speak Chinese, such a person has no culture and is too Americanized. Sometimes the native-born retaliated by calling their foreign-born peers *China-born* and *Jook kok* — "node of a bamboo." Since this is the thickest part of the plant, it implies stupidity or thickheadedness. It seems that these terms have been replaced by *ABC* and *FOB*.

Derogatory terms within an ethnic group are not unusual and any antagonistic feelings that exist in China between people of different regions and dialect groups have been brought to this country. When a visiting film director from mainland China was recently interviewed, he was quoted as saying: "I grew up in Northern China, which is a totally different culture from the south. Asian Americans are mostly from Canton, the south. I'm basically not fond of them, originally in China." Many educated Chinese who came to this country after 1949 were known to shun the Chinatowns because "they were neither merchants nor the descendants of coolies."

Because the native-born descendants of the early immigrants tend to lack the ability to speak Chinese and are not purists in observing Chinese traditions, they have been severely criticized. They have been depicted recently in some scholarly journals and books as being filled with self-hatred, as having rejected Chinese culture and, despite a craving for assimilation into white society, as still being shut out of the mainstream. As Dr. L. Ling-chi Wang points out, some of the criticisms leveled against them include moving out of the Chinatowns, dyeing their hair, and even Anglicizing their family names.

In contrast to these opinions, Professor Wolfram Eberhard of the University of California once wrote that many Chinese Americans in California are descended from "adventurous" businessmen. Recent research by Dr. Sucheng Chan confirms this: "By allowing merchants to have their wives with them, the [exclusion] laws made it possible for them to reproduce themselves biologically more readily than could other groups. That meant they could reproduce themselves socially as well, since the vast majority of the second-generation Chinese Americans were children of merchants who grew up in family settings with a petit bourgeois orientation."

Counting by Generation

The early Chinese immigrants, however, were relatively slow as a group to establish family life in this country. They strongly believed in following Chinese family customs which, at the time, dictated that a wife should stay home to care for her husband's parents when he left to seek a living elsewhere. Family life was also delayed because of the Chinese exclusion laws. The resident laborer could not send for his wife or children from China, and it was not until 1900 that it was judicially determined that the merchant could bring his family from China.

Most of the early immigrants were married and many made trips back to China periodically to see their families. Many sent for a son to join them in this country. When the son reached marriageable age, he usually returned to China to marry and started a family before coming back. This pattern was repeated when the son sent for his son. Betty Lee Sung, the sociologist, described this as a "predominant form of family life" that lasted until 1946.

A recent genealogical report by David Hom, a college student, illustrates this form of family life. His great-great-grandfather was an herbalist who arrived in Los Angeles in 1870, at age 28, leaving his wife and children behind in China. In 1882, a son — Hom's great-grandfather — joined him in this country, and left his wife behind. He returned to China in 1892, coming back in 1912 to Los Angeles, bringing a young son with him. Then this son — Hom's grandfather — went back to China in 1923 to marry except that his wife came with him on his return to this city. Subsequently, nine children, including Hom's father, were born to them.

Due to this pattern of family life, some Chinese Americans have difficulty in identifying themselves by the number of generations in this country. There is not the neatness of counting by generation as Japanese Americans do, such as describing the immigrant generation as *Issei* or "first generation," the native-born children as *Nisei* or "second generation," and the next native-born generation as *Sansei* or "third generation," and so forth. The early Japanese immigrants, who came two decades later than the Chinese, were more quick to establish family life because the Japanese government encouraged them to send for a wife and settle in this country.

How would one count Hom's family by generation? Is his father the second generation? Or was his great-great-grandfather the first generation? Or should his grandfather who established a family here in this country be counted as the first generation?

Counting by generation can be confusing to some families. A manager of a Chinese restaurant in San Francisco once proudly stated that he is of the "fifth generation" because his great-great-great-grandfather came to work on the railroad. But he himself was the first in the direct line of descendants to emigrate to America! Another man who came as a teenager from China with his parents, referred to his own child, who was born in this country, as "third generation." If one were to follow the Japanese American way of counting by generation, then grandparents, parents and children who emigrate at the same time are all "first generation."

Thus the term *1.5 generation* was coined. It came into usage during the 1970s when Korean Americans, who emigrated in family groups, discovered that the immigrant who came as a child had the same kinds of experience growing up in America as the native-born or second generation. Then there is the mixed generation parentage. Judge Delbert Wong and his wife Dolores, of Los Angeles, are "third-generation" and "fourth-generation," respectively. Both of their fathers were born in China. Judge Wong's mother was born in Weaverville, California, and Mrs. Wong's mother and grandmother were born in San Francisco. (Both mothers lost their American citizenship when they married their foreign-born husbands, regaining it only by becoming naturalized citizens after the Chinese exclusion laws were repealed.) Therefore, counting from Mrs. Wong's side of the family, their grandchildren are sixth-generation Americans.

First generation American is a term that has been used by Euro-Americans in referring to the native-born children of immigrant parents, according to a volunteer at the Mormon Family Genealogy and Research facilities in Los Angeles. However, this term would not have been by native-born Chinese Americans or Japanese Americans prior to World War II. As was just mentioned, it was taken for granted that only white people were Americans. Given the change in today's social climate, the native-born children of Asian immigrant parents could now use this term.

While Chinese Americans may still be in the process of defining themselves, evidently being Chinese in China is "culturally much easier today than it ever was in the past." This is because, according to Dr. Myron Cohen, being Chinese "no longer involves commonly accepted cultural standards." Dr. Cohen also points out that ruling officials in the past accepted the fact that districts all over China tend to have their own particular customs. Moreover, Chinese society itself has long accepted the concept that one dimension of being Chinese is to "have an origin from somewhere in China."

Whether Chinese Americans use the word "Chinese" as an adjective or as a noun, whether they speak Chinese or not, or whether they regard themselves as being culturally Chinese, surely that "origin from somewhere in China" is clearly stated by the surname character to their American surnames.

7. A GREAT VARIETY IN DIALECT SOUND AND SURNAME SPELLING

Thrice happy he whose name has been well spelt..."
Byron, *Don Juan*, viii, st.18

"How do you pronounce *Ng?*" Many people have difficulty with its pronunciation. Then there are surnames beginning with *Hs*—"How do you pronounce Hsiao?" Since the 1980s, immigrants from China have brought the surnames *Cui*, *Qi*, and *Xue*, which even Chinese Americans have difficulty pronouncing.

Most people acquiesce to their surnames and, for Americans of Chinese ancestry, this means the surname character along with its spelling. Spelling could have come from a clerk at the immigration office, a teacher, or a family member. A new immigrant may have looked it up in a Chinese-English dictionary. Sometimes individuals change the spelling of their name when they see one they like instead, one that suits their own personal whim.

The initial letter of these predominantly monosyllabic surnames can be any letter of the Roman alphabet. These names usually end in a vowel, the semi-vowel *y*, or a particular consonant (only certain ones are used, such as *h*, *k*, *m*, *n*, *p*, *r*, *t*, and *w*). The last letter "g" is always preceded by the letter "n" as in *ng*.

Spelling can vary for the same surname because the same sound can be phoneticized by different combinations of letters, as in other American names. For example, there are 9 ways to spell Jones, such as Joans, Johns, Johnes, Joahns, and Jhonse. The following are spelling variants for the same family name of Chinese origin:

Selected surname spellings	Surname character
Chew, Chiu, Jeu, Jew, Jue	趙
Chiang, Jiang, Kiang	江

Selected surname spellings	*Surname character*
Heui, Hoo, Hooey, Huey, Hui, Huie	許
Ni, Nie, Nieh, Nyi	聶
C'tol, Seto, Seeto, Szeto	司徒

Spelling for the same surname varies because of the wide differences between Chinese dialect sounds. The first surname 趙, mentioned above, is additionally spelled *Chao, Tio,* and *Zhao.* Some surnames have great differences in dialect pronunciation, such as the family name 謝 which is spelled *Char, Chea, Dare, Dear, Der, Hsieh, Ja, Jair, Jay, Shieh, Sia, Tse, Xie,* and *Zia.*

In contrast, the surname 李 —*Lee, Li, Ly*— has few spelling variants because it sounds almost the same in the different Chinese dialects. Even though it is pronounced "lay" in standard Cantonese, the spelling Lee prevails among Americans of Chinese ancestry of this dialect background. Consequently Chinese Americans have many more surnames than were actually brought to this country.

On the other hand, different family names may have the same spelling or spelling variants because of similarity or a close resemblance in dialect sound. For example, the spelling *Lu* represents four different surnames: 呂, 陸, 魯 and 盧. Two different family names, 吳 and 伍, are spelled *Eng, Ng,* and *Ung.*

The reason the same surname character can have such different dialect sounds is because Chinese written characters are aphonetic, like Arabic numbers. The number 10, for example, can be pronounced "ten," "diez," and "shi," without changing the meaning. As Mario Pei, author of *The Story of Language,* points out, words in the Chinese system of writing symbolize thought rather than sound. And it is the sound that is transcribed into the Roman alphabet.

Ever since the written language was standardized in the Qin dynasty (220–206 B.C.), there has been only one Chinese written language. This helped to wield the disparate regions of China into one country and shape the thoughts of people so that, despite disparities in the spoken language, there is one common culture, albeit with regional and local variations.

Since the late 1950s, a simplified form of writing has been used in the People's Republic of China. The longer, traditional script is still used in Taiwan, Hong Kong, and, at present, by most Chinese Americans. Regardless of which script is used, Chinese Americans have a permanent and stable symbol of identity in the ideograph to their surname.

Some of the differences between Mandarin and Cantonese are seen in the following surnames:

Mandarin	Std. Cantonese	Surname character
Chen, Zhen	Yan	甄
Chia, Jia	[Gah], Ka	賈
Hu	Woo, Wu	胡
Jen, Ren	Yum	任
Kong, Kung	Hong, Hung	孔
Weng	Yung	翁

It may possible to identify the dialect sound for a spelling variant if you know the surname character, as in the following renditions for the common family name 陳:

Selected spellings	Dialect represented
Chen, Tchen	Mandarin
Chan	Standard Cantonese
Chun	Chungshan
Chin, Chinn	Cantonese Four Districts
Ching, Chhin	Hakka
Ding, Ting	Foochow (Fuzhou)
Dzung, Zung	Shanghai
Tan	Amoy-Swatow

K, M, P, and T endings

A key difference between Mandarin and the southern dialects lies in the consonant ending of words. The final consonants *k*, *m*, *p*, and *t* do not occur in Mandarin. According to Dr. Chao, these sounds are remnants of the ancient Chinese language that have been preserved in Cantonese — which is akin to the language spoken during the Tang dynasty (618–907) — and in the Amoy-Swatow and Hakka dialects. You can follow the loss of the final *m* for the surname 林: it is *Lum* and *Lim* in Cantonese and Hakka, respectively. It becomes *Ling* in North Min and Shanghai before it changes into *Lin* in Mandarin.

The table below compares a few surnames that have *k*, *m*, *p*, and *t* endings with their Mandarin pronunciation:

Cantonese, Hakka, etc.	Mandarin	Surname character
Ip, Yap, Yep, Yip	Ye, Yeh	葉
Kwak, Kwock, Kwok	Guo, Kuo	郭
Nip	Nie, Nieh	聶
Sam, Shem, Shum	Cen, Tsen	岑
Seit, Sit	Hsueh, Xue	薛
Wat	Chu, Qu	屈
Yick	Yi	易

Actually the final consonant is merely hinted at. For example, the final *k* in *Kwok* is not as clearly sounded as one would enunciate the *k* in the surname *Cooke*. However, in the Union romanization system for the Shanghai dialect, the final *k* consonant — as in *Kok*— is not meant to be enunciated at all because it is a linguistic device to indicate that the preceding vowel has a long sound.

Transcribing Mandarin: Wade-Giles and Pinyin

Differences in spelling the same name occur as well because numerous methods were devised to transcribe or romanize almost all the major Chinese dialects (or languages) into the Roman alphabet. For many decades, the best known transcription method for Mandarin has been the Wade-Giles. It was devised in China by two British diplomats: Sir Thomas Francis Wade and Herbert A. Giles. Wade developed it in 1859 and Giles modified it for his *Chinese-English Dictionary* of 1912. Although the Wade-Giles system was never officially recognized in this country, it was used extensively in American newspapers and by librarians in cataloguing Chinese language materials. It is still used for spelling the names of immigrants from Taiwan.

Most romanization methods for the Chinese dialects fairly bristle with apostrophes and other diacritical marks for indicating pronunciation. Because diacritical marks are usually omitted in American names, names of Chinese origin tend to take on spelling pronunciation. Still, one is apt to mispronounce names unless one knows the key to the phonetic spelling of a romanization system.

For example, the Wade-Giles system does not use the letters *B*, *D*, and *G* for words beginning with these sounds. The sound values of these letters are represented by the letters *P*, *T*, and *K*, respectively. Thus *Pan* (班) is pronounced "ban," *Tu* (杜) is "du," and *Kao* (高) sounds like "gao." The usual sound values for *P*, *T*, and *K* are indicated by an apostrophe: *P'* as in "pea," *T'* as in "tee," and *K'* as in "kay." Therefore, even when the apostrophe is removed, it makes no difference in the way such surnames as *P'an* (潘), *T'ang* (湯), and *K'ung* (孔) are pronounced.

Surnames that begin with the letters *Ch* are also apt to be mauled. In Wade-Giles, *Ch'* sounds like the *ch* in "church" but *Ch* without the apostrophe is closer to a *j* sound. Since it is not always possible to know the intended pronunciation, many surnames take on spelling pronunciation. The following family names spelled *Chang*: 姜, 張, 曾, 章, and 鄭 are all pronounced with the sound of *ch* as in "church" even though they do not have this sound in Chinese.

The surname *Jen* (任) is easily mispronounced because in the Wade-Giles system, the letter *J* represents the "r" sound. Surnames that begin with the letters *Hs* have the sound of *sh* as in "shield." Thus *Hsu* (徐) sounds like "shu" and *Hsiung* (熊) sounds like "shiung."

For accuracy in pronouncing names spelled according to the Han Pinyin system for romanizing Mandarin, it helps to know its key features. Pinyin was officially adopted in 1958 in the People's Republic of China although it was not until January 1979 that it was used for sending official news dispatches abroad. Shortly thereafter, this system of spelling was recognized by our State Department and is now widely used in newspapers and by scholars for spelling place-names and names of personages in mainland China.

Pinyin uses almost every letter of the alphabet for the initial letter of a word except for *i*, *u*, and *v*. The table below compares Pinyin and Wade-Giles spelling for the following names:

Pinyin	*Wade-Giles*	*Surname character*
Bao	Pao	包
Cai	Ts'ai	蔡
Cui	Ts'ui	崔
Cheng	Ch'eng	程
Diao	Tiao	刁
Guan	Kuan	關
Ji	Chi	紀
Qiao	Ch'iao	喬

Pinyin	Wade-Giles	Surname character
Quan	Ch'uan	全
Ru	Ju	茹
Xiao	Hsiao	蕭
Zhou	Chou	周
Zou	Tsou	鄒

Incidentally, the surname *Quan* for Chinese Americans of Cantonese background is the same surname listed above as *Guan* and *Kuan*.

The Yale system for Mandarin, which was devised during World War II at the University's Institute of Far Eastern Languages, should be mentioned even though it has had a negligible influence on name spelling for Chinese Americans. One of its features is the substitution of *Sy* for the *Hs* of Wade-Giles. Hence the surnames Hsia, Hsiao, and Hsueh are spelled *Sya*, *Syau*, and *Sywe*, respectively, in this spelling system. The surname 黃 is transcribed as *Hwang* in the Yale system, but this spelling was used early on in the 19th century by Robert Morrison in his romanization system. Morrison was the first Protestant missionary in China, having arrived there in 1807 from England. The surname *Chow* (周) is also reminiscent of Morrison's method.

Romanizing Cantonese

During the 19th century, missionaries in China, especially English and American missionaries, were very active in romanizing the Cantonese, Foochow, Amoy, Hakka, and Shanghai dialects. Even though their endeavors were in aid of teaching Christianity, they must be credited with introducing the idea of writing Chinese alphabetically. Many American surnames of Chinese origin are reminders of the romanization systems that they devised.

The surname *Ng*, for example, is a legacy of the method designed by Samuel Wells Williams (1812–1884), an American Presbyterian minister, for romanizing Cantonese. This spelling is meant to convey the nasal sound of "ng" as it occurs in the word "singing." Other Cantonese-sounding names that are seen among Chinese Americans can be found in Williams' 1865 *Tonic Dictionary*: Ch'an (陳), Cheung (張), Chiu (趙), Fung (馮), Kwan (關), Kwok (郭), Lam (林), Lau (劉), Leung (梁), Ng (吳, 伍), Tang (鄧), Ts'oi (蔡), and Yeung (楊).

Features in Hakka and Shanghai Romanization:

The spelling "Ch'an" was meant to be pronounced "chhun," according to Williams, because the extra "h" signifies the usual aspirated sound for words beginning with a "ch" sound, as in "chair." This double "h" clue actually appears in Hakka-sounding names spelled according to the German Basel Missionary system, as in the surnames *Chhin* (陳) and *Chhang* (鄭). Even though the "h" in *Phang* (彭) signals the pronunciation "pang," this surname is often pronounced as "fong."

In the Shanghai dialect romanization, the letter "h" appears at the *end* of a word to indicate that the preceding vowel has a short, abrupt sound, as in the surname Kwoh (郭). Another feature is the use of *Ky* at the beginning of a name to denote a *j* sound. Therefore the surname Kyi (紀) is spelled *Ji* in Pinyin and *Chi* in Wade-Giles. The letter *Z* figures prominently in several Shanghai-sounding surnames:

Shanghai romanization	*Character*
Zak	石
Zau	邵
Zen, Dzen	全
Zi, Zee	徐
Zie, Zia	謝
Zung, Dzung	陳

Tones

All Chinese dialects are spoken in "tones" — a tone is like a musical pitch. Mandarin has four and Cantonese is said to have more than seven tones. Since the Chinese spoken language is rich in homophones, tones help to differentiate meaning for words of the same sound. For example, *ma* means "mother" in one tone and "horse" in another tone. Even though different words may have the exact same sound and tone, meaning is differentiated by context, in much the same way that English speakers can tell whether one is talking about the sea or the letter "c." But spelling cannot differentiate between the tones of Chinese words.

Almost all Chinese romanization systems use diacritical marks to indicate the particular tone for a word. Wade-Giles uses a numerical superscript, as in

Ma³; others use accent marks. These, however, would not be used in name spelling. The National Romanization System (Gwoyeu Romatzyh or G.R.) for Mandarin is distinct in its incorporation of the tone in the spelling. For example, the letter "r" in the surnames *Chern* (陳) and *Shyr* (石) means that Chen and Shih are pronounced in the second tone. The final "h" in the surname *Duh* (杜) says to pronounce Du in the fourth tone. Doubling of the "n" in *Fann* (范) also indicates the fourth tone, but the double vowels in *Luu* (魯) signal the low, third tone.

Spelling Spillover

Since the Chinese spoken language teems with homophones, surname spelling spills over from one dialect to another. *Wu*, for instance, is the spelling for several Mandarin-sounding surnames: 巫, 烏, 鄔, 吳, 伍, and 武. *Wu* is also the spelling for the Cantonese-sounding surname 胡—which is pronounced *Hu* in Mandarin. Most of the early established Chinese American families spell this surname *Woo*. To those who hail from the Shanghai area, *Woo* is the spelling for the fourth surname (吳) that is mentioned above. The Amoy-Swatow speaker spells this name *Go* or *Gouw* but the Cantonese speaker spells it *Ng*. The Hokkien dialect speaker thinks of *Ng* as the spelling for the surname 黃, which most Chinese Americans spell *Wong*. Our heads can swivel around, trying to follow the surname variants from one dialect to the next!

Other Romanization Influences

Other romanization methods have also left their mark on American surnames of Chinese origin. The surname *King* (金) comes from the Maclay/Baldwin method for the Foochow dialect. The surnames *Bae* (梅) and *Be* (馬) are based on Amoy-Swatow romanization. Interestingly, these surnames have an initial *m* sound in Mandarin and Cantonese.

Surnames such as *Djie* and *Tjhie* (徐) reflect Dutch spelling influence—Indonesia was under Dutch control until after World War II. The surnames *Tchen* (陳) and *Tchang* (張) owe their spellings to French orthography while the insertion of the letter "s"—as in *Tschen* and *Tschang*—is indicative of German spelling. The influence of the French and Portuguese languages is much more apparent in Vietnamese names, and this is seen in the names of the ethnic Chinese who fled to this country after the end of the Vietnam War: names such as *Hoang* or *Huynh* (黃), *Nguyen* (阮), *Tran* (陳), *Truong* (張), and *Trinh* (鄭)—the letters *Tr* have a *j* sound.

Dialects and Chinese American History

Actually this rich variety in dialect sounds and surname variants for Chinese Americans is of recent vintage. It occurred in stepwise fashion, synchronizing with U.S. immigration policy toward Chinese immigration and the migration patterns of the Chinese to this country.

The first hundred years of Chinese immigration — from the mid–nineteenth century to 1950—saw most surnames spelled according to Cantonese dialect sounds. When the first Chinese exclusion law was enacted in 1882, the Chinese who were in this country at the time were predominantly from Guangdong province; Hakka speakers comprised a small percentage. This was the first American law to exclude by racial group.

Chinese laborers were no longer welcomed although Chinese merchants, teachers, students, and visitors — called the exempt classes — could apply for entry. Subsequent laws extended the 1882 exclusion law and these governed Chinese immigration until their repeal in December 17, 1943. It was because China was our ally during World War II that this occurred and that the privilege of naturalized American citizenship was granted.

The exclusion laws essentially kept the Cantonese as the predominant dialect group and froze the variety of dialect spelling for surnames belonging to Chinese Americans. Another effect was the drop in population size. In 1890, there were 107,000 Chinese in this country; less than 62,000 were counted in the 1920 census, of whom 30 percent were counted as native-born. Few Chinese from other areas in China came as immigrants during the exclusion period. But a few thousand were encouraged to come as college and graduate students because of the influence of American-sponsored colleges in China and the availability of funds from the 1900 Boxer Rebellion indemnity payments which the U.S. government turned over to China for educational purposes. Thus, before World War II, many students came from different parts of China to attend colleges and universities, especially on the East Coast and the Midwest states.

Restrictions on Chinese immigration still existed after the exclusion laws were repealed. In keeping with American policy to limit immigration from Asia, China was granted a quota of 105 immigrants a year — almost all countries within the so-called Asia-Pacific Triangle area had an annual quota of 100 immigrants. Moreover, restrictions were due to the national-origins provision in the general immigration law that stipulated all Chinese persons must apply for admittance to America on the minuscule China quota. It did not matter where they were born or whether they were considered full Chinese or part Chinese. An ethnic Chinese born in France, for example, could not come on the quota for France. The national-origins system ended when the general immigration law was revised in 1965.

Yet, despite these laws, thousands of Chinese were admitted as non-quota immigrants and as refugees. About 6,000 war brides arrived between 1946 and 1950, the first time in Chinese American history when such large numbers of women came. When the People's Republic of China was founded in late 1949 — nearly 5,000 students and other foreign-born Chinese who were in this country at the time became permanent residents under the Displaced Persons Act. The 1950s and early 1960s saw thousands more being admitted as refugees.

The year 1950 marks the beginning when large numbers of surnames spelled according to Mandarin, Shanghai, and Foochow dialects became part of American family nomenclature. To be sure, surnames based on Mandarin and other dialect sounds existed in this country prior to this date except that these were greatly outnumbered by the Cantonese-sounding surnames.

The new wave of Chinese immigrants who came from different countries after 1965 added more surname variants to the pool of Chinese American names, which reflect their particular dialect sounds. Moreover, certain dialects tended to be brought from certain countries: the Hakka dialect from Malaysia and Indonesia, the Hokkien dialect from the Philippines and Indonesia, the Teochiu dialect from Bangkok and Malaysia, and the Hainan dialect from Singapore.

Spelling for American surnames of Chinese origin thus reveals the layered history of this ethnic group. Therefore it is important that each surname variant is regarded as a name in its own right. As name expert Elsdon Smith once observed, the owner of a name is the one who is "most intimately concerned with its shape and form and is accorded the authoritative voice." This advice should be applied as well to the individual's choice in name style.

8. A CHOICE
OF NAME STYLES

"A name is a kind of face whereby one is known."

Thomas Fuller

One traditional Chinese celebration that is often reported in an English language Chinese-American newspaper is the "Red Eggs and Ginger Party." The Chinese refer to this as *man yue* or "month-old" baby celebration. Traditionally, after a baby is one month old, relatives and friends are invited to a banquet so that the family could proudly introduce their newest family member. Red-dyed, hard-boiled eggs and thin slices of sweet pickled ginger are customarily included in the festive offering of food; red being the color of happiness, and eggs the ubiquitous offering in traditional observances. The Chinese believe that, in their *yin* (cold) and *yang* (hot) philosophy, ginger adds warmth to the nutritional needs of the new mother who becomes tired and weak — or too *yin*— after giving birth. In very ancient times in China, this debut of an infant was the occasion for conferring the given name.

All the infants mentioned in these American-style announcements have American given names. Usually they have two, as in *Kendrick George Dea* and *Ashleigh Noelle Lee*, which indicates that their parents are in the mainstream of American name practices. The fact that they are observing the *man yue* tradition is a clue that the honored guest is likely to have a Chinese given name too. Sometimes it is part of the full name, as in honoree *Brittany Ngon Lee*'s name and honoree *Deanna Laimun Low*'s name.

Names of parents and grandparents are also mentioned in these Red Eggs and Ginger Party announcements but are not usually presented in full. For example, the parents of little Christopher Michael Woo are the Bryon Woos and his grandparents are Mr. and Mrs. Howard Woo and Mr. and Mrs. Hom Gok. One set of little Marissa Rebecca Wong's grandparents are Dr. and Mrs. K.C. Wong. Limited as the name styles are in these announcements, we can see the influences of both Chinese and American cultures on Chinese American personal names.

Name styles refer to the way we write or state our names, and there are seven distinct American name styles according to Elsdon Smith. For instance, if Stephen Louie has only one given name, he may write his name as (1) *Stephen Louie* or as (2) *S. Louie*. Or he may call himself (3) *Steve Louie*. If he has a middle name, he has three more options in structuring his name: as (4) *Stephen John Louie*, as (5) *Stephen J. Louie*, or as (6) *S.J. Louie*. If he decides to be known by his middle name, he'll write his name as (7) *S. John Louie*. The fifth name style — the name with one middle initial between the given name and surname — is in particular an American custom.

These names styles are used by Chinese Americans whether their names are composed of a Western given name only, a Chinese given name only, or a combination of both names. Because the Chinese given name is structured in different ways when it is transcribed into Roman script, most name styles observed by Chinese Americans fall into three main categories, the second having four subcategories:

1. names consisting of Western given names only;
2. names consisting of Chinese given names only —
    a. written as separate words,
    b. written as initials,
    c. written as hyphenated names,
    d. written as one word;
3. names incorporating Western and Chinese given names.

The surname always follows the given name in the first and third categories, according to American name traditions, and it may appear before the given name in the second category, as in Chinese custom.

Names Consisting of Western Given Names Only

Generally speaking, most Americans possess two given names. Leslie Dunkling, author of several books on names, observed that 95 percent of American men and 92 percent of American women have a middle name. This American custom was influenced by the early German immigrants but it was not firmly established until the middle of the nineteenth century. Up to then, most Americans had only one given name. This is even illlustrated by the names of our presidents: from George Washington to Calvin Coolidge, only nine of the thirty presidents had two given names.

By the end of World War I, in 1918, it was presumed that every American had a middle name. According to George Stewart, author of *American Given Names*, if it had not been bestowed, a person could adopt one or just add a middle initial, as President Harry S Truman did. Many Euro-Americans bestow the mother's original surname to a child for a given name.

In all likelihood, most Chinese Americans do not have two American given names because of the high percentage of the foreign-born. One impression I had, while growing up in a Chinatown, was the rarity of native-born second generation Chinese Americans having two American names. Moreover, the one American name was often conferred or suggested by a doctor, a nurse, a missionary, a teacher, or an older native-born child.

Unlike the immigrant parents of my friends who tended to hold on to their Chinese names, both my parents, who emigrated from China during the early 1920s, selected an American name for themselves. As they later explained, this made it easier for non–Chinese people to remember them by name. My mother, who worked as a waitress, chose *Flo*, because it was suggested by a co-worker; my stepfather chose *Allen* because he was told it matched the sound of the first syllable of his Chinese name. It was only at work, though, that their American names were used because Chinese-speaking relatives and friends always called them by their Chinese names.

The 1920s and 1930s seem to have been times when some Chinese Americans gave themselves a second American given name. As one friend admitted, she and her friends did so while attending junior high school because they thought everyone in America had to have a middle name. In her posthumously published autobiography, Louise Leung Larsen charmingly related how she received hers. She was named *Mamie Leung* at birth. When she was in college during the 1920s, her best friend was Eleanor Chan, whom she thought was "more Americanized." As Larsen writes: "Eleanor's full name was Eleanor Ransom Chan, which I thought sounded most elegant. She said I must also have a middle name; we finally, after much argument, settled on 'Louise.'" This later became the name Larsen used professionally instead of *Mamie*.

Regardless of who suggested the American name, Chinese-speaking parents usually bestowed the Chinese given name — undoubtedly every child in a Chinatown possessed one. However, this was seldom used unless one attended a Chinese language school. Nor did the Chinese-speaking parents of my friends call them by their Chinese names. But whenever my mother called out my Chinese name, I knew immediately that I was in trouble!

No doubt these pre–World War II name experiences are being repeated today among the new immigrants. Not long ago, a young college student who was born in Vietnam said that he finally decided to call himself *Craig* after living here for several years. He thought it would make life easier in the workplace, adding the observation that none of his family or relatives would ever call him by this name.

The middle name for a Chinese American married woman, however, may represent her original surname. Although American women today may opt against adding the husband's surname to their personal name, women in mainland China consistently retain their own name after marriage. This custom, as mentioned earlier, is an ancient Chinese name tradition.

Names Consisting of Chinese Given Names Only — Written as Separate Words

Before proceeding further, a brief review on the composition of a Chinese personal name seems to be in order. Most Chinese names belonging to Chinese Americans consist of three words: one for the surname and two for the given name. Some names consist of only two words, such as *Lei Lai*. Some have four words, such as *Ow Yang Wai Ling* which represents a double surname and a disyllabic given name. The characters to the name *Chow Kwan Kam Oi* reveal that the first two words are surnames: *Chow* is the husband's surname and *Kwan Kam Oi* is the woman's full name.

When Chinese immigration began during the mid–nineteenth century, the prevailing name style was to write each syllable of the usual Chinese name as a separate word. This is still in popular use today. This name style, however, has generated the most confusion over the surname. One can never be sure at which end of a name lies the family name.

If you saw a name like *Yee Wah Tong*, for example, you would be hard-pressed to tell whether *Yee or Tong* is the surname. A name like *Chi Li* can keep you guessing as well. If it were not for the Chinese characters to a name like *Joe Fong Tuey Kwan*, you would not know that this is the name of a married woman: *Joe* is her surname and *Kwan* is her husband's; her Chinese given name lies in between. This name combines both Chinese and American name practices.

Prior to World War II, almost all foreign-born Chinese wives in this country had the traditional marriage name that consisted only of her original surname followed by the word Shee, as in *Gee Shee*. If her husband's name were placed last, as in *Gee Shee Woo*, this follows American name practices.

The early immigrant men were quite consistent in keeping the family name first in their Chinese names. Certainly the literature on Chinese American history is replete with such names as *Ng Poon Chew, Joe Shoong,* and *Soo Hoo Nam Art,* in which the surname comes first. Students and scholars from China also tended to keep the surname first.

Evidently by the 1930s, this practice was beginning to change. As Arthur E. Bostwick, a librarian in St. Louis, Missouri, commented in 1932, "Until very recently, the family name was always placed first and there was, therefore, no trouble in recognizing it. Recently, however, many Chinese have adopted the western plan of placing the family name last." He added the thought that if the Chinese would uniformly agree on the position of the surname in a name, confusion could be avoided.

The U.S. Census Bureau must have had difficulty ascertaining the surname in Chinese names. In the Soundex — an alphabetical listing by surname — to the 1900 federal census, for example, Soo Hoo Toy's name is listed under *Soo*, under *Hoo*, and under *Toy*. (*Soo Hoo* is most likely the surname.) The card for Chow Tai says, "See also Tai." As a result, the number of surnames of Chinese origin in the census records is greatly exaggerated. (This method is still used in indexing when the surname is unknown.)

Confusion over this name style must still occur. Several years ago, at a photographic exhibit about the Chinese in the small town of Locke in central California, a Mr. Wong Buck and his wife were identified as *Mr. Buck* and *Mrs. Buck*. The Chinese characters on the captions reveal *Wong* to be the surname. More recently, legal notices about fictitious business names show that some Chinese who want to keep the surname first are placing a comma after the surname. For example, a Chinese fast-food place owner signed his name *Liang, Gesheng* and the owner of a computer service store signed his as *Lu, Waymond C.*

It is due to the ambiguity in spelling Chinese names that so much confusion has occurred: many family names have the same spelling as given names of the same sound. And the number of Chinese words having the same spelling can be quite large. For example, at least 45 different characters are spelled Li. Therefore, it is only when Chinese characters are available that you can be sure of the position of the surname in a Chinese personal name.

This name style has been used by Chinese Americans in all socioeconomic levels. Dr. Yuen Ren Chao, who was internationally renowned, consistently preferred this name style and always placed his surname last. He also liked to initial his given name, as in *Y.R. Chao*.

Names Consisting of Chinese Given Names Only — Written as Initials

The surname usually follows the given name in this name style. Apparently, in the early decades of this century, it was quite a fad among students and scholars from China to initial the Chinese given name. A 1905 issue of *The Dragon Student*, which was published (possibly in San Francisco) by the Chinese Students' alliance of America, shows that many had such names as *C.S. Chan* and *Y. Wen*. Perhaps this American name style was adopted because it saves the trouble of spelling the Chinese given name in full. Or perhaps it spared one the pain of constantly hearing one's name being mauled and mispronounced. Or perhaps it was in emulation of prominent Americans in certain business and social circles, such as *J.D. Rockefeller*. Many missionaries in China had the habit of initialing their names: *D.H. Davis* and *D. MacIver* were among the authors of Chinese-English dictionaries.

This name style was apparently still popular two decades later as shown by the names in *The Chinese Students' Monthly*, published in 1920. By 1943, however, this name style had evidently lessened in popularity, judging from a *Directory of Chinese University Graduates and Students in America*. Unquestionably there was severe criticism coming from high Chinese quarters about the adoption of Western name customs. In 1936, a Chinese author wrote: "Certainly the use of initials in place of the given name is a most un–Chinese custom, while the adoption of a foreign given name may be regarded as an evidence of denationalization, a despoliation of the country's spiritual heritage."

Evidently he was castigating the students who were attending missionary-sponsored schools in China since he went on to scold: "For more than anything else is the name an index of nationality, and the fact that this practice of using foreign names arose in connection with missionary education merely makes matters so much worse."

As he pointed out, the Ministry of Education in China had issued an order in 1933 that forbade students to use initials before the surname and to adopt "foreign" names. Moreover, names were to be romanized in full, according to Mandarin. These orders were made so as to "obtain uniformity in the English rendering of Chinese names, and to preserve the wholly satisfactory and logical method of Chinese nomenclature."

In the 1943 Chinese students directory just mentioned, the names of most students from China were romanized according to Mandarin, ironically to the Wade-Giles system that was devised by foreigners. And the most popular name style was the hyphenated disyllabic name, as in *Sun Yat-sen*. The hyphen also occurs in disyllabic surnames, as in *Ou-yang Yi*.

Names Consisting of Chinese Given Names Only — Written as Hyphenated Names

The hyphenated name can be attributed to Giles, whose *Chinese Biographical Dictionary*, published in 1898, served as a model for structuring the Chinese name in this manner. The purpose of the hyphen is to distinguish between family name and given name since most family names consist of one character and most given names have two characters. It should be pointed out that Giles intended for the name after the hyphen to be lowercased — as in *Yat-sen*, not *Yat-Sen*.

Apparently it took many years before Giles' method became standard practice. A case in point is the name of Wu Ting Fang, who was appointed Chinese Minister to the United States in 1896. When this was announced by *The New York Times*, Wu's name was spelled *Wu-Ting-Fang*, with hyphens between each word. These were quickly removed in subsequent reports. In 1907, the *Times* began spelling his name *Wu T'ing-Fang*. By 1920, the Giles method was used except that *Wu Ting-fang* was spelled without the apostrophe. Interestingly, before his appointment, Wu went by the name *Ng Choy*, which reflects his native Cantonese background.

Most Chinese Americans tend to capitalize the initial of the name after the hyphen, as in *Di-Hwa Liu* and *Yo-Yo Ma*. Some place the hyphen between the two initials of the Chinese name, as in *S.-Y. Pi*. Some remove the periods after the initials, as in *Dr. Ricci Y-C Chan*. Sometimes one period is removed, as in *William S-Y. Wang*. The Chinese writer, who was just quoted, thought that capitalizing the initial of the second name is "more logical and in accordance with the nature of the Chinese characters."

First Name? Middle Name? Dithemic Name?

What then, exactly, is the nature of a two-character Chinese given name? One opinion is that the first character is equivalent to the American "middle name" and the second character is like the "first name." Another perplexing explanation is that the Chinese generation name is a "middle name" when we know that it can be represented by either the first or second character of a disyllabic given name. This may explain why some Chinese Americans write their Chinese name backwards. For example, the Chinese characters to Ching Tien Chay's name show that his given name is really *Tien Ching*.

When Shao Er Kuang came to America several years ago, the immigration officer who processed her admittance papers was of the belief that the first syllable of a Chinese disyllabic given name is a "middle name." Therefore she is now known as *Er Shao Kuang*. This is like having a Susie write her name as *Siesu*. On the other hand, two sisters and their brother discovered that they received the same "first name" because their two-character Chinese given names begin with the word Poh. They were told by an immigration officer that the first character is considered a "first name."

It seems that the use of American terminology to explain the Chinese two-character given name has not clarified any questions about its nature and evidently has caused changes instead in the actual names of some individuals. Incidentally, the Chinese two-character family name has not been described as two separate names. This is probably because it is usually regarded as one name that consists of two characters.

It seems logical to regard the two-character given name as a "dithemic" name, as one name composed of two words. As a reminder, the meaning for a Euro-American dithemic name, such as William, is composed of two elements.

Names Consisting of Chinese Given Names Only — Written as One Word

"The mystification over Chinese names is entirely due to our own making," Lin Yutang wrote in 1935 — the "our" referring to the Chinese themselves. He believed that the two-character Chinese name is like any polysyllabic name and should be written as one word. As an analogy, we would not write David as *Da Vid* or Johanna as *Jo Han Na*.

Dr. Lin also advocated adhering to the Chinese tradition of placing the surname first. The artist Dong Kingman, whose surname is *Dong*, has structured his name accordingly. This name style of writing the disyllabic name as one word is currently observed in the People's Republic of China and is used in all official news dispatches. This may not be true of names belonging to new immigrants from mainland China. Even though they may spell their names in Pinyin, they may or may not observe this name style after settling down in this country.

Names Incorporating Both Western and Chinese Given Names

The desire to retain the Chinese identity in a name is quite strong today among Chinese Americans and has led to the name style of juxtaposing both Western and Chinese given names, as in *Ryan Chieh-Chion Lee*. This name style has become very popular since the 1970s. Chinese student directories of previous decades indicate that this was adopted by some foreign-born students when they assumed American names. Evidently, Chinese Americans in Hawaii used this name style long before World War II. In comparison, it was never a popular name style for the native-born Chinese American on the U.S. mainland. If the Chinese given name were included as part of the name in English, only one syllable was usually presented, as in *Martin Foon Wong*.

Sometimes the Chinese given name comes first, as in *Vi-Kyuin Wellington Koo*, who was the first diplomat to sign the United Nations Charter in 1945. Dr. Koo also wrote his name as *V.K. Wellington Koo* and *V.K.W. Koo*. (That final name style composed of three initials has more of a British look.) Usually the Chinese name serves as a middle name, as seen in following names: *Walter Yuen Ng, John Kuo Wei Tchen, Paul Kuang-pu Huang, Janet Jen-Ai Chong, Kenneth Chiache Sze, Theodore H.C. Chen*, and *Ginger Y. Chiu*. All the methods for structuring the Chinese disyllabic name can appear in this name style. Yet it would be difficult to be consistent in writing down two initials for the Chinese given name because there is usually only room for one initial on most American legal forms.

On the other hand, when a double-barrelled name is simplified to one initial, it may be due simply to the dynamics of living in America. Victor Chuan recalls that when he first came to America as a college student during the early 1940s, he was advised to spell his Chinese name in full, as *Lu-chi Chuan*. Since he was named *Victor* when he was born, he decided to use the name *Victor Lu-chi Chuan*. As time went by, he reduced his Chinese name to two initials, at times writing it as *V.L.C. Chuan*. Finally, he dropped the second initial and legalized his name to *Victor L. Chuan*.

These particular name examples point out that nothing should be taken for granted about the middle initial in a Chinese American name. It can stand for a Chinese monosyllabic name, a Chinese disyllabic name, a Western given name, or a surname.

Due to interracial and interethnic marriages, there are now many multiethnic name combinations. For example, *Yi Ling Chen-Josephson* and *Yi Pei Chen-Josephson* are undoubtedly part–Chinese. *Araceli W. Tamayo-Lee* combines American, Filipino, and Chinese name practices, with the *W* standing for *WaiYun*. *Marcus Wing Yen Murray* was born to a sixth-generation Chinese American married to an African-American. The name *Taylor Jean Sachiko Nakayama* combines American, Japanese, and Chinese names. These are all truly American names.

Placing the Surname in the Middle

One more name style that is seen occasionally should be mentioned because it involves placing the family name in the middle of a name, as in *Harry Dong Lai Kay*. The family name acts like a fulcrum in keeping the order of the name in English as well as in Chinese: Harry Dong's name says that his Chinese name is *Dong Lai Kay*. It seems practical except that the last word in the name could be mistaken for the surname, a subject that will be discussed in Chapter 15.

This name style appeared as early as the 1870s in California. Billy Ho Lung was listed in the 1880 federal census for Sacramento, California, as a labor contractor and, according to the 1878 Wells Fargo Directory of Chinese Business Houses, *Ho Lung* was his Chinese name. Mary Wong Ching, who came to this

A name style in which the surname (Fong) appears in the middle of the name.

country during the mid–nineteenth century, was the matriarch of the Lee Bowen family that settled in Oakland, California; the oldest of her five children was born in 1876. *Wong* was her family name. This name style can be seen in some of today's names: *Cecelia Tang Shu-Shuen, Henry Hoesie, John Liu Fugh,* and *Jose Wong On,* among many others.

Ten More Popular Name Styles

Because of this synthesis of both Chinese and American name traditions, Chinese Americans observe, in addition to the seven American name styles, ten more name styles, listed here with typical examples:

1. Chinese name with the surname first: *Lou Sheng, Lin Hui Ling,* and *Chen, Pei-Ying;*
2. Chinese name composed of three or more separate words: *Ieoh Ming Pei, Kwai Yung Chui Ja.* The given name may be reversed as in *Ching Tien Chay;*
3. Hyphenated Chinese disyllabic name, with a lowercased second syllable: *Wing-cheung Ng;*
4. Hyphenated Chinese disyllabic name, with an uppercased second syllable: *Han-Sheng Lin;*
5. Disyllabic Chinese name as one word: *Renqiu Yu;*
6. Combination American given name and a Chinese middle name: *Jean Yun-Hua King.*
7. Combination Chinese given name with an American middle name: *Sao-ke Alfred Sze;*
8. Two initials for the disyllabic Chinese given name: *Tracy S.Y. Wong;*
9. One initial for the disyllabic Chinese given name: *Robert T. Poe* (the *T* is for *Ta-Pang*);
10. Family name in the middle of the name: *Abraham Ng Kamsat.*

This variety of name styles for Chinese Americans can be attributed to a greater tolerance in America for multiethnic and multicultural expressions in names. The desire to retain ethnic name traditions and to have a unique name is strongly felt today by many Americans of different ethnicities. Nevertheless, as we shall see in the next part of this book, Chinese American names have been greatly influenced by the American way with names.

PART III

CHINESE AMERICAN NAME CUSTOMS

"Louie? Is that a surname? What kind is it? Is it Italian?" "Is your husband Caucasian?" "Aren't all surnames in China pronounced in just one syllable?" It is not at all unusual for Chinese Americans to encounter such questions. On the other hand, Chinese Americans may assume that because a surname looks Chinese, it must belong to a person of Chinese ancestry or else interracial marriage must have taken place.

Mrs. John Ong of Pasadena, California, first learned that her surname also belongs to Chinese Americans when her hairdresser, a Chinese American, expressed surprise upon seeing her blue-eyed, blond husband instead of an Asian-looking man. A Mrs. Chew of San Jose, California, once had to ask the Chinese Students' Club at the local college to stop sending her meeting notices because neither she nor her husband is Chinese in ancestry.

The fact that Americans of Chinese descent have many surnames in common with Americans of other ethnic origin is largely due to their ancestors settling here at a time when all foreign names tended to be spelled or respelled to fit the American language. The Americanization of names and the synthesis of Chinese and American name traditions are part of the dynamics of living in America. Acquiescing to the American way with names is one means of accommodating to life in the newly adopted country.

Evidently there is an adjustment period because many immigrants want to retain their name traditions. For example, parents may try to duplicate the *Pai-hang* naming system when selecting American given names for their children. In adhering to their name traditions, many parents acquiesced to part of their Chinese names becoming the new surnames of their children. Some parents attempt to apply American naming practices to strictly Chinese names.

Part III is an explanation of how the Americanization of names has worked for Americans of Chinese ancestry. But the clustering of surnames of Chinese origin in certain parts of the United States indicates that changes are taking place in this ethnic population.

9. CHINESE NAMES IN
EARLY OFFICIAL RECORDS

"Zhang San Li Si"
 — an old Chinese saying that means "the common people"

On February 28, 1855, the *Douglas City Gazette* published an account of a Chinese New Year celebration held at the Chinese temple in the nearby town of Weaverville. This mountainous pine-covered area of Northern California, where the Trinity Alps loom tall in the background, once boasted over 2,500 Chinese, most of whom were miners. This temple still exists, having been rebuilt after the original building burned down in 1872, and its official name is the *Weaverville Joss Temple State Historic Park*. Its Chinese name is *Won Lim Miao*— as pronounced in Cantonese — which means "Temple amidst the Forest beneath the Clouds." It is one of the numerous landmarks in the state that bear testimony to the presence of the Chinese in the late nineteenth century.

Names of the donors who contributed money to rebuild the temple have also been preserved. They have been immortalized in hand-written Chinese characters on the wooden plaque that states this temple was "auspiciously built the second time" in the Emperor Guangxu's Third Year. This would be 1877 since the emperor began his reign in 1875.

Over 1,000 names were recorded; some are store names and only a few are names of women. Sixty-three different surnames were counted. Interestingly, the southern custom of prefixing the vocative *Ah* to a given name shows up in about 20 percent of the names — as in [*Wong Ah Gow*]. There are no names that consist of a monosyllabic given name, so perhaps the *Ah* was inserted to fill in the spaces. You may recall that disyllabic given names characterized 80 percent of all Chinese names by 1900.

Closer to San Francisco is the Bok Kai Temple in Marysville, California. It too has preserved the names of several hundred donors who contributed to rebuilding it in 1880. This temple was founded in 1854 and, after the old building was destroyed by fire, it was relocated closer to the Yuba River. Its name appropriately means "North mountain stream temple." Today, relatively few people of Chinese descent live in Marysville but the temple is still used for religious observances and its famous Bomb Day celebration is still held after the lunar new year.

The usual Chinese name — family name followed by a disyllabic given name — prevails on two donor name plaques. Only one name [Leong On] is composed of a monosyllabic given name. The family name is missing from nine percent of the names, as in [Ah Sam] and [Leen Oi] — the latter being a two-character given name. Altogether, 76 family names were counted. In comparison to the list of donors to the Weaverville temple, many more store names are listed in the Bok Kai Temple name plaques.

These late–nineteenth century Chinese records tell us that the vast majority of the early emigrants had the usual Chinese name; however, this is not indicated in the early American official records, such as ship passenger lists and federal census records. The Ah type of name and names that consist of only two words prevail instead, suggesting that the early emigrants were either reluctant to reveal their full name to strangers or they found it more convenient to use only part of their name.

Non-Chinese clerks and census takers undoubtedly recorded a Chinese name according to the way they heard it pronounced or thought it was pronounced. Therefore, nineteenth century American official records can provide a picture of what can happen to the usual Chinese name when neither Americans nor the Chinese knew much about one another's name traditions. By 1900, however, the usual Chinese name appears with greater frequency when recorded in English.

Ship Passenger Lists

Masters of ships were required by federal law, since 1819, to file passenger lists with the collector of customs upon arrival at a port of entry. (There were no standard immigration procedures until the passage of the first general immigration law in August 3, 1882, which was enacted several months after the first Chinese exclusion law.) Although ship passenger lists for San Francisco were destroyed by fires in 1851 and in 1940, a reconstruction of these lists from 1850 to 1875 shows that Chinese names were rarely recorded. Most Chinese came as steerage passengers and therefore their arrival — like that of all steerage passengers — was recorded by the number per boatload.

The passenger list for the ship *Brant* that docked in February 1852 — after a voyage of 90 days from Hong Kong — mentions three Chinese passengers but their names were partially recorded. It shows that "Mr. Wang Ching (Chinese)," "Miss __ Asee (Chinese lady)," and "Miss __ Ayum (Chinese lady)" landed in San Francisco along with 359 unidentified passengers. In contrast, the cargo for two Chinese men is described in far greater detail in another ship passenger list for March 1852: 1,000 eggs, 5 cases of silk were consigned to "__ Look (a Chinaman on board)." And 400 bags rice, 10 pkgs. dried fish, 50 bags rice flour, 6 chests tea, 8 boxes shrimp, 1 pkg. indigo, 4 boxes eggs were consigned to "__ Yesing (a Chinaman on board)."

(Interestingly, in the early 1850s, steamships from Hong Kong did not just stop in San Francisco. They plodded up rivers, dropping off passengers nearer to the gold mining areas. Ships sailed up the Pacific coast as far as the Columbia River, where passengers disembarked at Astoria and Portland.)

Chinese names on the two ship passenger lists submitted at the 1877 Congressional hearing on Chinese immigration could have been written by the same person since all consist of only two words. Most seem to include a surname and a monosyllabic given name. A sampling of the ship passenger list for the S.S. *Victoria* that arrived in Port Townsend, Washington, in 1900, reveals that the usual Chinese name was still vastly underrepresented: out of 39 names, only five consist of the usual Chinese name.

Federal Census Records

Federal census records, in comparison, are a veritable gold mine of information on Chinese name traditions. The 1850 federal census for California, in which several hundred Chinese names are listed, is the first for this state, having joined the Union that year. Unfortunately, records for San Francisco, Contra Costa, and Santa Clara counties were destroyed by fire. Fire also destroyed almost all of the 1890 census schedules, and none exist for the Western states where the vast majority of the early Chinese immigrants settled. Nevertheless, random samplings of census schedules from 1850 to 1900 for a few Western states indicate that the Chinese tended to respond in certain ways to questions about their names.

The 1850 census for California is especially valuable because it provides a baseline on the recording of Chinese names. Although the number of Chinese names greatly increases in the later nineteenth-century census records, the same kind of name recording usually occurred. The 1850 census shows, for example, that when the Chinese did not reveal their surnames, they identified themselves by their given name in three different ways: 1) by a monosyllabic name only — as in *Ging*, 2) by the vocative *Ah—* as in *Ayat*, or 3) by a disyllabic given name — as in *Ki Siong*. When a surname was recorded, it is usually followed by a monosyllabic given name, as in *Che Pang*. Only a few names in this census look like the usual Chinese name, such as *We Longho*.

Generic names, such as *Chinaman, John Chinaman*, and *Chinese*, were evidently used when the census taker was unable to obtain any information — these terms should not be considered as racist in intent. As one census taker in Eldorado County wrote, "I found about 80 Chinese men in Spanish Canion who refused to give me their names or other information." Other groups are identified by generic terms as well, such as *Spaniard* and *Kanaka*, which refers to a Hawaiian.

John Chinaman is another generic term that was used by the census taker to describe a Chinese person — like *John Doe*, it refers to a person whose name is not known. *John* even occurs as a given name for several Chinese in the 1850 census; among those listed are *John Awa, John Ching, John Jake*, and *John Wheelan*. The word *Chinese* appears as a surname for *Chinese, John; Chinese, Chow; and Chinese, Songton*. Nationality has long played a role in shaping surnames, such as *English, Deutsch*, and *French*; however, there is no evidence that *Chinese* occurs as a surname for Chinese Americans. Even though *China* is used as a given name by a few Americans, it would be rare indeed — if it occurs at all — to find this word as a name for a Chinese American.

The 1850 census, in addition, contains some rather unusual names for the early Chinese emigrants. A few Spanish names are listed: *J. Miguel Gomez, Jean Archeo*, and *Pedro Arquano*. (It is not unusual to find Spanish given names among Chinese Americans today, such as *Luis Esquerra Yee* (余) and *Jose Mak* (麥). A couple of names of indeterminate origin are recorded, *Cha Anchordar* and *Aho Cendenderham*, and a couple of American-style names. *Joseph Goo* and *Charly Tysian*. A few are identified by a single American given name only, such as *Jack* and *Samuel*.

Some surnames that are seen for white Americans could be easily mistaken for Chinese names. For example, two men from Germany had the surnames *Chen* and *Sing*. A man from Ireland had the surname *Han*. The following were recorded for white Americans from other states: *Ding, Ing, Ming, Shum*, and *Tan*. And *Cathay* was the surname for three white men.

As larger numbers came from China to America in subsequent decades, the types of names that were recorded for the Chinese in the 1850 census simply increased in number in later census schedules. Random samplings for California, Idaho, Oregon, and Washington show that an entire census page could contain the generic term *Chinaman* instead of personal names. Sometimes *Chinawoman* is recorded for the relatively few Chinese women. Sometimes only a single Chinese name, such as *Tong*, is recorded for an individual. Certainly whole pages are filled with names prefixed by the word *Ah*. Sometimes it is followed by a disyllabic name as in *Ah Ok Sam*. Sometimes it accompanies an American given name, as in *Ah Charley, Ah Bill* and *Ah Georgee*. Not surprisingly, the ubiquitous *Ah* is listed as a surname in the *Soundex*, the alphabetical listing of surnames for a decennial federal census.

Occasionally, a nickname such as *Shinbone* is recorded, as seen in the 1860 Oregon census. American names, such as *Jenny Susan* and *Anna Susan*, are recorded for the few Chinese women listed in the 1870 Portland, Oregon, census. (Although those who settled in rural towns were called *China Mary*, this generic name did not appear in these census samplings.) And John continues to be recorded as a name for the Chinese as they moved northward, as shown in the 1870 Washington territory census sampling.

Charley is another American name that stands out for the early Chinese emigrants. *Lee Charley* is the name for a seven-year-old boy born in Oregon and *Charley* is the name of a cook. Apparently this name became very popular among the Chinese who settled in the New England states, New Jersey, and New York. According to a 1930 Chinese business directory, many an owner of a laundry was named *Charlie*. Sometimes this was spelled *Chas*, as in *Chas. Wong* and *Chas. Sing*.

Sometimes the name of a Chinese store was recorded instead of the owner's name. For example, *Wa Chung* is listed as a merchant in the 1870 census for Seattle but this was the name of the store owned by Chin Chun Hock, the first Chinese merchant in this city. The 1880 San Francisco census lists *Quan Wo* as a shoe manufacturer and *Poy Kee* as a ladies' shoe maker, whereas these are names of shoe manufacturing factories as listed in the 1878 *Wells Fargo Business Directory*.

Apparently it was not considered unusual for a store name to be recorded as a person's name. Ah Jack, a witness for a Chinese merchant planning for a trip to China in 1911, admitted under interrogation that the name *Lun Ying* on his certificate of residence was actually the name of the store that he managed. Ah Jack undoubtedly identified himself in this way because white customers in those days often assumed that the store name was the owner's name. As Pardee

In the matter of the Application of :
                                       :
    W I N G   S I N G   :
                                       :
Domiciled Chinese Merchant, member   :   Port Townsend, Wash.,
of the firm of Yet Wo Company, Port   :   November 7, 1911.
Townsend, Wash., for preinvestigation :
of status.   :

                Tom L. Wyckoff, Immigrant Inspector, Examiner,
                Henry A. Myers, Immigrant Inspector, Stenographer.

        AH Jack, duly sworn, testified as follows: (Alien speaks
English).

Q. What are your names?
A. Ah Ying is my baby name; married name is See Foon; Ng is my
    family name; American name is Jack.

Q. How old are you?
A. Forty- three (43).

Q. Where were you born?
A. Sing Chong village, Sunning District, China.

Q. When did you come to the United States?
A. I came to Port Townsend in K. S. 5.

Q. Have you a certificate of registration?
A. Yes. (Witness exhibited Certificate of Registration No.
    143084, issued in the name of Lun Ying, person other than
    laborer, residence Port Townsend, Wash., dated at Portland,
    Ore., Feb. 2, 1894, signed by H. L. Pittinger, Chinese In-
    spector, Washington, D. C., Jan. 4, 1904, issued in lieu of
    Certificate No. 44510.).

Q. Were you ever known by the name of Lun Ying?
A. I was manager of the Lun Ying Company at that time and was
    registered under that name.

Q. What is your present business?
A. Manager of the Yet Wo Company, Chinese Merchants of this city,
    306 Washington Street.

Q. When was the Yet Wo Company organized?
A. K. S. 34, 6th month.

Q. How many members are in the Yet Wo Company?
A. Ten (1 0) altogether.

Interrogation of Ah Jack, a witness for Wing Sing, a merchant applying for permission to go on a trip abroad. Ah Jack admitted to using store name as personal
name. (Courtesy of the National Archives — Pacific Northwest Region.)

Lowe pointed out in his book *Father and Glorious Descendant*, his father owned a store called *Sun Loy* and white customers called him "Mr. Sun Loy"—much to the amusement of his children.

In Chinese tradition, the name of a store is selected for a propitious meaning. *Man Lee & Co.*, for example, which was in business in San Francisco in 1868, means "Ten Thousand Profits Company." Many Chinese Americans today follow Euro-American custom in naming their stores after themselves, but if there are several owners then they may still follow Chinese tradition when naming their store.

During the Chinese exclusion period, a Chinese store may have had many more owners than was expected of a small business because being a merchant was a viable way of making a living in this country and to being able to bring a wife from China. For example, in 1906, the Man Jan Company in San Francisco listed 29 partners and the Peking Bazaar listed 18 partners in 1916. No doubt some were laborers who were partners in name only because this was the only way they could bring their families to this country. (After the role of a Chinese merchant was defined in 1893 (28 Stat. 8), immigration authorities required Chinese stores to submit partnership lists so that they could keep track of those claiming this exempt classification.)

The early census records show an almost endless variety in the spelling of Chinese names — one almost longs for Chinese characters to decipher each one. Yet some seem to belong together as the same name: the double surname *So Ho*, *Sho Ho*, and *Slo Ho*; the surname *Lee*, *Li*, and *Ly*; and the surname *Yee*, *Yi* and *Ye*.

The prevalence of monosyllabic Chinese given names in these records was undoubtedly due to the omission of one syllable from a disyllabic given name. Huie Kin, a Presbyterian minister in New York City, wrote that it was a matter of convenience when he dropped part of his full name, which was *Huie Kin-Kwong*. Nevertheless, as the reader may recall, omitting the generation name when signing a legal document was permitted in traditional China.

Chinese Name Customs in Census Records

The gradual increase in the usual Chinese name toward the end of the nineteenth century seems to be tied to the establishment of family life because it is in the names of children that it is usually found. (This sampling of federal census records shows a few Chinese were born in California since the 1850s.) Most

In the matter of the application of :

    A H   Y E U K

for admission to the United States :   Port Townsend, Wash.,
as a returning domiciled Chinese :
merchant, member of the Sing Chong :   February 26, 1910.
Lung Company of Port Townsend, :
Washington. :

Tom L. Wyckoff, Asst. Inspector in Charge, Examiner.
R. D. Gould, Inspector,   Reporter.
F. H. Tape,   Interpreter.

Witness sworn.

Q. What is your name?
A. Eng Yee Tung is my married name; Ah Keung was my baby name;
   Eng is my family name.
Q. What is your age?
A. Forty-seven.
Q. Are you at the present time a member of the Sing Chong Lung
   Company of this city?
A. Yes.
Q. Are you the manager of that company?
A. Yes.
Q. Has there been any changes in the membership of the company
   since October 1, 1908?
A. No.
Q. How many partners in the company at the present time?
A. Eleven.
Q. Name them and write their names in Chinese characters.
   (Below are the names given and written by the witness)

Ah Cing,   伍敬

Ah Pak,   伍柏

Ah Yeuk,   伍郁

Ah Poy,   伍培

Ng Woo,   伍護

Wong Sing,   黄勝

Ng Sue Tow,   伍士藻

Ng Lun Fong, 伍倫芳

Case of Ah Yeuk-- Testimony of Eng Yee Tung-- Page (2)

Ah Lung,　　　　　里龍　　　　　　　　　　　　　　　　.

Pon Jung,　　　　洋中　　　　　　　　　　　　　　　　.

Eng Yee Tung,　　伍子瓊　　　　　　　　　　　　　　　.

Q How long have you been manager of this Company.
A Since K. S. 27, Eleventh month.
Q What is the interest that each partner has in the Company.
A $700.00 each.
Q Give the present whereabouts of each member of the Company.
A Ah Lung, Ah Ging, Ng Sue Tow, Ng Lun Fong, Wong Sing, Ah Poy
  and myself work in the store; Ah Pak in Port Townsend but not
  working in the store; Ah Yeuk now in China; Ng Woo in Portland,
  Ore. for past two or three years; Pon Jung working in Boise,
  Idaho.
Q Has Ah Yeuk disposed of his interests or any part thereof
  since he has been in China.
A No Sir.
Q Do you recognize this photograph (exhibits photgraph attached
  to applicants papers.)
A Yes, that is Ah Yeuk.

　　　(Eng Yee Tung) *Ng Yee Tung* 伍子瓊　　　　　　　)

　　　(Ah Keung) 甚子琛　　　　　　　　　　　　　　　　)

　　　(Eng) 伍　　　　　　　　　　　　　　　　　　　　)

Subscribed and sworn to before me this 26th day of Feb. 1910.

　　　　　　　John L. Styckoff
　　　　　　Assistant Inspector in Charge.

Above and opposite: Witness for a merchant seeking reentry. Note his married and baby names. K.S. 27 is the year of the Emperor Guangxu's reign — Kwong Suey in Cantonese. (Courtesy of the National Archives — Pacific Northwest Region.)

of the Chinese families listed in a sampling of the 1900 census for San Francisco followed the traditional *Pai-hang* system in naming their children. For example, the Chinese names belonging to the three sons of Wong Sow Shu and his wife consist of the word *Dick;* and the word *Tai* appears in their names of their three daughters. Only a few families ignored the *Pai-hang* system, and the children of a few families had American given names.

Astonishingly, though, parents of several families bestowed the same generation name to their sons and daughters. For example, the two daughters and one son of Chow Hoy and his wife have the generation name *Gum* in their names. All six sons and one daughter of Jee Gam and his wife have the same generation name *Shin*. Jee Gam was a devout Christian and preacher, which may explain this revolutionary act in treating sons and daughters equally in their names.

In several families the generation name for the daughters was changed, usually when a third daughter was born. A very interesting example is seen in the names of the seven daughters — two of whom were twins — of a Tong family. The first three daughters have *Sue* for their generation name but the next three daughters did not have any generation name — they have entirely different names. It was in the name of the seventh daughter that the word *Sue* appears again — as if the parents had resigned themselves to having yet another daughter and were welcoming her wholeheartedly to the family.

If we recall, it is not unusual for a Chinese woman to have a name that expresses the wish "I-want-a-son-the-next-time." Perhaps this desire was being expressed when the early immigrants changed the generation name for a newborn daughter. A friend thought that this could account for the fact that she and the next sister have a different generation name from the one bestowed to her two younger sisters. She knew that her father had fervently hoped for a son, and this may have been expressed in the change in the generation name for the last two daughters.

This sampling of the 1900 census for San Francisco also shows that the Chinese faithfully followed the tradition of identifying a married woman by her *shi* or original surname. (In contrast, the given names of wives were listed more often in the sampling of earlier census records.) *Shi* is variously spelled *Shee, Sea, See,* and *She,* as in *Yang Shee.* Curiously, one census taker prefixed the word "mon" to the names of several wives, as in "Mon Gung She." This word (門), which means "door," represents yet another name custom for women except that it usually appears on gravestones and the husband's surname would always precede this word. For example, the name *Loo (men) Yuen Shee* indicates that this woman of the Yuen clan had entered the house of the Loo clan in marriage.

If this sampling of the 1900 San Francisco census is any indication, extremely few interracial marriages took place among the Chinese. Only several are listed, one of whom is Charles Laiyow who married a Russian woman. The percentage of Chinese men taking non–Chinese wives was probably much higher in New York's Chinatown. Louis Beck, whose book was published in 1898, wrote that out of 84 married couples, 48 wives were white women and, in 30 families, both husband and wife were born in China.

All of these irregularities in name recording, and the variations in surname spelling which occur in these early official records, are also found in the identification certificates required of the Chinese during the exclusion period. The exclusion laws not only regulated Chinese immigration, they instigated an identification and certification system for the Chinese in this country. Thus, this raises the question of whether these laws had a particular effect on stabilizing surname spelling for Chinese Americans.

10. STABILIZING SURNAMES

"Yet leaving a name, I trust, that will not perish in the dust."
Robert Southey, *My Days Among the Dead Are Past*

Registration of various kinds helped to stabilize surname spelling among Americans in general, Howard F. Barker noted in his articles about names in the United States during the 1920s and 1930s. The beginning of surname stabilization is attributed to World War I (1914–18) when veterans discovered after the war that, in order to enjoy the benefits of their service, they had to adhere to the spelling of their name as it appeared on official records. Prior to that war, Americans were in the habit of changing or respelling their surnames in favor of ones that took their fancy. It was not until 1940 that family names became more stable as more Americans registered for an insurance policy, a car license, or for home ownership.

Since the Chinese exclusion laws required the Chinese to obtain special certificates to ensure their right to be in this country, it follows that these laws should have had an effect on stabilizing their surnames. From 1882 to the end of 1943, Chinese immigration was administered under a plethora of complicated rules and regulations. There were certificates for gaining admittance to this country and for leaving this country if the applicant wanted to be readmitted from a trip abroad. After 1892, the resident laborer, who was here before the 1882 law was enacted, had to register for a certificate that entitled him to remain a legal resident.

Identification Certificates

Four main types of certificates were issued: the "Section 6" Certificate, the Return Certificate (or Certificate of Departure), the Certificate of Residence, and the Certificate of Identity. "Section 6" referred to the particular section of the 1882 law that described this document issued to the exempt class, such as the

In the matter of the application of   :

    U N G S O O K E E

registered Chinese laborer, (Certifi- :   Port Townsend, Wash.,
cate of Residence No. 55797), for a :   Nov. 12, 1910.
return certificate.

        Tom L. Wyckoff, Immigrant Inspector, Examiner,
        Henry A. Myers, Immigrant Inspector, Stenographer.
        Lan On Tai, Chinese Interpreter, (sworn).

  UNG SOO KEE, having been duly sworn, testified as follows:

Q. What are your names?
A. Soo Kee is my baby name; Ung is the family name; Jim Kee
   is my American name.

Q. How old are you?
A. Fifty-two.

Q. How long have you lived in the United States?
A. Thirty years.

Q. What occupation do you follow for a living?
A. Gardener.

Q. You allege in your application for return certificate that
   Len Chung owes you $1,000.00, money which you loaned to
   him. When did you lend him the money?
A. K. S. 34, 1st month, 2nd day.

Q. Where were you when you loaned the money?
A. Dungeness, Wash., at the McAlmond ranch.

Q. What kind of a paper did Len Chung give you to show that
   he owes you $1,000.00?
A. He didn't give me any.

Q. In the past two years has he paid you any interest or anything for the use of the $1,000.00?
A. No, not yet.

Q. Do you know what Len Chung borrowed the money for?
A. To plant potatoes.

Q. What does Len Chung do for a living?
A. He is a gardener, renting land from McAlmond at Dungeness.

Interrogation of Ung Soo Kee, a resident laborer applying for a return certificate so he could go abroad. Note his baby (or milk) name and American name. K.S. 34 equals 1909. (Courtesy of the National Archives — Pacific Northwest Region.)

merchant. But it did not guaranteed admittance. Any conflicting information obtained through intensive interrogations conducted by immigration officers could have resulted in a denial of entry.

If a resident of Chinese ancestry wanted to take a trip abroad, he had to apply at least a month in advance for written permission and for a Return Certificate from the immigration department. The traveler even had to return to the same place from which he departed in order to be readmitted. No Chinese person could take a trip outside of this country on the spur of the moment — not even to Canada or Mexico — without jeopardizing his status.

Merchants, teachers, and students had to apply for the Exempt's Certificate (Form 431); the American-born citizen applied for the Native's Return Certificate (Form 430); and the resident laborer obtained a Laborer's Return Certificate (Form 432). After 1909, immigration authorities issued a Certificate of Identity for both admission and readmission purposes.

Prior to the 1937 Sino-Japanese War, the early established families customarily sent their children to China for schooling or for marriage purposes and the identity certificate paved the way for their return. Some families discovered that they had to safeguard their certificates while in China, otherwise they would be stranded if these were lost or stolen.

Chinese Americans also found that planning a weekend visit to Canada or Mexico was like planning a year's trip to China. For instance, in 1940, when my husband, who lived in Seattle, decided to visit friends in Vancouver, Canada, for the first time, he almost forgot he had made such plans by the time he received permission to do so. However, after being instructed to apply to the Canadian government for permission — Canada had similar Chinese exclusion laws — he abandoned his plans.

Certificate of Residence

Beginning in 1892, all resident laborers had to register for a Certificate of Residence (called a "chock gee" in Cantonese) or face deportation (27 Stat., 25). Although the law did not stipulate it, many merchants registered for one because, from time to time, immigration authorities conducted raids in Chinatowns across the nation to arrest the person found without this certificate for the purpose of deportation. A sampling of these certificates from the holdings of the National Archives in Washington, D.C., included some issued to a merchant's wife, a native-born child, and a six-day-old infant born in San Francisco! In 1900, the

Example of a Certificate of Residence issued to a "Person other than a Laborer."
(Courtesy National Archives, Washington, D.C.)

registration law applied to the Chinese in Hawaii since the islands had become a U.S. territory.

At first the Chinese protested the 1892 registration act, but the Supreme Court upheld its constitutionality. Another law (the McCreary amendment) extended the registration period because it would have cost several million dollars to deport the thousands of Chinese who had refused to register. Ironically, in 1922, when immigration authorities first proposed registration for all aliens in this country, they cited the registration of the Chinese (Fong Yue Ting test case [149 U.S., 698]) as giving this right to Congress.

Earlier, in 1907, immigration authorities had wanted to reregister every Chinese person in this country for a Certificate of Residence, claiming there would then be better administration of the exclusion laws. Fortunately, their recommendations were not acted upon. In looking back, the exclusion laws not only discriminated against Chinese immigration, these laws set up a special system of identification and certification that singled out the Chinese from immigrants of other ethnicity.

Name Recording on Identification Certificates

Yet the special certification system did not result in a sudden regular reporting of the usual Chinese name. A sampling of nearly a hundred return certificates and certificates of residence reveals that names were similar to those recorded in the federal census records. What proved to be most helpful in deciphering Chinese names were the Chinese signatures on many of these documents. This indicates

Certificate of Identity issued only to Chinese residents or persons of Chinese descent under the Chinese exclusion laws.

that many surnames are still commonly seen today—*Lee, Wong, Lem, Yee,* and *Lew*—and that variations in spelling the same surname could change over time. For example, the spelling variants *Leo* and *Louie* are not usually associated today with the family name that is spelled Lew (劉).

The Chinese signatures on some certificates of residence disclose the fact that the disyllabic given name was indeed recorded without the family name. Otherwise, such names as *Ching Hoy, Doo Lun,* and *Wen Chung* are easily mistaken for a surname and a monosyllabic given name. In one certificate, only the given name *Hing* appears. When the family name was recorded, it was usually followed by a monosyllabic given name, as in *Wong Ham.* In a sampling of return certificates, the vocative *Ah* appears in many of the names, such as *Ah You, Ah Yuk,* and *Ah Frue.* As explained earlier, these are partial names without the surname.

It was quite amusing to note the Chinese signatures of Charley Sing and Charlie Kee on their return certificates because both had merely phoneticized the sounds of their adopted names into Chinese. In this way, they succeeded in keeping their full Chinese names a secret. Such irregularities in name recording undoubtedly occurred because the exclusion laws required the Chinese applying for a certificate to have two white persons testify on his behalf. Therefore, if a white person had only known *Charlie Kee* by this name, it makes no sense for Charlie to record his actual Chinese name on his identification certificate. He might have been deported. Besides, it was just as practical to phoneticize the American name into Chinese — what are the chances of a white person from a small town knowing that the Chinese signatures of Charlie Kee, Ah You, and Ching Hoy, are not their actual or full Chinese names?

Chinese Habeas Corpus Cases

In comparison, the index to Chinese *habeas corpus* cases — which were tried in San Francisco from 1882 to 1904 — indicates that the usual Chinese personal name was recorded with greater frequency toward the turn of the century. This may have occurred because these cases — appeals made by those who were denied entry — took place in a city where there would be more familiarity with Chinese names.

Still, unusual surname variants abound, as in the census records. The vocative *Ah* still appears in many names except that it is usually preceded by a surname — as in *Leo Ah Yee.* Interestingly, the usual Chinese name appears with great

111

consistency for the young men identified as sons of merchants. Not surprisingly, some names are spelled differently from one document to the next. For example, Lam Young Doar had his surname respelled as *Lane* and Leong Din had his respelled as *Leng*. There are some instances of children having surnames that are differently spelled from the father's name. One father has the surname *Hom* and his son's is spelled *Tom*. Another father has the surname *Hor* although his daughter's is spelled *Ho*.

There is every reason to believe that spelling stabilized gradually for the Chinese rather than as an immediate result of the exclusion laws. Irregularities in name recording for the Chinese undoubtedly occurred because names were not as carefully recorded as they tend to be today. Also, the population itself was not stable in the early decades of the exclusion period. An attrition of surnames would have taken place because many Chinese left this country and did not return. Moreover, most laborers, who comprised a large segment of this population during those decades, did not have families in this country. As we shall see in the chapters ahead, new surname variants would arise when more families were established.

Some of the factors that helped stabilize American surnames prior to the 1940s had a negligible effect on surnames of Chinese origin. Before World War II, relatively few Chinese owned their own homes and even fewer possessed insurance policies. But illegal immigration was likely a strong factor in stabilizing surname spelling among the early immigrants.

11. IT'S ONLY
A "PAPER" NAME

"Sometimes true and false family relationships became hopelessly entangled..."
Betty Lee Sung, *The Story of the Chinese in America*

The first time I heard the term "paper name" was in Chinese language school. A girl had come up to me and said, "You know, of course, that your surname in Chinese is not the same as your surname in English." Of course I was not aware that both ought to match up in sound. Fortunately, there was a classmate who had two different surnames. When I asked her for the reason, she merely replied abruptly: "It's a paper name." It meant nothing to me at the time but it sounded like the perfect answer to give to anyone else who commented on my name.

"Paper name" — or *ji ming* as it is called in Chinese — is a euphemism for the name of an illegal immigrant who had purchased a falsified certificate for the purpose of gaining entry to this country. The name on the certificate was perforce adopted by the individual and, later on, if he married and had children, the "paper" surname was handed down to them. For example, a Miss Dong may tell you that *Dong* is her "paper" surname and *Law* is really her surname.

The "paper name" was always a Chinese name that had been transcribed into English, but its owner's true identity was revealed by the characters of his actual Chinese name. His actual family name would also appear in the Chinese names of his children. A few individuals managed to purchase a certificate that had the same family name, and occasionally one comes across a family with a father having one "paper surname" while his son has a different one. Because of his illegal status, the individual with a "paper" name, in all likelihood, did not deliberately respell or change his name.

Paper Sons

Despite the legal and social discrimination against them during the exclusion period, many Chinese were still desirous of emigrating to this land of freedom and economic opportunity. Since few qualified for the exempt classification, surreptitious means were used to gain entry. It was usually young men who came to this country on falsified papers. They came as students, as sons of merchants or as sons of U.S. citizens. The young man who came as a merchant's son was called a "mah-jeen son" by the Chinese speakers. And the young man who claimed to be a son of a citizen was commonly known as a "paper son."

The most popular deceptive practice was to claim being a son of an American citizen. (American law grants derivative citizenship status to a foreign-born child of an American citizen.) His certificate of identity was often purchased through the so-called "slot system," a fairly simple yet long-term project. The "slot" was created when a Chinese, returning from a family visit abroad, reported to immigration authorities that his wife in China had given birth to a son (daughters were rarely reported) even though it may not have been true. In this way, a certificate became available to relatives or could be sold years later to a family who had a son old enough to leave home and work to repay the debt incurred in its purchase. The usual price of a certificate during the 1930s was about $100 per year of age.

For many years, the immigration department required all Chinese who made trips home to give detailed information about their families in the belief that this could prevent evasion of the exclusion laws. It later dawned upon some officers how well the Chinese appreciated the opportunity to lay a foundation for a family of sons, complete with fictitious names.

However, the "paper son" had to pass some tricky cross-examinations by immigration officers that could bar his way to living in America. It was well-known to the Chinese that interrogations were designed so as "to trap or trick a person into giving contradictory information so that he would expose himself" as a fraudulent case. Any discrepancies in answers could lead to deportation. The Chinese also knew that the immigration authorities knew about the slot system.

As a result, the "paper son" was coached on responding to questions and had to memorize information about his "family" before being interrogated. Sometimes an unscrupulous immigration officer demanded money for approving admittance. Unfortunately, those with legitimate claims could be denied entry because they either refused to pay the bribe or did not know the exact answer to such questions as, "How many steps to the attic?"

Citizenship

Citizenship of the father of a "paper son" was another questionable matter. The Burlingame Treaty of 1868 between America and China recognized that Americans and Chinese had a right to emigrate to each other's country, but the exclusion laws specifically denied the Chinese the privilege of becoming naturalized citizens. (Incidentally, Burlingame, California, was named for Anson Burlingame, who negotiated this treaty.) Therefore a Chinese had to be born in this country in order to claim American citizenship, a status that was officially recognized by the U.S. Supreme Court in the 1898 Wong Kim Ark case (169 U.S. 649).

Many Chinese were able to claim American citizenship after the 1906 San Francisco earthquake and fire, since birth records and other documents had been destroyed. This in turn enabled many more young men to come as a "son of a citizen." Nonetheless, immigration authorities wondered about the extraordinary number of "sons" versus "daughters" who were born to Chinese families.

"Confession" Program

Although it was common knowledge in the close-knit Chinatowns across this country that many individuals had a "paper name," the threat of deportation made it necessary to be cautious about revealing this information lest it reached the ears of immigration authorities. Any leakage about one person's "paper name" could have a domino effect on others caught in this same situation. This was not always understood by the native-born generation because many parents did not discuss such matters in their presence. The prevalent stance was: the less you know, the better for us all.

In 1959, a program was launched by the U.S. Justice Department and Chinese community leaders to encourage all those who came under cloudy circumstances to reveal their true identities. And they were to inform authorities of others who had entered illegally. Over the next decade, about 8,000 "confessions" were obtained in San Francisco alone. Since then, some Chinese Americans discarded their "paper" surnames and reverted to the true family name. Most people, however, continue to acquiesce to their accidental surname.

The "paper name" even follows its owner to the grave. It may be detected on gravestones because the "paper name" will not match up in sound with the Chinese characters of the deceased's actual name. So, even in death the "paper

Gravestone reveals that Toy is the "paper" surname for a Wong family.

name" prevails. It was not until the 1970s that Chinese Americans became more comfortable about revealing in public that they had a "paper" surname. Although it serves as a reminder of the illegal status of a family's progenitor, the "paper" surname can be regarded as a symbol of his adventuresome and intrepid spirit.

12. ATTEMPTS
TO STANDARDIZE
CHINESE NAME SPELLING

"Lack of uniformity in the English spelling of the names of Chinese persons has been a prolific source of confusion..."

David D. Jones

In American law, the sound of the name is considered more important than its spelling, in recognition that spelling variations exist for the same name. Even today, when surname spelling has been stabilized for Americans, names are still inadvertently misspelled, which we might find amusing. During the exclusion period, Chinese immigrants faced the threat of deportation if their names were respelled. As a result, at least two attempts were made in this country to standardize spelling for Chinese names.

The David Jones Spelling System

David Jones, an immigration officer and interpreter for the Chinese, had noticed that the lack of a standard spelling system caused some serious problems. If, for example, a resident laborer applied for a replacement of his identity certificate and the name on his application did not match that on the original document, he could be deported. A merchant could be blocked from reentering this country from a trip abroad if the name on his passport was spelled differently from that on his original identity certificate. All original documents were kept in the files of the immigration department.

Some habeas corpus cases undoubtedly occurred because names were respelled. Fong Shue Jon's name was respelled *Kwong Sow Jan* on his China passport by Chinese authorities. They probably thought that Mr. Fong's name should have been spelled according to standard Cantonese except that in doing so, it changed

117

the pronunciation. This also happened to Jone Kon Kum whose name was respelled *Choong Hung Kam.*

So, in 1904, Jones established a Chinese name spelling company in San Francisco in hopes that his method of spelling would prevail. Names would be transcribed according to the two Cantonese subdialects spoken by most Chinese in this country at the time. These were the *Sam Yup* and *Sze Yup* dialects, which the author spelled as "Saam Yup" and "Sz Yip," respectively. *Sam Yup* means "Three Districts dialect," which is akin to standard Cantonese, and *Sze Yup* means "Four Districts dialect."

The table of pronunciations below illustrates the differences in sound between these two dialects as they are still heard in Chinese American communities today:

"Saam Yup"	*"Sz Yip"*	*Surname character*
Dang	Ang	鄧
Gwaan	Gwaan	關
Jeng	Jeang	鄭
Jue	Jee	朱
Ley	Lee	李
Lue	Looy	雷
Lum	Lem	林
Mooy	Moy	梅
Tsoy	Toy	蔡
Wun	Woon	溫

Suffice it to say, Jones was not successful in his attempt to standardize spelling except to add a few more surname variants. Some surnames, such as such as *Wong, Chin,* and *Yee,* were already popular spellings.

J. Endicott Gardner's Listing

A few years later, in 1909, John Gardner, a Presbyterian minister who was also a Chinese interpreter, compiled a longer list of surnames with their transcriptions according to the "Cantonese or Sam Yup," "Sz Yup," and "Mandarin" dialects. It has over 1,900 family names, including 177 double surnames and 10 triple character ones. A column of "various U.S. popular spellings" was added. His compilation was made at the request of the Bureau of Immigration and Naturalization.

Gardner modified the Jones method for the Four Districts dialect but used the J. Dyer Ball romanization system for the Three Districts dialect. The S.W. Williams system was selected for Mandarin transcription — Williams, as mentioned earlier, was an American Presbyterian minister who served in China. The following table gives the spellings in Gardner's book for the same family names in the order that they are listed above:

D. Jones "Sz Yip"	Ball's "Sam Yup"	"Popular U.S. spellings"	S.W. Williams Mandarin
Ang	Tang	Tang, Dung, Dang	Tang
Gwaan	Kwan	Kwan, Qwan, Gwaan	Kwan
Jing	Ching	Ching, Jing	Chin
Jee	Chu	Chu, Jue, Chee, Jee	Chu
Lee	Lei	Lay, Lee	Li
Looy	Lou	Lou, Looey, Luey, Luie	Lei
Lem	Lam	Lam, Lum, Lem, Lim	Lin
Moy	Mui	Mui, Muie, Mooy	Mei
Toy	Tsoi	Tsoi, Choi, Toy	Tsai
Woon	Wan	Wan, Wen, Woon	Wun

It is difficult to understand, however, the source for Gardner's "various popular spellings" for each family name because less than ten percent of the names listed were brought to this country. Only two double surnames — *Sze To* (司徒) and *Au Yang* (歐陽) — had been brought by the early immigrants. Even today, double surnames rarely occur among Chinese Americans. A few more have been seen recently, such as Chu Ke (諸葛) and Twanmoh (端木). As for triple character surnames, these belong to ethnic minority groups in China. One can concede, though, that some "popular spellings" could be given names since the Chinese, like other peoples, use family names as such.

Undoubtedly many of Gardner's "popular spellings" fell by the wayside as family life was established. For example, *Quan* and *Quon* are seen among the early established families rather than *Gwan* or *Gwaan*. The spelling *Gee* is seen more often than *Jee*, and *Choy* occurs more frequently than *Choi* or *Tsoi* for fourth and later generations of Chinese Americans.

Certain Dialect Features

Before going further, one outstanding difference between the Three Districts dialect and the Four Districts dialect should be pointed out. The initial "T" sound that is heard in the Three Districts dialect is usually transformed into an "H" sound in the latter dialect. For instance, the surname *Tom* is pronounced as *Hom* in the Four Districts dialect. Four other surnames reveal this dialect trait:

Selected Spelling	*Four Districts sound*	*Character*
Sze To	Soo Hoo	司徒
Tian, Tien, Tin	Hen	田
Tang, Tong	Hong	唐
Tang, Tong	Hong	湯

The Chungshan dialect is another significant Cantonese dialect that was brought by the pioneer immigrants and it is still a dominant dialect in Hawaii. Since the initial "Y" sound that is heard in the other two dialects is usually dropped, the surname *Yu* (余) sounds more like "eu." Four other surnames show this tendency:

Selected Spelling	*Chungshan*	*Character*
Yiu	Iu	姚
Yim	Im	嚴
Yoon, Yuen	In, Inn	袁, 阮
Yip	Ip, Ipp	葉

Rules on Chinese Name Spelling

Gardner's listing, however, was not mentioned in any of the rules and regulations that enforced the Chinese exclusion laws. In 1917, a rule on the "Spelling of Chinese Names" appeared for the first time. As Rule 26 stated: "It is practically impossible to use any general and uniform method of spelling Chinese names. Such names are supposed to be rendered in English according to the science of phonetics, but there is a great divergence of opinion as to the letters of the English alphabet that ought to be used to represent certain sounds." The only advice given to the immigration officer was to spell the name or sound *Lui* according to these three letters and not as "Louis, Louie, Looey, etc." Evidently this advice went unheeded because *Lui* was never a popular spelling for this family name among the early immigrants and their descendants.

Telegraphic Code

There may have been one other government attempt to romanize the Cantonese dialects, but whether it had any direct bearing on surname spelling is not clear. For some reason, the Chinese Telegraphic Code was transcribed according to Mandarin, Cantonese, and "Toyshan" sounds. "Toyshan" or Toishan is a subdialect of the Four Districts dialect group that was spoken by the majority of the pioneer immigrants from Guangdong province. Unfortunately no information could be obtained about this U.S. government publication — it may have been compiled during the 1940s — or about the spelling method used for the Cantonese dialects. The Wade-Giles was apparently used for the Mandarin transcription.

Numbered codes have been used for sending telegrams in the Chinese language since the late 1800s — the telegraphic system was established in China in 1881. It is the only accurate way for sending messages in the Chinese language by wireless communication since a message sent in alphabetical script can be easily garbled in translation.

The British government found the Chinese Telegraphic Code to be very useful for identifying Hong Kong residents by name. A friend, who lived in Hong Kong when it was still under British rule, recalls that each resident had to carry an identification card on which the personal name appears in English spelling, in Chinese characters, and in telegraphic code number. For example, the architect I.M. Pei's name would be coded as 6296 5124 6900.

If the Chinese Telegraphic Code had indeed been transcribed for name spelling purposes in this country, then the following surnames might be spelled accordingly:

Mandarin	Cantonese	"Toyshan"	CTC number	Character
Chao	Chew	Jell	6392	趙
Chen	Yun	Jin	3914	甄
Han	Horn	Horn	7281	韓
Su	So	Thloo	5685	蘇
Tseng	Chung	Dong	2582	曾

The transliteration *Thloo* for the Toishan dialect is particularly interesting because the initial *S* sound is quite similar to the Welsh *Ll* sound which is represented in such names as *Llewellyn*. By the 1940s, surname spelling among Chinese Americans had become quite stabilized just as this was taking place among Americans in general. And many family names were Americanized as family life grew in this country.

13. AMERICANIZATION
OF NAMES

"Everybody has a name anybody has a name and everybody anybody does what he does with his name feels what he feels about his name, likes or dislikes what he has to have with having his name, in short it is his name unless he changes his name unless he does what he likes what he likes with his name."

Gertrude Stein, *Four in America*

What one perceives to be a surname of Chinese origin may be based on the way it looks—it looks Chinese. Or it may be due to association—you know that its owner is of Chinese ancestry. But looks can be deceiving.

Tong, for example, is an English name that looks Chinese. *Ching* and *Yuan* resemble Chinese names as well, yet these are Cornish or Welsh names. Who would believe at first glance that *Wang* and *Wong* are old English names—*Wang* means "a piece of meadowland." Here in America, surnames such as *Ing*, *Lew*, *Ling*, *Ming*, *Pan*, *Tso*, and *Yow* belong to Americans of different ethnicity as well as to Chinese Americans.

On the other hand, some American surnames of Chinese origin look Euro-American, such as *Fann*, *Juan*, *Lang*, and *Lau*. Some Anglicized names can be traced to personal whim. As William Tann explained, his surname was originally spelled *Tang* (鄧). His father came to this country for his college education during the 1930s. It was not until he returned home to China to reside in Shanghai, that his father Anglicized his surname by dropping the "g" and added the extra "n."

Americanized surnames of Chinese origin are mostly phonetic renditions of Chinese dialect sounds. Most occurred because the early immigrants from China came at a time when the names of all foreigners were subject to respelling. If they did not speak English, their names were spelled for them, according to the way it was heard or thought to be heard. Usually names were Americanized because it was common practice "to alter an unfamiliar name into a familiar name or word with a similar sound." As Elsdon Smith points out, this was also done to please the American eye and ear, causing many foreign names to look "more like English names."

Howard Barker, who wrote about surnames in the United States in the late 1920s and 1930s, observed that many polysyllabic European names were relentlessly reduced to one or two syllables so that they could conform to the English language. Americanizing a name was sometimes made deliberately for economic and psychological reasons. These include, according to Louis Adamic, author of *What's Your Name?* the difficulty in being hired when one had a "foreign" name, the painful experience of having one's name continually mispronounced and the shame of having a foreign background.

For Chinese Americans, though, an Americanized name would not spare an individual from any kind of racial discrimination since facial and other physical features cannot be hidden. An employer or landlord could take one look at a Chinese American applicant and lie about the job being filled or that the apartment or hotel room had just been rented.

This brings to mind the following story once told by a friend: During World War II, a Chinese American woman wanted to rent a place in Sacramento, California, in order to be near her husband who was a serviceman. She spent several days futilely setting up appointments in response to ads about available housing to rent only to be told, when she showed up in person, that it was just rented. Finally she broke down and wept. When her young daughter asked why she was crying, she sadly replied that it must be because of their race that they were turned away. The little girl mulled over what she heard. Then she said, commandingly: "Mommy, next time don't tell them we're Chinese!"

Having a name that was acceptable in appearance was another reason to Americanize a name. In places where relatively few Chinese American families lived, having an unusually spelled name or one that could be turned around in meaning was liable to attract unwanted attention and could subject its owner to ridicule. Herbert Moe, whose family was one of the early established Chinese American families in Portland, Oregon, recalled that his surname was spelled *Moo* before it was respelled. Henry Chann and Ernest Chann of Oakland, California, said that their older sister added the extra "n" to their family name when she enrolled them in public school. She happened to meet someone with this surname and liked the way it looked.

As a result of acquiescing to the American way with names, Chinese Americans have a large number of Euro-American family names in common with Americans of other ethnicities. These include *Hugh* (丘), *Jew* (周, 趙), *Knapp*

(聶), *Lewis* (羅), *Lord* (陸), *Luke* (陸), *Sidney* (薛), *Towne* (湯), and *Zane* (曾). Incidentally, the surname *Jew* is not of Jewish origin. According to Robert Rennick of Kentucky, this surname existed in England before the fourteenth century, among families in the Devonshire area who were not of Jewish faith. British surnames are well-represented in the names of Chinese Americans and are, surprisingly, quite close to their Chinese pronunciation. *English* names especially abound, such as *Chew* (趙), *Chin* (陳), *Dear* (謝), *Gee* (朱), *Gum* (甘), *Hall* (何), *Huey* (許), *Joe* (周), *Law* (羅), *Lee* (李, 利), *Leo* (廖), *Lock, Locke* (駱), *Lum* (林), *Marr* (馬), *Thom* (譚), *Tong* (唐, 湯), and *Young* (楊).

Some are *Irish* names: *Dea* (謝), *Dunn* (鄧), *Dwan* (段), *Hoey* (許), and *Quan* (關). And some are *Scottish* names: *Don* (曾), *Huie* (許), and *Mar* (馬). The spelling *Ing* (伍, 吳), however, is derived from the *Welsh*, whereas the spelling *Eng* is Scandinavian in origin.

Among the *German* names represented are *Jung* (曾,張, 蔣, and 鄭), *Lang* (梁),* *Lau* (劉), *Leon* (梁),† *Mau* (毛), and *Yung* (容, 楊, and 翁). Incidentally, *Jingling, Yingling,* and *Yuengling* are not surnames of Chinese origin; these are spelling variants for Swedish or German names.

Some surnames of Chinese origin speak of other nationalities:

> *Dutch*: *Bock* (白), *Jong* (鍾), *Look* (陸);
> *French*: *Char* (謝), *Louis* (雷), *Lung* (梁, 龍);
> *Italian*: *Pei* (貝, 皮); and
> *Norwegian*: *Eng* (伍, 吳), *Moe* (巫).

And so the list of "American" surnames among Chinese Americans can go on.

Adoption of "American" Surnames

Although *Smith* is the most common American family name, the Chinese did not adopt it for a surname as did many people of different national origins; undoubtedly because there is no initial "sm" sound to words in the Chinese language. However, there is an old story about a Chinese who received the name *John Smith*. When asked about how he came by his unusual name, John replied that an immigration officer gave it to him. He was standing in line behind a man who answered "John Smith" when the officer asked for his name. When it came to his turn to give his name, he told the officer that it was *Sam Ting*.

---

*Lang can be English or Scottish.   †Leon can be Spanish.

Actually, very few Chinese immigrants discarded their Chinese name. Lieaou Ah-See was probably the first to do so. He was one of several Chinese students who attended a foreign mission school in Connecticut between the years 1818 and 1828 and is considered the first Chinese Protestant convert in this country. Lieaou adopted the name *William Botelho* to honor his patron.

Charles Jamison was the name of a Chinese who married a Miss Ah Quy in one of the first Chinese weddings that took place in California during the 1860s. Yo Hing, a cigar store owner in Los Angeles, adopted the name *Joseph Hinton* in 1873 and during the 1890s, another local man, O.Q. Tow, a vegetable vendor in Santa Ana, went by the name *Jimmy Craig*.

In the records of the Chinese Women's Home in San Francisco, a haven for women and girls sponsored by the Presbyterian denomination beginning in the late nineteenth century, the surnames *Johnson*, *Harley*, and *Watson* were mentioned as belonging to Chinese men who had married white women. The explanation for the surname *Watson* is found in H.K. Wong's book, *Gum Sahn Yun*. It arose in 1891 when the eldest son of Jow Wat and Frances Waters was baptized as James Edward Watson in Old Saint Mary's Church in San Francisco.

Interestingly, one of the women in the Home married a white man who was called *Ah Bo*! These records mention a *Susie Runyon* but it turns out that her husband, *Ah Yow*, had leased a fruit ranch from a Mr. Runyon. Being known by the name of the white employer was probably fairly rare among the early Chinese immigrants. A study of the Chinese in Idaho reveals two Chinese men in Idaho City were identified by their employer's name: *Kirtley Sam* worked for a Mr. Kirtley and *Martinelli Sam* was a janitor in Martinelli's saloon.

Richard Lym of San Francisco recalled his mother, Rose Ford Chung, telling him that her father was known as *Billy Ford* and that later he went by the name of *William Ford*. Lym's maternal grandfather came from China in the late nineteenth century and settled in Tonopah, Nevada, where he worked for William or "Billy" Ford — the Fords were a prominent family in town. Although the family name *Chung* was retained, his grandfather gave each of his children the name *Ford* for their middle name. (This seems to be an application of the *Pai-hang* generation naming system, a subject that will soon be discussed.)

The Rev. Edwar Lee, a Methodist minister, thought that there was a vogue, about the turn of the century, among the early Chinese Christians to adopt "American surnames." Nevertheless, they risked being ostracized by other Chinese who regarded it as an act of "forsaking the family name" and a sign of "denationalization." One will recall that "denationalization" was one of the criticisms against students in China adopting Western name customs.

126

Usually people are strongly influenced by their original name when they deliberately change their name. Jee Man Sing who came to America in 1872, for example, took the name *J.M. Singleton* while living in New York City. He was in charge of a Chinese Christian mission in Brooklyn and worked as an interpreter as well. His colleague, Yee Kai Man, also an interpreter, went by the name *Guy Maine*.

Chin [Doo Wah], who settled in St. Helena, California, in the late 1880s, was another Christian who took an American name. He was known as *Frank Chandler*. The family attended the Napa Methodist Church, according to his daughter, Stella Chandler Louis of San Luis Obispo, who had married into another Chinese pioneering family in California.

Conversion and Respelling

Surnames are Americanized in several ways, according to Barker. It is by conversion, respelling, translation, abbreviation, or ornamentation. Conversion takes place when the spelling of another name is adopted because of similarity in sound. Many of the surnames mentioned above are such examples. Additional ones are *Dean* (丁), *New* (牛) and *Stowe* (司徒). Incidentally, the Dean Lung Chair of Chinese at Columbia University was named for a Chinese servant. Dean was a valet to General Horace Carpentier who, in 1901, donated $100,000 to establish a department on Chinese studies to honor his faithful servant. Dean himself gave his life's savings of $12,000 to the University.

Respelling of names commonly occurs when individuals want to improve on the appearance of their name. Kay Jum Ng of Lewiston, Idaho, changed his name to *George Eng*. (The Chinese in the Pacific Northwest have leaned towards the spelling *Eng* rather than *Ng*.) A report in the book *Chinese Argonauts*, about the Chinese of Santa Clara County in California, mentions that Tom Wang Yuet at first altered his name to *Thomas Tom*, then to *Thomas Thom*. After realizing the possibility of being known as Tom Tom, he took the name *Edward T. Thom*.

My husband's family name, Louie (雷), was previously spelled *Loui* and *Louis* before it settled down to its present form. Joseph Jein, who grew up in Santa Barbara, California, recalled that his father adopted this spelling after becoming a Christian — the family name was originally spelled Gin (甄). This surname is also Americanized as *Gene, Ginn,* and *Jean*.

Americanization led to the removal of the final "g" in a few names:

Spelling	*Character*
Don instead of Dong	曾
Jan instead of Jang	曾, 鄭
Leon instead of Leong	梁

Two unusual Anglicized versions exist for the double surname Ou-yang 歐陽: *O'Yang* and *O'Young*. These Irish-looking names brings to mind the time when a friend played hookey on St. Patrick's Day. Her surname was Young. When she showed up in class the next day, her teacher laconically asked: "Well, Miss O'Young, did you have a nice day?" I recall chortling over a cartoon strip called *Tumbleweeds* in which an Indian had captured a Paddy O'Chang. "Where you from?" asked the chief. The reply: "Eastern Ireland!"

Abbreviation and Translation

Abbreviations and translations were often made to bring what were considered awkward and difficult names into line with the English language. A Mrs. Wang said that her husband's name was originally Wangsensteen. Mrs. John Ong of Pasadena, California, said that her husband's family name is an abbreviation of *DeJong*, which was brought here from England and that all the men in their family are blue-eyed blonds. Abbreviation has been unnecessary for the monosyllabic names of Chinese origin, although a double surname like *Soo Hoo* (司徒) might be shortened to either *Hoo* or *Soo*.

Translation is another rare occurrence for surnames of Chinese origin. But there is at least one example: Dr. Mary Stone, one of the first women who came from China around the turn of the century for a college education, had translated her surname *Shih* (石) to accommodate classmates who had difficulty pronouncing her name.

Ornamentation

Ornamentation, on the other hand, is quite common for Chinese American names. This includes doubling the final consonant, adding or substituting letters to an otherwise plain name. Somehow the tendency of Americans to add a final "s" to a short surname did not occur for Chinese Americans. The surname

Jones (鍾) may be one exception — the original spelling could have been *Jone*. Jones was the surname of an early established Chinese family in Portland, Oregon, and is also seen in the San Francisco Bay area.

The following surnames are examples of doubling the final consonant:

Spelling	Character
Chann, Chenn, Chinn, Chunn	陳
Ginn	甄
Jann	鄭
Lamm, Limm, Linn, Lynn	林
Marr	馬
Nipp	聶
Tongg	鄧
Yapp, Yepp	葉

The silent "e" ending seems to round out the appearance of the name:

Spelling	Character
Choye, Toye	蔡
Dere, Jaire	謝
Funge	馮
Goe, Koe	高
Lowe	劉
Moye	梅
Soe, Sue	蘇
Wye	韋

There are other ways to ornament a name:

Spelling	Character
Doung instead of Dong	曾
Johe instead of Joe	周
Lamb instead of Lam	林
Lym instead of Lim	林
Pond instead of Pon	盤
Tain instead of Tan	譚

The letter "r" was added to several surnames:

Spelling	Character
Char, Dair, Dare, Der, Dere, Dear, Jair	謝
Harm, Tarm	譚
Hor	何
Lor	羅
Mar, Marr	馬
Mark	麥, 莫
Shyr	石
Yorn	袁

There is no "r" sound when pronouncing these names in Chinese, but this letter could have been inserted as a clue to a broad "a" or "aw" sound. Or, if the surname is spelled according to Chao and Yang's romanization system for Mandarin, the "r" indicates the correct tone to use. As mentioned in a previous chapter, the "r" in the surname Chern is a clue to pronounce it in the second tone in Mandarin.

Sometimes when an individual respells his family name, this results in family members having different surnames. Richard Lym mentioned that other members of his father's family kept the original spelling *Lim*. David R. Chan of Los Angeles observed that each of the three brothers in his father's family spelled the family name differently. The original spelling was *Chin*. One brother kept it, his father changed it to *Chan*, and another brother changed it to *Chen*.

To be sure, an Anglicized name is not always indicative of Americanization. Due to the influence of the English language in different countries, a Chinese immigrant may arrive with an Anglicized surname. Henry Gaw of Southern California, who emigrated from Hong Kong during the 1980s, recalls that when his family lived in Burma, their surname was spelled *Ngaw* (吳). His father dropped the initial letter "N" after moving to Hong Kong because he felt that people have difficulty pronouncing the "ng" sound. Incidentally, *Gaw* is another surname of English origin that is found among Chinese Americans. It happens to mean "foreigner" or "stranger."

It seems that the Americanization of surnames of Chinese origin is no longer as prevalent a practice as it was prior to World War II. The use of Chinese-English dictionaries, a strong sense of being Chinese, a better social climate in

America, and the tolerance for differently spelled surnames have all contributed to an even greater multiethnic representation in name spelling for Chinese Americans. And, as we shall see in the next chapter, immigrants tend to seek ways to transfer their name traditions even if they acquiesce to the Americanization of their names.

14. TRANSFERRING
NAME TRADITIONS

"Giving a name, indeed, is a poetic art..."
Thomas Carlyle, *Journal*, May 18, 1832

It was the usual legal notification of a name change that has been appearing regularly in a Chinese-American English language newspaper since the late 1980s. However, it was eye-catching in its statement. Yuk Hing Low and Augusto L. Siu had petitioned the court to change their son's name from Dragon Tin Loong Siu to *Kevin Tin Loong Siu*. Those of us who were born and raised in America can understand why a boy named *Dragon* would want to change his name. It may be a popular name in Chinese naming traditions but it bellows for attention — unwanted attention — in this country. Chinese names are rarely translated but now and then one comes across a *Lotus*, a *Jade*, and a *Tiger*.

The translation from "loong" to Dragon and the father's name of Augusto suggest that the parents are recent immigrants. As Leslie Dunkling, author of *Our Secret Names*, observed, newcomers might well not have a precise image of American name fashions and might think that any English-sounding name can be used in the English-speaking world at any time. On the other hand, Dragon's parents could have wanted their son to have a unique name; *Dragon* is not likely to be repeated. Americans can empathize with the desire to have a unique name.

According to George Stewart, naming practices began to change during the 1950s and the old familiar names — such as *Mary* and *John* — were rejected in favor of new names or differently spelled names, especially for girls. Today one is apt to meet a *Cindi* or *Syndi* instead of a *Cindy* and a *Viki* instead of a *Vicky*. Yet most Americans tend to follow the same name fashions. For instance, there was a *J* craze in the selection of names. Beginning in the early 1970s, *Jennifer* was the most popular girl's name, then *Jessica*, and this carried over into other *J* names, such as *Joelle* and *Jenna* for girls and *Jason* and *Jared* for boys.

Stewart attributed the rise in manufactured names and the search for originality in names to the "flight from old social customs." Leonard Ashley, another onomastician, believes this is due to African-Americans and other ethnic groups seeking "stronger cultural identities." However, unusual manufactured names, such as *Bendrew*, *Citania*, *Czarina*, *Dragona*, and *Kenjohn*, that are found for Chinese Americans could be attributed to Chinese naming practices. As a young woman who emigrated from Taiwan explained, she chose the name *Mirage* for herself because she wanted to have one that is uniquely hers, just as her Chinese name makes her feel like a special person. This same sentiment was echoed by a friend who emigrated from Hong Kong—she named herself *Cassandra* because it is not a common name for American women.

Some very creative names belong to the siblings of a Honolulu family: eight daughters were named after the musical scale and two sons received the names of planets. According to one story, a General Tai—he is *Robert Tai* in Elsdon Smith's version—named seven of his daughters *DoDo*, *ReRe*, *MiMi*, *FaFa*, *SoSo*, *LaLa*, and *TiTi*; he named the eighth daughter *Octavia*. The sons were named *Uranus* and *Saturn*. This story may sound apocryphal, yet a LaLa Tai was selected Narcissus Queen during the 1969 lunar new year celebration in Honolulu.

Naming After Placenames

Certain other Chinese name traditions have been transferred in the selection of an American name, such as naming a child after a placename. Courtland Chow was named after his birthplace, a small town located south of Sacramento, California. He was almost named *Woodland*, after a town that is located north of Sacramento. His father had wanted a name to match up in sound with the Chinese name he had already selected for his first-born son. When the doctor heard about this, he felt he had to take a hand in the matter. He said to Mr. Chow: "Why don't you name your son after our town? Nobody knows where Woodland is."

A girlhood friend was named *California* by her father—we called her *Cal*. A schoolmate, who was born in Twin Falls, Idaho, was named *Usa* in honor of the United States of America. A foreign student, who came from Shanghai during the late 1930s, was named *Utah* but he may have acquired the name of this state quite inadvertently because it is a transcription of his Chinese name. His brother or cousin, Makepeace Uho Tsao, also has the letter "U" for his generation name.

Naming After Respected Persons

Another Chinese naming practice is to name a child after someone the parents admire and respect. Jefferson Shannon Kitt, who was born in 1867 in Fresno, California, was named after his father's good friend and business partner, Jefferson Milam Shannon. According to a family member, his father Leong Ah Kitt — *Leong* is the family name — came to California during the 1850s and became a blacksmith; Shannon, who was well-known in local politics, joined him later in the blacksmithing business.

Jee Gam, a preacher and member of the Congregational Mission in San Francisco, who was mentioned earlier, named all of his children after leaders of this Protestant denomination. Although the 1900 federal census for San Francisco County lists only their Chinese names, their full names are in the 1894–1895 annual report of the California Chinese Mission. His sons are *Jee Shin Wong Linforth, Jee Shin Fwe Pond Mooar, Jee Shin Yien Luther McLean, Jee Shin Quong Henshaw, Jee Shin Min Benton,* and *Jee Shin Hong Howard Lovejoy*. His daughter was named *Jee Shin Mae Felt Blodgett.*

Doctors, especially obstetricians, have also been honored in the names of some native-born Chinese Americans. Munson Arthur Kwok of Los Angeles received his middle name from the surname of the doctor who delivered him. His given name, however, is a phonetic rendering of his Chinese name.

Naming After Famous People

Some Chinese Americans were named after state governors and American presidents. It seems that many a young man who grew up in an American Chinatown before World War II had the name *Roosevelt, Calvin, Lincoln,* or *Hoover.* A friend said he was named after a president but it was also the name of the ship that his mother sailed on to reach America. No doubt the names of famous Americans were selected in hopes that the namesake would live up to the expectations of the name.

Pardee Lowe wrote that his father had named his oldest child, a daughter, after the obstetrician. But when he was born — being the first-born son — his father wanted the name of a more famous person. The doctor suggested *George C. Pardee,* who was Governor of California at the time. After that, his father aspired even higher in the names of the next children: the girls were named *Alice Roosevelt* and *Helen Taft,* and the twin boys were named *Woodrow Wilson* and

Thomas Riley Marshall— after the president and vice president who were in office (1913–1921) at the time.

The name of another California governor lives on in the name of Gage Wong, Jr., of Los Angeles. His grandfather, who worked for Governor Henry T. Gage (1898 to 1902), named his son *Gage Wong* in his honor. Calvin Lee and Dawes Lee of Los Angeles were named after President Calvin Coolidge and his vice president, Charles G. Dawes, respectively, on the advice of the doctor who delivered them. The same doctor suggested naming their sister, *Annie*, after Annie Oakley, the rifle sharpshooter.

Louise Leung Larson relates in her book, *Sweet Bamboo*, that her brother Lincoln, who was born in 1917, was originally named *Bismarck* after the German chancellor whom her father greatly admired. Since this was during World War I, and Germany was our enemy at the time, he received advice that he should not be naming his son after a famous German.

Naming after a famous foreign leader brings to mind the name *Wellington* because it is such an eye-catching name for a Chinese American. The Chinese diplomat V.K. Wellington Koo (1887–1985) seems the logical role model for such namesakes. However, Dr. Koo himself may have selected this name to honor the Duke of Wellington (1769–1852), a statesman who was one of England's greatest soldiers.

Even though names are part of a nation's language and culture, it seems that Americans did not — some still do not — always understand why Chinese Americans have American or Western given names. (It would be similar to an American in China adopting a Chinese name.) H.L. Mencken, the iconoclastic author of *The American Language*, thought that the juxtaposition of a Western given name and a surname of Chinese origin represented "somewhat bizarre combinations." He also commented that the Chinese who were in a higher social level took on "more pretentious names" than the laundrymen who had such names as *Frank*, *George*, and *Jim*. No doubt such ridicule makes it difficult for a non–English speaker to feel confident about selecting an American name. As it is, there is a pattern of gradual adoption of American names in most minority groups, according to Elsdon Smith; men being usually slower in doing so.

Names Selected According to Their Sound

Even though Chinese-speaking parents may tend to retain their Chinese names, most are amenable to their children having American names. And selecting one that matches the sound of the Chinese name facilitates matters. As was mentioned, Munson Kwok's parents chose this name for this reason. Teachers often use this method. In 1895, when Ahhanga and Ahhung began attending school in Pierce City, Idaho, their teacher named them *Arthur* and *Albert*, respectively. He probably selected these names to match the vocative *Ah*. He gave the name *May* to their sister, Ahmee. Ruby Ling Louie, who was born in Chicago, recalls that her elementary school teacher selected this given name because it sounded like the second syllable of her Chinese name.

Even university students have received American names by this method. When Professor Henry Tiee, who taught at the University of Southern California in Los Angeles, came to this country in the 1960s, one of his professors at a university in Texas gave him this name. The professor thought that *Henry* sounded almost like Tiee's Chinese name, which he thought was too difficult to remember.

School teachers may even have asked their students to choose their own American name if they wanted one. One young man, who emigrated from Guangdong, China, during the 1960s, recalls choosing the name *Robin* because he happened to like watching the *Robin Hood* series on television. Yet, in looking back, he didn't really understand who Robin Hood was.

Marion Fong noticed that most of her students rarely used their Chinese names as a reference point when selecting their American names, even though they were in an ESL (English as a second language) program. They tended instead to choose a name they could pronounce — even checking to see if their friends could pronounce it — and which they liked in other ways before making the final choice.

Nonetheless, this method of having both American and Chinese names match up in sound may remind the Chinese American who does not speak Chinese of the pronunciation for the Chinese name. As it is, the non–Chinese speaker may maul the Chinese name out of recognition. When my stepfather was asked to name one of his great-grandsons, his first suggestion was rejected because when my daughter tried to pronounce it, it sounded more like "roast pig" than "Introduce, Knowledge," its intended pronunciation.

Lorraine Dong, who teaches at San Francisco State University, decided to ask her father to select the Chinese name first before she and her husband chose the American name for her first-born child. Actually, some Western names are transcribed consistently into certain Chinese characters. For example, George is phoneticized into two characters that sound like "tso gee." David is phoneticized as *da wei*, Martin as *ma ding*, Henry as *hin lay*, and Anna as *ah na* or *ahn na.* In fact, it is not unusual to find the characters for a phoneticized American name listed, say, in the membership directory of a Chinese organization when the individual's Chinese name is not known.

The desire to bestow a child with a name that is a visual reminder of the Chinese given name undoubtedly gave rise to the popular name style in which the Chinese name acts as a middle name. However, this is not always be appreciated by a young person. For instance, a change-of-name notice announced that the father of Andy Jun-Dong Ng had petitioned the court for approval to have his son's name changed to plain *Andy Ng.*

The Sr. and Jr. Name Custom

In this cross-fertilization of American and Chinese name customs, some Chinese Americans have adopted the American custom of naming a child after his father and placing *Jr.* after the name. Such names as *Dong Kingman Jr.*, *Wellington Koo Jr.*, and *George Ow Jr.*, are now more commonly seen. Nor is it surprising to read about Mr. and Mrs. Robert Yick III hosting a Red Eggs and Ginger banquet. However, it is unusual to see the Jr. added to a Chinese personal name, as in *Hing Owyang, Jr.*, and *Moon Shao-Chuang Chen, Jr.*

None of these men are likely to be Juniors in their Chinese names. For example, the Chinese characters on a large tombstone located in a New York cemetery show that *William Fong, Sr.*, and *William Fong, Jr.*, had different Chinese given names. In this strictly American name custom, a man is a "Jr." only when father and son have the exact same name. If Peter John Doe's father were Peter James Doe, then the son cannot be a "Jr." It is highly unlikely for a Chinese American father and son to have the same Chinese name because of the *Pai-hang* naming system and because the Chinese practice has been to avoid the repetition of names in the same family.

Transferring the Pai-hang System

If you recall, many Chinese Americans follow a simple horizontal *Pai-hang* in bestowing their children with a generation name. And some parents have been quite ingenious in transferring this name tradition to the selection of American given names for their children. Since it is not always possible to find several names with the same initial sound or with the same final syllable that could act as a generation name, American names have to be selected for their approximate similarity in sound.

The daughters of a Wing family that lived in Evanston, Wyoming, have names that begin with the letters *Li*: they are *Lily, Lilac, Lillian*, and *Lilia*. Two brothers in a Sacramento, California, family were named *Bill* and *Billy*. Three sisters in a Chicago family received the names *Marianne, Mary*, and *Rosemary*. The sons of a Mu family in Los Angeles are all Stans: *Stanley, Stanton*, and *Stanford*. The names of three sons in a San Francisco family illustrate the fact that the generation name can be the second syllable of a two-character name — they are: *Raymond, Edmund*, and *Gilman*.

Today's Chinese practice of bestowing sons and daughters with the same generation name has been transferred as well. For example, the parents of Victor Chuan, who was born in Paris, named their next child *Victoria*. In a Hom family in Los Angeles, the daughter is named *Sylvin* and her two brothers are *Alvin* and *Kevin*. Surely these names are the ultimate expression in synthesizing ancient and new Chinese naming practices with American name traditions.

Nicknames

Chinese names are also a rich source of nicknames because the high number of homophones in the Chinese language invites the punning and translation (sometimes undesirable) of names. As I recall, one good-natured schoolmate at our Chinese language school was known by the nickname "intestine" because a slight change in the tones for the two characters of his name produced this description. Another boy endured being called *Dog* in English because his name was similar in sound to the Chinese word with this meaning.

All through her life, Frances Chin of San Francisco was known as *Crispy* because her Chinese name had the same sound as the word meaning "crisp." The "y" sound is often added on directly to the Chinese name and this has created such nicknames for their owners as *Sunny* from Sun, *Bunny* from Bun, and *Toony* from Toon. Many names belonging to Chinese Americans have thus been created or re-created by the combination of Chinese and American name traditions.

15. NEW PATRONYMS
AND OTHER NEW NAMES

"Xing bu geng ming; Zuo bu gai xing"
(Walking, I won't change my name;
Sitting, I won't alter my family name.)
                                    an old Chinese saying

When Ella Wing accepted David Wing's proposal of marriage, there were no outcries from their families, no stern lectures about Chinese tradition forbidding persons of the same surname to marry. This is because Ella's actual family name is *Joe* and David's is *Yee*. *Wing* happens to be their new patronym, their new surname that arose in this country. I call these "new patronyms" because some surnames of Chinese origin arose in antiquity from a father's or grandfather's given name and Chinese Americans trace their patronyms to the progenitor who established family life in this country.

Adherence to Chinese traditions led to the creation of these new names but white Americans have been blamed, too, for misunderstanding Chinese name customs. Yet some parents must have known that the father's given name had become the surname for their children, especially if they had more than one child. It's more probable that they acquiesced to the change in name. For example, all five children of the Rev. Ng Poon Chew and his wife received the patronym *Chew* although *Ng* is their family name. The Rev. Ng was ordained a Presbyterian minister in 1892, the first person of Chinese ancestry on the West Coast to achieve this position. The Chinese-language newspaper he founded in San Francisco at the turn of this century existed until late 1950.

In another early established family in California, some children of Leong Way and his wife received *Way Leong* as their patronym while the others received *Leong Way*—*Leong* is the family name.

Even today, new patronyms are being adopted. A Chinese American college professor recalled that when his family emigrated here during the 1960s, his father's given name became their surname. The family has never tried to correct the mistake, and he believes there is no reason to do so since everyone in the family knows the actual family name. His acquiescence may explain why the early established families kept their new patronyms.

Andy Anh, an ethnic Chinese from Vietnam, also kept his given name as his surname. He was *Nguyen Anh* when he arrived in America after the end of the Vietnam War. He inadvertently turned the order of his name around when he placed *Anh*, his given name, in the space marked "Last name" and *Nguyen*, his surname, in the space marked "First name," not realizing at the time what these terms mean to Americans.

Some of the early immigrants merely tacked on the Chinese given name when they adopted American names, such as Charlie Kee and Charley Munn. Norman Assing, a colorful character who lived in San Francisco during the early 1850s, may have been one of the first to do so except that he added the vocative *Ah*. The Chinese who had names like Jim (詹) Hoy, Tom Garden, and Joe Den didn't have to adopt American names because their surnames — the first word in their names — could easily be mistaken as such.

It seems that the new patronyms adopted here in America symbolize the founding of a new branch to the old clan. As you may recall, during the Zhou feudal dynasty, a new clan name or *shi* was usually adopted when a new subclan was formed.

New patronyms generally fall into the following four categories:

1. An ancestor's monosyllabic given name prefixed by *Ah* or *A*,
2. An ancestor's monosyllabic given name,
3. An ancestor's disyllabic given name, and
4. An ancestor's family name plus his monosyllabic given name.

Monosyllabic Given Name Prefixed by "Ah" or "A"

Anyone who has mingled among the southern Chinese will have heard the vocative *Ah* used when a person is called by name: "*Ah Margie ah!*" "*Sam ah!*" "*Ah Ralph!*" As mentioned earlier, Chinese names prefixed by *Ah* fill page after page in federal census records for the West Coast states. Despite the prevalence of this name custom, the *Ah* was rarely included in the new patronym for Chinese Americans born on the U.S. mainland.

Among the old-time families in California is the patronym *Ah-Tye*. It came from their progenitor's name, Yee Lo Dy — *Yee* is the family name. At first it was spelled "Ah Dy" but the spelling was later changed by one of the sons. The Ah-Fong family of Boise, Idaho, trace their patronym to C.K. Ah Fong, an herb doctor, who settled there in 1900. The letter "C" stands for *Chuck*, his family name.

The *Ah Louis Store* in San Luis Obispo, California, is a state historical landmark that honors Ah Louis, a pioneer entrepreneur and labor contractor who came in this country in 1860. Actually Ah Louis —*Ah Luis* was the original spelling— was a sobriquet given to Wong On by a white American employer. *Wong* is the family name. Nonetheless, *Louis* became the patronym of his eight children — the "Ah" was never used.

This syllable was also not used when *Quin* became the patronym of the twelve children of Tom Quin, who was the first Chinese to establish family life in San Diego. He arrived in 1879 and was better known as *Ah Quin* — *Tom* is the actual family name.

In comparison, patronyms prefixed by *Ah* or *A* arose frequently for the early Chinese families in Hawaii, such as *Achong*, *AhChick*, and *Ah-Sam*. This is attributed to the Hawaiianization of Chinese names. The actual family names to some patronyms are listed below:

New patronym	Family name	Character
Achu	Hee	許
Afong	Chun	陳
Ahee	Mock	莫
Ah Leong	Lau	劉
Ahpong	[Ng]	吳
Aloiau	Wong	王
Asing	Hu	胡

The letter *a* appears at the end of some patronyms:

New patronym	Family name	Character
Aana	Seu	蕭
Ahana	Wong	黃
Akana	Yim	嚴
Akina	Tang	鄧
Awana	Yin	袁

Monosyllabic Given Name

The monosyllabic name is the predominant patronym for the native-born on the U.S. mainland and one of the earliest examples is *Tape*, as seen in the 1885 San Francisco school segregation case, Tape v. Hurley (66 Cal. 473). Mamie Tape's father was Jew Dip, a Christian, who took the name *Joseph Tape*. Jew was his family name and *Tape* was the Americanization of Dip.

An article about Richard Wing, a renowned restaurateur of Hanford, California, reveals that *Wing* came from his grandfather's name: *Chow Gong Wing*, who settled in this area in the late nineteenth century. *Gong* is the family name which happens to be placed in the middle of the progenitor's name.

Because *Wing* is such a very popular Chinese given name, not all Chinese American Wings are related: *Fung* is the family name of the Wing family in Vallejo, California; *Wong* is the family name of the Wing family in Evanston, Wyoming; and *Lew* is the family name of the Wing family in Seattle, Washington. It so happens that a daughter of the Vallejo Wings married a son of the Evanston Wing family.

Kim or *Gim* is another favorite Chinese given name. Again, there may be no relationship between those bearing this new patronym. *Joe* is the family name of the *Kim* family in Marysville, California, and *Ng* is the family name of the *Kim* or *Kimm* family in Bakersfield, California. *Kim*, as mentioned earlier, is a common Korean surname. Chinese Americans and Korean Americans have many other surnames in common, such as *Chang, Hong, Kwon, Lee, Lim, Ma*, and *Yue*. Historically, the northern section of Korea was part of the Chinese empire during the Han dynasty and, consequently, many Han surnames were adopted by Koreans.

Other popular Chinese given names that have become new patronyms are *Bing, Bow, Fat, Ging, Hing, Hoy, Loy, Kay, Kee, King, Sing, Suey, Wah*, and *Yook*. As with the Wings and Kims, Chinese Americans bearing these surnames may not be related at all.

During the decades when there were relatively few Chinese American families, Chinatowns were like small towns where everyone's family name was known to everyone else. For example, those in the Chinese community in Oakland, California, generally knew that *Joe* was the family name of the *Shoong* family. Joe Shoong was a successful businessman and philanthropist who owned a chain of department stores, called National Dollar Store, located in several cities and towns.

Other new patronyms with the actual family name are given, along with the locality where the family once settled, as follows:

New patronym	Family name	Character	Locality
Fat	Dong	鄧	Sacramento, CA
Got	Lowe	劉	San Francisco
Jig	Wong	黃	Washington, D.C.
Jone	Yee	余	Chicago
Kee	Huey	許	Fresno, CA
Moon	Wong	黃	San Francisco
Nahme	Lee	李	Washington, D.C.
Schoon	Gee	朱	Los Angeles
Ten	Lew	劉	Los Angeles
Yook	[Siu]	蕭	Seattle

Family members may have different versions about the origin of the new patronym. A friend, who met a member of the Ten family, was told that the grandfather received this surname because he thought the immigration officer had asked how many children he had. A decade later, I met another member of this family and his explanation seemed more plausible: his grandfather, Lew Din, at some point in time, changed the spelling of his given name to *Ten* and this became the patronym of his fifteen children.

Curiously, some Chinese American businessmen, like C.K. Ah Fong, adopted the name style of initialing the family name and spelling the given name in full. No doubt this unwittingly led to many new patronyms. A Chinese business directory published in 1946 provides several examples:

Name	Family name	Character	Locality
C. Chock Hing	[Cheng]	鄭	Honolulu
N.L. Ting	[Ng]	伍	New York City
J.H. Lett	[Joe]	周	Boyle, MS
L. Hing	[Loo]	盧	Sledge, MS
C.Y. Wing	[Chu]	趙	Memphis, AR
W. Sai-Chun	[Wong]	黃	Stockton, CA
O.S. Mow	[Ong]	鄧	Phoenix, AZ

The Chinese who adopted this name style could have been emulating American businessmen who initialed their given names — a name style that was favored in certain American business circles.

143

The name in Chinese shows that the initial "O" stands for the surname.

Due to the ambiguity of Chinese names, the spelling for a new patronym can easily be mistaken for a family name. For example, *Chew* could be a patronym or the same spelling as the common surname (趙). The patronym *Ai*, for a Honolulu family, has the same spelling for a family name of Mandarin sound (艾). Sometimes a new patronym may indeed be a family name that was used as a given name. Among the more popular ones that are used are *Moy* (梅), *Hong* (洪), *Lum* (林), *Lee* (利), and *Young* (楊).

Disyllabic Given Names

Disyllabic patronyms, in comparison, are one of a kind. When the actual family name is added, there you will have the full name of the family's progenitor. Unlike the monosyllabic patronym, a disyllabic one is usually associated with a specific family because of the highly individualistic nature of the Chinese two-character given name. It may be written as one word, as two separate words, or with a hyphen between.

The following patronyms belong to four old-time families of Seattle and Portland, Oregon:

New patronym	Family name	Surname character
Jower	Wan	溫
Monwai	Wan	溫
Tsoming	Wong	黃
Yaplee	Soong	宋

Patronyms arose elsewhere:

New patronym	Family name	Character	Locality
Bo-Linn	Wong	黃	Houston, TX
Bowen	Lee	李	Oakland, CA
Doshim	Wu	伍	New York City
Garbern	Yee	余	El Paso, TX
Glenchur	Chong	張	San Francisco
Saiget	Kong	江	Astoria, OR
Tinloy	Kan	簡	Grass Valley, CA
Typond	Lee	李	New York City

145

Other new patronyms include *Anshon* (Chou 周 is the surname), *Bing-You* (Wong), *Hipon* (Wong), *Jinhong* (Eng), and *Mooncai* (Wong).

Family Name Followed by Monosyllabic Given Name

In this category, the family name is included and it almost always comes first. *Kimlau* is an exception in that the surname *Lau* follows the given name. Evidently it arose in San Francisco but it is also found in New York City. Usually the family name and given name of the progenitor are written as two separate words.

A well-known example is James Wong Howe, the famous Hollywood cinematographer. His father was Wong How who settled in Pasco, Washington — *Wong* is the family name. As the story goes, when James came to this country as a child, his name was *Wong Tung Jim*. When he entered public school, his teacher mistook *Jim* as a nickname for James and changed it accordingly, while adding and Americanizing his father's name.

Victor Sen Yung (or Young), the late Hollywood actor, inherited his father's name for his patronym — *Sen* (冼) is the family name. Victor gained fame as "Number 2 Son" in the old Charlie Chan movies and later as the cook in the television series *Bonanza*.

The old-time families in Oregon and Washington seem to have a high number of new patronyms, which include the following:

New patronym	Family name	Surname character
Lew Kay	Lew	劉
Loo Kay	Loo	盧
Louis Kay	Louis	盧
Quan Foy	Quan	關
Goon Dip	Goon	阮
Jewell	Jew	趙

This type of patronym arose as well in different places:

New patronym	Family name	Character	Locality
Chu Lin	Chu	趙	Glen Allen, MS
Chun-Hoon	Chun	陳	Honolulu

New patronym	Family name	Character	Locality
Goo-Sun	Goo	古	Honolulu
Hong Sling	Hong	湯	Chicago
Jen Kin	Jen	鄭	Chicago
Lai Mye	Lai	黎	Oakland, CA
Landon	Leong	梁	San Francisco
Leong Ming	Leong	梁	Bakersfield, CA
Mammon	Ma	馬	San Francisco

Two placenames in Bakersfield, California, honor Mr. Leong Ming for his numerous civic activities: *Ming Road* and *Ming Lake*. His full Chinese name is *Leong Yen Ming*. Many of the early immigrants shortened their name, as mentioned earlier. Mr. Lai Mye had also shortened his name which, according to his daughter, Rosebud Lai Mye Quong, was *Lai Cheung Mye*.

Dr. James Jen Kin, of Long Beach, California, recalls that when his father came to America in 1918, he spelled his surname as *Jung* and later as *Jeng*. Then, during the 1930s, when he became a businessman in Chicago, he settled upon *Jen Kin* as his name. But his white American clients often mistook his surname for *Jenkin* or *Jenkins*, an error that continues to this day for Dr. Jen Kin.

Other new patronyms of this category include *Chin-Bing, Chin-Park, Der-Bing, Gong-guy, Goonyep, Lee Sing, Levy, Mafong, Marfoe, Mark Gate, Wongham,* and *Yee Quil*.

Not all new patronyms have remained intact, however. The next generation might use only the initial of the family name rather than spelling it out in full, as in *Albert L. Hing*. Or the next generation might drop the actual family name altogether. Some monosyllabic patronyms may have started out with the family name before it was discarded. As mentioned earlier, a given name that has one character is not supposed to be stated alone; it would be mentioned with the family name or with the vocative *ah*.

Other Changes in Surnames

Other unusual surnames developed for various other reasons. Howard Yuen, of San Francisco, who grew up in Grass Valley, California, recalls how some of his cousins came by their surname *Fore*. Their father was called *Uncle Four*, a translation of the Chinese kinship term, because he is the fourth brother in the family. Later, Uncle Four took the name *Yuen Fore*, changing the spelling "four" in the process.

Many a Chinese businessman was called by the name of his store which, traditionally, does not consist of the owner's name. Mrs. Grace Wong Chow, who was a prominent Los Angeles businesswoman, recalled that as a child she was often called *Gracie Hi Loy* because *Hi Loy* was the name of the family store located in Fresno, California. Her father, Wong Dun, was called *Mr. Hi Loy* by his customers.

In actual practice, though, the store name rarely became the surname of the owner's children. One example is *Kaikee*, the surname of an Oakland, California, family. This was the name of their family store that was located in the small town of Ione in the Mother Lode country. Their actual family name is *Cheng* (程).

The *Lee* in Moon Lim Lee's name came from the name of the restaurant that his father owned in Weaverville, the town in northern California where the Chinese Joss Temple is located. The name of the restaurant was *China Restaurant* but the townspeople knew it better as *Sam Lee*, which was its name in Chinese. They also called Moon's father *Sam Lee*. By the time his children attended school, teachers had assumed that *Lee* was their surname. Their actual family name *Lim* was preserved as Moon's middle name.

Accidental surnames occurred as well for the Chinese in other countries. Some have been brought here in recent decades, such as *Ah-Tung-Oing, Hing Fay, Man-Son-Hing, Tankhim,* and *Woo-Sam.* The Man-Son-Hing family emigrated from Guyana; and Edward Tankhim, who came from Singapore, said that his actual family name is *Tan.* Eleanor Hing Fay, whose actual family name is *Louie*, emigrated from Queensland, Australia, where there is a cluster of Louie families. Most have patronyms, she said, just as her family does. Louies have also clustered in certain places in this country and, as we shall see in the next chapter, this phenomenon occurs for all common surnames.

16. SURNAME CLUMPING AND FAMILY ASSOCIATIONS

"...common surnames tend to clump in distinct regions."
H.L. Mencken, *The American Language*

All common American family names tend to clump, dominating in distinct patterns in certain areas of this country. For example, *Smith*— the quintessential American surname, has headed the list of common surnames in New York City and San Francisco but it has been second to *Johnson* in Milwaukee and Chicago. The sociologist Rose Hum Lee noticed that when Chinatowns were formed during the late nineteenth century, usually one family name dominated. And even if three or more different surnames were present at the beginning, one usually will dominate over time. Nevertheless, what may be a common surname in one area may be rarely seen in other parts of a country.

Wong, Lee, and *Chan*— long considered the most popular surnames for Chinese Americans — have tended to cluster in certain cities. *Wong* evidently is the most common American surname of Chinese origin and it ranked 457 in the 1984 Social Security file of over 5,000 common surnames in the United States. It has been a dominant name in San Francisco, placing fifth in the ten most common surnames of this city during the 1960s. Wongs also clustered in such cities as Boston, Minneapolis, and Honolulu. A friend once remarked that Wongs were so numerous in Los Angeles, it was called "Wong town."

The surname *Lee* ranked number 26 in this listing but, unfortunately, there is no information as to the percentage of Lees who are of Chinese descent. As mentioned earlier, *Li*— the same family name — is the most popular name in China and it could very well be the leading surname for Chinese Americans, considering the influx of new immigrants from mainland China and Taiwan. *Lee* was the dominant name in the Chinatowns of Philadelphia and Washington, D.C, whereas the surname *Chin* clustered in the Chinatowns of Chicago, Denver, and Seattle.

The surname *Moy*, however, dominated Chicago's Chinatown and clustered as well in Washington D.C. The surname *Tom* clustered among Chinese Americans in San Diego and New York City. It was once estimated that the surname *Ong* or *Tang* (a spelling variant) belongs to two-thirds of the Chinese American population in Phoenix, Arizona. A 1946 Chinese business directory indicates relatively few Ongs settled further south in Tucson, where the names *Gin*, *Lee*, and *Lum* predominated instead.

Other clumpings of surnames have been reported:

Surname	Chinese character	City
Fong, Kwong	鄺	Sacramento, CA
Lee, Mah, and Wong	[李, 馬, 黃]	Stockton, CA
Leong	梁	Bakersfield, CA
Lew	[劉]	Baltimore
Louie	雷	Cleveland, OH
Ng	伍	San Antonio, TX
Yee	余	Detroit, Santa Barbara

Sometimes surname clustering in an area can be traced to certain individuals. For example, T.C. Moy, who arrived in Chicago in 1870, is believed to be the first Moy to settle in this city. Chin Sou Lin, who worked as a gang boss for the Central Pacific Railroad, was the first Chin to establish family life in Colorado. His daughter, Lily Chin, was born in this state in 1873. Astonishingly, Chin was described as a 6'2" tall Chinese, with "blue eyes." Another Chin, Chin Chun Hock, was the first Chinese merchant in Seattle, arriving there in 1860. Along with *Chin* (陳), there are small clusters of Chinese Americans surnamed *Eng* (伍), *Lew* (劉), *Woo* (胡), and *Mar* (馬).

Surname clustering has been traced as well to a particular *heung* located in the Four Districts dialect area of Guangdong province. (A *heung* or *xiang* consists of a large grouping of villages.) For example, the Wongs of *Yin Gong Heung* emigrated to Boston; the Tom clan of *Bak Seui Heung* went to New York City; and the Ma clan of *Bak Sah Heung* settled in Wichita, Kansas, and its environs. Clustering of surnames occurs in states where relatively few Chinese immigrants settled. According to the 1946 business directory that was just mentioned, *Chew* or *Chu* (趙) was the most popular surname for store owners in Arkansas, and the surname *Joe* (周) dominated in Mississippi, followed by *Pang* (彭) and *Seit* (薛).

Family Associations

A good indication of surname clumping in an area is the presence of a clan or family association, because membership is based strictly on surname. You don't have to be directly related to any other member because of the belief that people of the same family name are all descendants of a common ancestor. Family associations are usually found in metropolitan areas, but not all surnames that were brought to this country are represented by one; it depends on interest and leadership as in any organization.

Historically, family associations were first established in California but, according to Him Mark Lai, these were not formally organized until about 1870. It was one of three types of organizations that were founded by the early immigrants from Guangdong province; the other two are the district association and the *tong* or fraternal group.

Interestingly, family names played an important role in the election of the top officers for the large and powerful Ning Yung Association that was organized in 1853 by immigrants from the Toishan district. Because of the dominance of the Wong and Lee clans, a plan was devised at some point in time that enabled other clans to be represented on the board. These two family names and 28 others were placed on a 26-year rotation schedule for the top three offices. For example, the president can be a *Wong* only six times in the 26 years; a *Lee*, four times; a *Chin*, three times; and a *Ng*, twice. "No Yees in Ning Yung," any Chinese American old-timer will tell you. It was in 1862, over a hundred years ago, that the Yee clans of this district split off after a dispute to form their own organization.

In the early decades, the family association was like a home away from home for the men who did not have families here. The early immigrants had a keen sense of clan solidarity and of family obligations since they came from the southern part of China where clans have been strong for many centuries and where clan rules guided proper behavior. These organizations provided a mailing address, a place for members to meet informally, and temporary housing. Clan elders arbitrated disputes, no doubt acting *in loco parentis* for the younger men.

Incidentally, one basic concern of the early immigrants was that, if death took place in this country, their bones would be returned to the home village for reburial. Bodies were exhumed in about ten years after burial so that the bones could be cleaned, then ceremoniously packed in a special box for shipment to China. Prior to the 1940s, shipments of bones were made regularly. (No

151

doubt the bones were reburied in large funereal jars since this was a common practice in southern China. However, bodies could be exhumed three years earlier since the coffin is not buried as deeply as it is in America.) This practice undoubtedly kept the Chinese cemeteries in this country from being overcrowded as this seems to be occurring today.

Family associations usually have a voice in local Chinatown affairs because many belong to the umbrella group of organizations, such as the *Chinese Consolidated Benevolent Association* that acts as a quasi-official governing body in most large Chinatowns in this country and in Honolulu.

"Tongs" and "Fongs"

The name of a family association may refer to it as a *tong* (堂), which means "ancestral hall." This word, for example, is seen in the name Leong Jung How Tong Association that was organized in St. Louis, Missouri. However, the Leong's Family Association in Boston, like many other family associations, eschew this word in English, using it only in the Chinese title. The avoidance of the word

Wong Family Benevolent Association in San Francisco on Waverly Place.

152

Chinese title on an older building includes the Wong clan's ancient territorial name and the word "tong."

tong may have occurred during the years when it often conjured up the image of "tong wars" and the violent means by which the fraternal tongs used to resolve their disputes prior to the mid–1930s.

Members of a large family association, such as the Wong Family Association, are divided into lineage groups called *fong* (房), which means "branch or subclan." The Gee How Oak Tin Association, which is composed of three clans — *Chan* or *Chin* (陳), *Woo* (胡), and *Yuen* (袁), has a separate *fong* or two for each. The Chans from Toishan district — being so numerous — have two *fongs*: one for the lower and one for upper part of this district.

By the early 1940s, over forty family associations, representing 47 different family names, had been established in 31 American cities. In 1976, there were over 50 associations and the large family associations had chapters in many cities. For example, the Wongs had organizations in 20 cities and the Lees in 16 cities. In comparison, the smaller associations are located in only a few cities, such as the Goon or Yuen (阮) family association that is found in New York City, Boston, and Chicago. The Locke's Family Association (駱) exists only in Seattle, and the Kams' Society (甘) only in Honolulu.

153

Territorial Names

Sometimes the name of a family association can be quite obscure because it does not always consist of the family name. For example, the name of the Soo Yuen Association, composed of the Louie (雷), Fong (方), and Kwong (鄺) clans, symbolizes instead three rivers swirling together. Or the name of the family association may include the name of the ancient territory—called *jun ming* (郡名)—that was associated with the clan name a few thousand years ago. The *jun*—spelled *chun* in Wade-Giles—was a forerunner of the prefecture and province in China. For example, *Lum Sai Ho Tong* is the name of the family association for the *Lum* (or *Lin*) clan and the words *Sai Ho* are the name of their ancient *jun*. The Lum clan also refer to *Sai Ho* as their *tang hao* (堂號) or "ancestral hall name." All the common Chinese family names are known by a particular *jun ming* or *tang hao*.

One hundred *jun ming* are listed in Giles's Chinese-English dictionary and the number of family names in each varies. For example, six other clans claim *Sai Ho* as their ancestral hall name. The Gee Poy Kuo Association for the *Gee* (*Chu, Zhu*—朱) clan is unique because it is the only family name associated with the territory of Poy Kuo.

In the following table, Pinyin spelling for Mandarin appears in brackets for the *jun ming* when it does not appear in the association's English title:

Jun ming	Surname in English title	Surname character
Chi Young	*Toy* (Cai, Tsai)	蔡
[Ho Nan]	*Luke* (Lu)	陸
Kao Young	*Huie* (Su, Xu)	許
Kong Har	*Wong* (Huang)	黃
Lung Sai	*Lee* (Li)	李
On Ding	*Woo* (Hu)	胡
[Qiao Guo]	*Chao* (Cao, Tsao)	曹
[Qing He]	*Chang* (Zhang)	張
Wing Chuen	*Chan* (Chen)	陳
[Zhong Shan]	*Hong* (Tang)	湯

There are other esoteric reasons for the name of a family association. The Lung Kong Tien Yee Association, for example, took the words *Lung Kong* from the name of a temple located in Guangdong province. The family association

The territorial name in Chinese for the Gee clan.

called *Lee On Dong* indicates an organization for the Lees from Toishan district. The Way Ben Association that exists only in Los Angeles took its name from the river once fished by their remote ancestor.

Multiple Family Associations

Some family associations represent two, three, or more family names and these were formed so that smaller clans could have a voice in local Chinatown affairs or for business purposes. But clans could not combine willy-nilly into one organization; they had to justify their union by "some blood or other significant relationship."

Three clans of the Soo Yuen Association all claim *Louie Gung*, also known as the "Thunder god," as their common ancestor. The three clans of the Gee How Oak Tin Association — Chan, Woo, and Yuen — trace their lineage back

155

Soo Yuen Benevolent Association in San Francisco is decorated for Christmas.

to the legendary Emperor Shun (ca. 2318 B.C.). The Wong's and Ng's Family Association in Baltimore evidently base their relationship on some significant incident. I recall my mother remarking how Wongs and Ngs always stand up for each other because, centuries ago, one provided help to the other who was in trouble.

Perhaps the most romantic history of all the multiple clan associations belongs to the Lung Kong Tien Yee Association, known colloquially as the *Four Families.* Their surnames are commonly spelled as Lew (劉), Quan (關), Chang (張), and Chew (趙). And their relationship dates back to the Three Kingdoms period (A.D. 220–265) when three young men, *Liu Bei, Guan Yu,* and *Zhang Fei,* met while answering the call to save the Han dynasty. They pledged themselves as "blood brothers" in Zhang Fei's peach garden, later immortalized as the "Peach Garden Oath." The addition of the fourth clan is because *Zhao Yun,* one of the five "tiger" generals, rescued Liu's baby boy from certain death. It was Guan who said: "He is as good as my brother."

Changing Role of the Family Association

Today, family associations have become more like social clubs since the decades of enforced bachelorhood brought about by Chinese family customs and the exclusion laws have long gone by. A member can drop in and while away the time or join in the daily mah-jong games that every family association now seems to host, an activity not limited to those of the same family name. In addition to the annual New Year or Spring dinners, some associations celebrate Thanksgiving and Christmas. Some present scholarships to their young people seeking higher education. Some hold national conventions. Some attend international ones because wherever the Chinese settled, they tend to organize themselves by surname and by locality.

However, a decline of these organizations was reported in the 1960s, citing the disinclination of the native-born as well as the new immigrants in becoming members. It is likely that some of the smaller associations that were once very active may no longer exist. On the other hand, a few new family associations were established, such as the Goo (古) Society that was founded in Honolulu during the 1950s and 1960s by second generation Chinese Americans. They wanted to perpetuate Chinese family customs and philosophy and to teach these to their young people. A Cheng (鄭) association was founded in San Francisco in the mid–1980s.

No doubt the larger family associations will continue to exist for a long time since they own valuable real estate property, like the Gee How Oak Tin Association, which can assure their survival. Therefore it may still be "too early to consign the clan to oblivion," as one author observed two decades ago.

New Patterns of Surname Clumping

Any changes in the existence of family associations undoubtedly are reflected in surname clustering patterns, which are expected to change because of the tremendous growth in population. When Professor Cavalli-Sforza of Stanford University conducted a study of surnames in several parishes in Italy, he discovered that surnames can become extinct in an area after ten generations and replaced by new names. (This would take about 200 to 300 years.) However, the professor noticed that the greater the number of people who own a surname, the longer it will survive.

Considering the extremely limited number of family names that have been brought from China since Chinese immigration began, Dr. Cavalli-Sforza's observation could be applied to the spelling variants for the same family name. Already the surnames of the early established families are being nudged aside by the names of newcomers who greatly outnumber the descendants of the early immigrants.

A few Mandarin-sounding names may be replacing the Cantonese-sounding names that used to prevail in some cities. In the 1983 telephone directory for San Jose, California, for instance, the surname *Chen*—a Mandarin-sounding name—filled a little over a column (about 120 names). Only 48 persons were surnamed *Chin*—most likely a spelling variant of *Chen*. *Wong* was the most popular surname since it filled over two columns.

However, a decade later, as the 1996-1997 telephone directory indicates, *Chen* had clearly replaced *Wong* as the leading surname: Chens had increased fivefold compared to the Wongs who had only doubled numerically. Incidentally, the main problem in using telephone directories as a resource for Chinese American names is the impossibility of counting the number of Chinese Americans who have the surname *Lee*. This in turn makes it impossible to determine its popularity as compared to the surnames *Wong* and *Chen*.

Nevertheless, two intriguing questions arise: Will the surname *Wong* be replaced as the dominant Chinese American surname? Is it really the dominant name if we take the surname character into consideration? It seems safe to say that the vast majority of Wongs write it in Chinese using the same surname character 黃 . Other common family names, unlike *Wong*—and *Lee*, for that matter— have numerous spelling variants, which can dilute their importance as leading surnames among Chinese Americans. Therefore, if the surname character were taken into consideration, the dominant family name may be different—even when one uses the combination *Wong* and *Huang* to boost the number of Chinese Americans having this common family name.

158

Leaving the combination of *Lee* and *Li* aside, the most likely contender is the combination of *Chan*, *Chen*, and *Chin* because these, in all likelihood, represent the same common family name 陳. Judging from the listings in telephone directories for several American cities, this combination is indeed a formidable challenger to the *Wong/Huang* combination as the dominant surname character in Chinese American names.

These five surnames were tallied up in a sampling of telephone directories from four cities that were selected because of the existence of their Chinatowns. The table below shows a slight decline of *Chin* in these cities, a surname that predominated for the early immigrants from the Four Districts dialect area. The rapid increase in the surnames *Huang* and *Chen* in ten years' time is far more startling and is undoubtedly the result of new immigration to these cities.

Wong/Huang combination:

1983–84	San Francisco	New York	Houston	Seattle
Wong	2,530	1,116	185	247
Huang	128	78	89	23
Subtotal	2,658	1,194	274	270 = 4,396

1995–96				
Wong	2,890	1,274	290	291
Huang	594	408	175	122
Subtotal	3,484	1,682	465	413 = 6,044

Chan/Chen/Chin combination:

1983–84	San Francisco	New York	Houston	Seattle
Chan	1,127	899	130	130
Chen	255	281	232	62
Chin	441	579	59	116
Subtotal	1,823	1,759	421	308 = 4,201

1995–96				
Chan	1,593	1,100	211	174
Chen	881	1,185	339	178
Chin	451	531	57	128
Subtotal	2,925	2,816	607	480 = 6,828

Overall, the *Chan/Chen/Chin* combination has surpassed the *Wong/Huang* combination in these particular cities, which may indicate that the family name represented by these three surnames may be the dominant one. Or it may be second in popularity if *Lee* predominates instead. Except for Houston, *Wong* has not yet been dislodged as the leading surname. And if the picture of Chinese American names in these cities is of any indication, *Wong* is still the leading name.

Nevertheless, these new patterns in surname clumping tell us that more changes are in store for Chinese American names. We can expect to see *Chen* and *Huang* increasing — perhaps by leaps and bounds — because the surname characters they represent are similarly transcribed in both Pinyin and Wade-Giles. At the pace this is occurring, we can expect to see more Mandarin-sounding surnames replacing the surnames belonging to the descendants of the early immigrants. And, as each generation becomes further removed from the ancestral hall in China, the non–Chinese speaking owner of a surname of Chinese origin is more likely to forget or lose the surname character that is represented by his surname.

PART IV

WHAT'S IN A SURNAME CHARACTER?

Although the language spoken by the immigrant is usually lost by the third generation, it is necessary that the Chinese ideograph for an American surname of Chinese origin be retained by its owner. Not only does the ideograph hold the key to family history; it is an integral part of the surname.

With the rapid changes taking place in the Chinese American population, there is an urgent need to document surname characters, especially for families who have been in this country for several generations. These are the families whose surnames are not usually found in Chinese-English dictionaries and whose actual surnames may have been changed when their ancestors settled in America.

The increase in interracial and interethnic marriages also makes it imperative for the owner of a surname of Chinese origin to hold on to the surname character. And it can never be assumed that the spelling represents a particular ideograph. Unfamiliarity with the Chinese written language easily leads to errors in writing the surname character and to mistaking another one for the actual family name.

The final part of *Chinese American Names* ends with a summary because there is no conclusion yet. The story of American surnames of Chinese origin is still evolving, and we are watching the transition take place.

17. PARSING THE CHARACTER

"The general rules are from top to bottom, from left to right and from the outside to the inside."
Florian Coulmas, *The Writing Systems of the World*

"What Wong are you? Are you a 'big-belly Wong'?—ai-oo Wong?"—asks a Four Districts dialect speaker of another. "Or are you a 'three-strokes Wong'?—a thlam-wahk Wong?" Those who grew up speaking this dialect were often amused by this rustic way of distinguishing between these two surnames (黃 and 王) that have the same Cantonese sound. The more refined way of inquiring after the first Wong character is to ask: "Are you a 'grass-head' Wong?" This refers to the radical that lies atop the character.

Inquiring after the surname character is commonplace in China because, in each dialect, two or more different surnames can sound alike or nearly alike. This is similar to asking an American to spell his or her name because of the variations in spelling: "Is it *MacInnes* with 'm-a-c' or 'm-c'?" "Is Stephen spelled with a 'v' or a 'ph'?"

There are several ways the Chinese use to describe the surname character aloud: (1) by taking apart its components and mentioning each separately, (2) by naming a famous person of the same surname, and (3) by stating another word with the surname character, which is quite similar to translating the name.

Parsing the Character

Most Chinese words are easily taken apart or parsed. As each main component is mentioned, the person hearing it should be able to picture the character and put it all back together mentally. As pointed out earlier, most characters are composed of a radical and a phonetic part and the radical in most surnames is found at the top or at the left side of the word. Some names have the radical on the right side or at the bottom; a few are radicals in themselves, like the "horse" Ma.

163

When the radical is at the top or bottom, the character is parsed crosswise; when it appears on the left or right side, the character is taken apart lengthwise. The radical is often described or sounded out first and then the rest of the character, depending upon its complexity, follows with its sound value. Sometimes the radical is not mentioned and only one component need be described. But the surname is always stated at the end of the description, as in the following examples.

Lee, Li (李), the most common family name in China, is neatly parsed crosswise as "*mu zi Li*," which is like saying "wood son Lee." The etymology to this character is rather charming: it depicts a child standing beneath a tree.

Chang, Zhang (張), the third most common Chinese family name, has the exact same sound and tone as another name (章). The first character is halved lengthwise and described as "*gong chang Chang*" or "long bow Chang"—the radical is a pictograph of a bow for shooting arrows. The other surname character is halved crosswise as "*li zao Chang*" which refers to the two components of this word. It is like saying "instantly morning Chang."

Louie stands for two American family names of Chinese origin: "Thunder Louie" (雷) and "Two mouths Louie" (呂). The first surname (also spelled *Lei, Louis,* and *Lui*) is often parsed as "*yu tian Lei*" or "rain field Louie" because the top half is the word for "rain" and the lower half is that for "field." Oftentimes it is easier for owners of this name to say "Thunder god Louie" because most people who inquire after it would know of this ancient mythical god. The description "Two mouths Louie" or "*shuang kou Lu*" (also spelled *Lu, Lui,* and *Ly*) is indicative of the ideograph itself—the lower component is simply written a little larger. The other meaning for the ideograph for "mouth" is "entrance."

Another family name (吳) that includes the word for mouth is "Mouth heaven Wu" or "*kou tian Wu.*" Its spelling variants are *Eng, Ing, Ng, Woo,* and *Wu.* Actually the lower half is not the ideograph for heaven, it only looks somewhat like it.

The popular surname *Chen* (陳) is described as "*er dong Chen*" or "Ear east Chen" because the radical on the left looks like the shape of an ear; the right half means "east." This ear-shaped radical, however, is the topographical radical for a "mound or embankment."

When this radical occurs on the right side of a word, it is the topographical radical for "city" or "district capital." It, too, is described as an ear. The surname *Cheng, Zheng* (鄭), for example, is parsed as "*dian er Cheng*"—the "dian" being the pronunciation of the left component.

The common surname *Woo* or *Hu* (胡) is described as "Old moon Woo" or "*gu yue Hu.*" The component on the left is the word for "old" except that the radical on the right really stands for "meat" or "flesh." Nonetheless, it looks more like the radical for "moon." Certainly, this is a far more pleasing description.

The rather cryptic description "Point ten thousand Fang" or "*Dian wan Fang*" is for the surname *Fang, Fong* (方). *Dian*—meaning "point" or "dot"—describes the top stroke and *wan* refers to the lower half of this character (万) because it refers to the simplified form of the word (萬) meaning "ten thousand."

Referring to a Famous Person

It helps to know a bit of Chinese history when inquiring after the surname character because the reply may be the name of a historic personage. For example:

Chao, Chew, Chiu, Zhao (趙), as in "*Chao Zulung.*" He was the famous tiger general of the Three Kingdoms period.

Guo, Kuo, Kwok (郭), as in "*Guo Zui.*" He was the renowned general who averted an attempt to overthrow the Tang dynasty.

Liu (劉), as in "*Liu Bei.*" He was the elder brother of the Peach Garden Oath.

Translating the Character

Even though most Chinese family names are ordinary words found in the common written language, the dictionary meaning is not usually used unless, as Dr. Y.R. Chao pointed out, one is making a pun. However, as mentioned earlier, it is easier for the non–Chinese speaker to use the dictionary meaning than another explanation. Below are a few more examples to add to the previous list:

Selected spellings	Dictionary meaning	Surname character
Cha	to investigate	查
Char, Der, Hsieh, Xie, Zia	to thank	謝

Selected spellings	Dictionary meaning	Surname character
Fu	teacher	傅
Ko	spear	戈
Soon, Sun	grandson	孫
Tso, Zuo	on the left side	左
You, Yu	to swim	游
Yuen, Yuan	a long robe	袁

Look-Alike Characters

Since it takes a practiced eye to notice all the particular strokes or components of a Chinese character, the American of Chinese ancestry who does not read or write Chinese has to be more careful in writing his or her surname in Chinese. Among the common errors are writing the wrong radical, adding one when none existed before, omitting a stroke or tacking on an extra stroke or more where they don't belong. For example, if you extended the center vertical line in the lower half of the ideograph for *Louie*—雷—you may end up with the word—電—that means "lightning" or "electricity"!

Errors in writing a surname character may produce the character for a different surname, which may result in family members barking up the wrong family tree. For example, *Yu* (于) and *Gan, Kan* (干) look alike except for the hook at the end of the ideograph for *Yu*. Unless you look carefully at the construction atop the character for the surname *Dong, Dung* (董), you can mistake it for the surname *Tong, Tung* (童).

One also has to be careful about adding or substituting radicals. The surname *Lung* (龍) becomes the surname *Pang* or *Pong* (龐) if the radical for "shelter" is placed over the dragon. This radical looks almost like the "cliff" radical that overhangs the surname *Li* (厲) except for the dot at the top. Removal of this radical results in the surname *Wan* or *Man* (萬).

Even the well-educated Chinese speaker finds that unless there is the opportunity to write in Chinese regularly, recollection of the simplest word can become rusty over time. Errors may even lead to a non-existing word. It seems that the eye cannot catch all the details of an unfamiliar word.

The following surnames further illustrate the need for accuracy in writing the surname character:

166

Spelling	Surname characters		
Au, Ou, Ow	區	and	歐
Chiu, Hew	丘	and	邱
Hou	侯	and	候
Ning	寧	and	甯
Pu	浦	and	蒲
Voo, Wu	烏	and	鄔
Wang	王	and	汪
Wei, Wy	韋	and	衛
Yu	俞	and	喻

The following table gives additional examples of different surnames that have the same spelling:

Spelling	Surname characters
Chin	金, 陳, and 秦
Fan	范, 樊
Fu	傅, 符
Ho	何, 賀
Lai	黎, 賴
Shih	石, 史, 施, and 時

As Ethel Williams, an author on genealogical research, once wrote, a surname is one's "most intimate possession, which symbolizes your personality, and forms the latest link in the historical chain of ancestral sequence." Surely the Chinese surname character is part of this intimate possession and is the link that confirms ancestry for the American who possesses a surname of Chinese origin. This is all the more reason for preserving it accurately for the sake of posterity.

18. PRESERVING
THE SURNAME CHARACTER

"...For my name and memory, I leave it to men's charitable speeches, and to foreign nations, and the next age."
Francis Bacon, from his Will, 1626

The American who owns a surname of Chinese origin will find that the surname character is not easily retrievable if it had became lost or it had not been documented. Most methods that were devised for transcribing the Chinese language into the Roman alphabet "work only one way and are not reversible," Dr. Yuen Ren Chao observed. In other words, you cannot state with certainty that the spelling for a Chinese word represents a particular ideograph. Dr. Chao's observation applies absolutely to Chinese American names because you cannot assume that the spelling for a particular surname stands for a certain surname character.

In every system of transcription — whether for Mandarin, Cantonese, Shanghai, or other dialects — two or more surnames can have the same spelling. As mentioned earlier, six different Mandarin-sounding family names and one of Cantonese sound are spelled *Wu*.

This brings to mind an incident that occurred during a conversation with a Mr. Ong about his name. He happens to be an ethnic Chinese from the Philippines. His surname reflects his Hokkien dialect background and it is the same character which is *Wang* in Mandarin. But when one of his employees happened to see the ideograph that was written, he exclaimed: "You wrote the wrong character! That's not the right name!" It turns out that the employee did not speak Hokkien and had assumed that *Ong* stands for another name of a different dialect sound.

Nor can one assume that the spelling of a surname represents the individual's actual dialect background. For example, a Mr. Chang, who came to America prior to World War II, admitted that he adopted this Mandarin spelling while attending college. He was a *Jeong* before his name change, a surname of

Cantonese sound. On the other hand, a Mr. Shek, who came from Fujian province in the 1930s to attend college, used to spell his surname *Shih* according to Mandarin sound. He respelled it after deciding to stay here permanently and because most of his associates were Cantonese. When a Mr. Chinn was asked if his family came from the Four Districts dialect area, he replied that his surname was originally spelled *Ching* according to the Hakka dialect; his father changed it because he liked the looks of *Chinn* better.

Sometimes surname spelling can offer a clue, though, as to the locality from which an immigrant departed for this country. For example, in earlier decades, those who came to this country through Shanghai had their names spelled according to this dialect. Those who emigrated from Hong Kong had their names spelled according to standard Cantonese if they did not know how to write their names in English. Immigrants from Taiwan tend to have their names spelled according to the Wade-Giles system; and today, the names of new immigrants from mainland China are uniformly spelled in Pinyin, regardless of speech origins.

However, many American surnames of Chinese origin do not follow academic methods of spelling, such as the Americanized names and those that were respelled to suit personal whim. While it is possible to guess the exact surname character for just a few names, the "paper" surname, the new patronym, or any other accidental surname do not even offer a clue to the individual's true family name.

Genealogy Records

Assuredly, there is a surname character for every surname of Chinese origin: it may represented by the spelling or it may be found only in the individual's Chinese personal name. The stories about how the spelling came about — or how the true name had to be hidden from public eye, or how it became lost in the misunderstanding of name customs — adds color to family history.

Many descendants of the early immigrants are now constructing their genealogies, no doubt realizing that some information may no longer be recoverable after the older Chinese-speaking generation is gone. Already the owners of a surname of Chinese origin may have few or no Chinese language skills, and many are describing themselves as being of mixed ancestry. Maintaining a genealogical record can therefore preserve the surname character as a visual reminder of ancestry, enabling future generations to tie their surname to its source that is somewhere in China.

Chinese American family history should start with the progenitor who established family life in America. As the renowned Chinese scholar Ou-yang Hsiu of the eleventh century instructed: "...one's family tree should begin with the progenitor who first settled in or moved to a place and raised his family there." New immigrants are bringing or sending for their clan genealogies — these are being published in Hong Kong, Taiwan, and elsewhere — and these trace the family name to its ancient sources and settlement in China.

Fortunately, for Americans of Chinese ancestry, there are some resources in this country which may assist in locating or confirming the exact surname character to the family name. Namely, these are gravestones, the immigration case files compiled during the Chinese Exclusion period, and the Indexes to villages and family names that are found in four particular districts in Guangdong province.

Gravestones

Gravestones can be a lucrative source when the information about the deceased is recorded in both English and Chinese, but these are not a reliable resource. (As mentioned earlier, many graves were disinterred prior to World War II and the bones of the deceased were sent to China for reburial.) Unlike the brief facts that are usually stated in English, the Chinese text may contain genealogical information when the place of origin is mentioned along with the name of the deceased and the dates of birth and death. The place of origin often includes the names of the province, district, *heung* (formerly an administrative cluster of villages), and village, and these are usually recorded in this order. (The Chinese place great value on naming larger things first, which is why the smallest unit is named last.)

It should be pointed out that dates of birth and death on gravestones may be stated quite differently in Chinese. For example, if the deceased were born in 1889, this could be recorded as "born in *Guangxu* 15," the fifteenth year of this emperor's reign. Dates may be recorded according to the year of existence for the Republic of China, which was founded in 1911. For example, "died *Min guo* 41" means that the year of death was 1952. Sometimes the lunar calendar is used for months and days.

The names of the district and village represent place of origin and not necessarily birthplace because the Chinese traditionally give this information even though they may be born elsewhere. Unfortunately, the place of origin is traditionally

Place of origin for the deceased's husband is translated into English on this gravestone.

omitted on the gravestone for the wife of an early immigrant and sometimes the husband's place of origin is recorded instead. Also, because of Chinese tradition, the names of the wives of the early immigrants consist only of the original surname followed by the word *shi* that is often spelled "Shee."

When this traditional name for a married woman is recorded in Chinese, the husband's family name comes first, followed by the word "door," and then

ORIGINAL *Teacher of Student*

Consular No. 20/22

FORM OF CHINESE CERTIFICATE.

In compliance with the provisions of Section 6 of an Act of the Congress of the United States of America, approved July 5, 1884, entitled "An Act to amend an act entitled "An Act to execute certain treaty stipulations relating to Chinese, approved May 6, 1882."

THIS CERTIFICATE is issued by the undersigned, who has been designated for that purpose by the Government of China, to show that the person named hereinafter is a member of one of the exempt classes described in said Act and as such has the permission of said Government to go to and reside within the territory of the United States, after an investigation and verification of the statements contained herein by the lawfully constituted agent of the United States in this country.

The following description is submitted for the identification of the person to whom the certificate relates :—

Name in full, in proper signature of bearer *Lau Kwan-hou*
Title or official rank, if any :
Physical peculiarities :

Date of birth: *1895 Sept 14d.*
Height : *5ft 3 inches*
Former occupation : *Student*
When pursued : *1913*
Where pursued : *Canton Christian College*
How long pursued : *6 years*
Present occupation : *Student*
When pursued : *1919*
Where pursued : *Peking National University*
How long pursued : *3 years*
Last place of actual residence : *Peking National University*
(NOTE.—If a merchant the following blanks should be filled out :)
Title of present mercantile business :
Location of said mercantile business :
How long said business has been pursued :
Amount invested (gold) in said business :
Present estimated value of said business :
Specific character of merchandise handled in said business :

(NOTE.—If bearer is a traveller the following blanks should be filled out :)
Financial standing of bearer in his own country : *10,000*
Probable duration of his stay in the United States :
Issued at Tientsin, China, on this *3rd* day of *June* 192*2*

Chulungyuan
Special Commissioner of Foreign Affairs.

I., the undersigned duly authorized consular officer of the American Government for the territory within which the person named in the above certificate resides, have made a through investigation of the statements contained in the foregoing certificate and have found them to be in all respects true, and accordingly attach my signature and official seal in order that the bearer may be admitted to the United States upon identification as the person represented by the attached photograph, over which I have partly placed my official seal.

Consul General of the United States of America.

$2 $2 $5
FEE STAMP

MISC.
SERVICE
No.
2191

her name, as in "Woo *men* Gee Shee." As mentioned earlier, it means that this woman of the Gee clan had entered the house of the Woo clan. This traditional method was used even if a Chinese American married woman had an American name. For example, Mrs. Elsie G.Y. Young Wong is identified on her gravestone as "Wong *men* Young Shee." Fortunately, the full Chinese name of a married woman is now being recorded regularly on gravestones. So, unless the early immigrant woman had documented her full Chinese name and her place of origin in China, this information can be lost to her descendants. On the other hand, conformity to Euro-American customs could eliminate all of this genealogical information that is found in the Chinese text. Therefore gravestones, despite their seemingly permanent quality, cannot be the only means for documenting vital information.

Immigration Case Files

During most of the Chinese exclusion period, from 1882 to the end of 1943, immigration authorities kept case files on every Chinese immigrant — even on those who were deported — and on the native-born who took a trip abroad or who sought permission to do so. Case files do not exist for the native-born who never left the country during this period of time. In recent years, the Department of Immigration and Naturalization Services transferred their massive accumulation of now defunct Chinese case files from their regional offices to the Regional Archives System of the National Archives and Records Administration, thus opening them up for research purposes.

These immigration case files are of immense value to the descendants of the men and women who came and settled in this country before the repeal of the exclusion laws, whether they came as laborers, merchants, students, or teachers. Copies of important papers can now be obtained for documenting family history. Many files contain documents with names written in both English and Chinese. In an article by Waverly B. Lowell, Director of the National Archives–Pacific Sierra Region office in San Bruno, California, many case files contain a map of the immigrant's home village, photographs, passport, and marriage certificate. Native-born Chinese Americans may find a copy of their birth certificate in their files. They may even rediscover how they or their parents replied to the questions that were asked by the immigration officers.

Opposite: Section-6 certificate for a man seeking entry as a teacher and student during the Chinese exclusion period. (Courtesy of the National Archives — Pacific Sierra Region.)

IN RE

LIST OF PARTNERS OF

MAM JAN & CO.,

625 Grant Avenue.

State of California,)
) ss.
City and County of San Francisco.)

GENERAL MERCHANDISE.

Choo Dee, being first duly sworn deposes and says:

That the photograph hereto attached is the photograph of affiant and that affiant is a merchant and manager of the firm of Mam Jan & Co., which said firm are engaged in business at 625 Grant Avenue, in the City and County of San Francisco, State of California.

That the following is a true list of all the members of the above named and their places if residence.

That the interest of each of the named members in said firm is $500.00 or more. That the capital stock of said firm is $15000.00, consisting of stock on hand and solvent credits.

NAMES	RESIDENCES	INTERESTS.
CHOO DEE (Manager) 陶地	San Francisco	$1,000.00
LEE FOR YONG 李火容	San Francisco	500.00
LAI LUN 黎倫	San Francisco	500.00
KOO FOO 高桃	San Francisco	500.00
LOCK WING PON 駱永邦	San Francisco	500.00
KOO JAN CHEW 高振朝	San Francisco	500.00

NAMES	RESIDENCES	INTERESTS.
CHEONG SING 張成	San Francisco	$500.00
WONG SHUN 英信	San Francisco	500.00
HOO LOOK 何六	San Francisco	500.00

陶地 (Choo Ka) $15000.00

Subscribed and sworn to before me this 16th day of July, 1909.

Notary Public, in and for said City and County of San Francisco, State of California.

Above and opposite: **Merchant partnership listing for Mam Jan & Co. in San Francisco. Names were required by INS to be written in English and Chinese. (Courtesy of the National Archives–Pacific Sierra Region.)**

Other kinds of files were generated as well by the Chinese exclusion laws, such as the *habeas corpus* case files and the partnership listings of Chinese stores. The file for a Chinese store consists of the names of merchants and partners written in both English and Chinese. The National Archives–Pacific Northwest Region in Seattle, for example, has a partnership listing of Chinese merchants who were in Portland and other parts of Oregon during the exclusion period. All of these case files and other documents comprise a largely untapped resource for Chinese American family history, containing nuggets of information waiting to be discovered.

Indexes of Villages and Family Names

During the 1960s, the American Consulate General in Hong Kong compiled indexes of *heung* and villages located in four particular districts of Guangdong province, namely: *Toishan, Hoiping, Sunwui,* and *Chungshan* districts.

Descendants of the immigrants who came from these districts may find them especially useful for confirming the Chinese characters to their surname and for the place of origin for their ancestors. Even though the pattern of Chinese immigration had changed by the 1960s, the sole purpose for compiling these indexes was for investigating possible illegal immigration because these were the areas from which the vast majority of the early immigrants emigrated to this country.

Surely authorities did not envision these indexes serving a different kind of investigation. The name of each *heung* and that of the village and its marketplace are recorded in English and Chinese, including the telegraphic code number for each ideograph. Family names are similarly recorded except that these are listed only when fewer than six different family names are found in a village. Only in Toishan district is every family name listed.

It is of interest to note that the double surname *Soo Hoo* or *Seto* exists mainly in the Hoiping district and apparently is not found in the Chungshan area. Instead, the double surname *Owyang* or *Au-yeung* occurs mostly in the latter district and apparently does not exist either the Hoiping or Toishan districts. In comparison, both these family names exist in Sunwui, the district that lies between Toishan and Chungshan.

Incidentally, according to the historian Him Mark Lai, 35 of the common family names in Guangdong province were brought by the first contingent of settlers who came from other parts of China. Because they came through a main route of migration in northern Guangdong, called the *Zhuji Xiang*, some clans consider it a matter of prestige to claim descent from an ancestor who traveled this route. No doubt this information is mentioned in many Cantonese clan genealogies.

Whether or not these various resources mentioned above can provide specific answers to questions sought by the American of Chinese ancestry, the best source of information remains, as in all genealogy research, other family members. A record on family history can be started, and the surname character can be documented, but it is still left to future generations here in America to maintain it and to keep the integrity of their family name intact.

19. SUMMARY

Chinese American names have been part of American family nomenclature for over a century and a half, adding to its multicultural spice and flavor. Still, these names belong to the continuum of Chinese name traditions, with the surname character as the visible link to origin in China. The story of Chinese American names is about observing traditions, and about the transitions that take place when two diametrically opposed name traditions of different cultures meet.

Nevertheless, no conclusion can be drawn about this story; a review and summary will have to suffice. There can be no doubt, though, that the picture of Chinese American names is being rearranged and that this will continue to evolve as new immigrants arrive. Names that used to be rare are now more commonly seen, and the surnames that were once most common are being overshadowed by the names of newcomers who now form the majority of this ethnic group. Perhaps in the next 150 years of Chinese American history, the surnames that belong to the descendants of the early immigrants will become like fossils of speech, reminders of the dialects that once formed the basis for name spelling.

As a group, though, Chinese Americans have kept the family names of their forefathers. Most names can be traced back to ancient times in China — thanks to the assiduousness of the Chinese in keeping historic and genealogical records and in keeping alive the myths and legends of ancient China. As a group, Chinese Americans have been faithful as well in bestowing their children and their children's children with Chinese given names even when they also confer American names. Generations born in the United States have tended to follow the name traditions that were brought by their parents or ancestors. The centuries-old *Pai-hang* naming system directed early immigrants to bestow a different generation name to their sons and daughters.

A few Chinese American parents, as shown by the 1900 census for San Francisco, repeated their generation name in the names of their sons and daughters, undoubtedly to signify equality in status. It was too early, though, and

177

perhaps too revolutionary, to go against the grain of tradition by modifying the *Pai-hang* system. Only in recent decades, with the influx of new immigrants, has the practice of conferring the same generation name to sons and daughters become popular. In contrast, newcomers from the People's Republic of China are bringing their name practice of bestowing a child with a one-character given name.

Chinese American names also reveal a synthesis of American and Chinese name traditions. Some parents transfer the *Pai-hang* when selecting American names for their children, and some adopt the American custom of naming a son after the father and adding "Sr." and "Jr.," even attaching these notations to transcribed Chinese given names. The popular name style that includes both American and Chinese given names indicates that the desire to retain the Chinese identity remains very strong.

At the same time, the mystification of Chinese names, which the writer Lin Yutang observed over 60 years ago, evidently has not been resolved. There is still confusion over the Chinese given name that consists of two ideographs. The name styles of Chinese Americans indicate this: it is being written as two separate words, as hyphenated words, and as one word; it is being inverted, with the second syllable written first in a name. There is also acquiescence in treating the first syllable of the two-character name as a "first name." If the two-character name stands for one name — as Chinese speakers seem to believe it does — then this has yet to be clarified when it is transcribed in English.

The fact that there are relatively few surnames of Chinese origin has facilitated the telling of this story about Chinese American names. About 300 family names have been brought to this country, though the proliferation in spelling variants has resulted in perhaps three times that many surnames. The increase is mainly due to differences in Chinese dialect sounds for the same family name and to the new surnames that came into existence when immigrant parents adhered to the Chinese tradition of placing the family name first.

Dialect representation in surname spelling is closely linked to Chinese American history and to the chronicle of laws that limited and governed Chinese immigration for almost a century. Each major dialect represented in a large number of names can be correlated to certain immigration or refugee laws. It is as though each new legislation after the repeal of the exclusion laws released names by batches according to dialect sound.

Chinese American names provide a bonanza of information about history, language, philosophy, and social habits and attitudes. To preserve that precious information, Chinese Americans must regard the surname character as an integral part of a surname of Chinese origin. For some Americans, a surname of Chinese origin may be the only visual reminder of having Chinese ancestors, and the only proof that the surname arose in China.

Moreover, there can be only one particular surname character that represents the family name that was brought to America. Therefore the American who bears a surname of Chinese origin is encouraged to preserve the surname character, whether by carving it in stone, by printing it in a family record, or perhaps by displaying it as a piece of beautiful calligraphy.

At the same time, the surname of Chinese origin belongs to American family nomenclature, reminding us who we are as Americans. Our names give a point of reference that can enable us to see who we have become. Because names are a part of a nation's language and culture, Americans are connected to one another through the American way with names. Names surely can be one way to learn about ourselves and about other peoples.

APPENDIX:
COMMON SURNAMES
AND THEIR
CHINESE CHARACTERS

This list presents some of the spelling variants and Chinese characters for over 100 common family names belonging to Chinese Americans. Some rarely seen family names are also included because of similarity in spelling or to demonstrate the diversity in dialect sound for the same name. Spelling for each family name is in alphabetical order. Because of limited space, many surnames cannot be listed separately. Those beginning with the letters Q, X, and Z, especially, can be found among surnames beginning with Ch, Hs, J, and K.

Ai, Ngai:	艾
Ang:	鄧, 洪
Ao, Gaw, Gore, Ngo:	敖
Au, Ou, Ow:	區, 歐
Auyang, Au-Yeung, Euyang, O'Young, Ou-yang, Ow Yang, Owyoung:	歐陽
Aw, Foo, Hu, Woo, Wu:	胡
Bae, Boey, Bui, Mei, Moy, Moye, Mui:	梅
Bai, Bock, Pai, Paik, Pak:	白
Ban, Pan:	班
Be, Ma, Maa, Mah, Mahr, Mar, Marr:	馬
Bei, Pei:	貝
Bong, Pang, Peng, Penn, Phang, Pong:	彭
Cai, Chai, Choa, Choi, Choy, Choye, Chua,Thai, Toy, Toye, Tsoi, Tsai:	蔡
Cao, Chao, Choe, Chow, Jow, Tow, Tsao:	曹
Cen, Chen, Sam, Shem, Shum, Sim, Sum, Tsen:	岑
Cha:	查
Chai, Chak, Zhai:	翟

181

Chak, Check, Cherk, Cheuk, Cho,
  Chock, Chuck, Zhuo: 卓
Cham, Chan, Chim, Jan, Jim, Zhan: 詹
Chan: 陳, 秦, 詹
Chan, Chann, Chang, Chen, Chenn,
  Chern, Chhin, Chin, Chinn,
  Ching, Chun, Chunn, Dzung,
  Tan, Tchen, Tschen, Ting, Tjhen,
  Tran, Tren, Zung: 陳
Chan, Chin, Qin: 秦
Chang: 常, 姜, 章, 張, 程, 鄭, 陳
Chang, Cheng, Jan, Jang, Jann, Jeng,
  Jhen, Jing, Jung, Tay, The, Trinh,
  Zheng: 鄭
Chang, Cheong, Cheung, Chong,
  Chung, Jeong, Jeung, Jong, Jung,
  Tchang, Tea, Tio, Trong, Truong,
  Zhang: 張
Chang, Cheng, Cherng, Ching, Tcheng,
  Trinh, Zung: 程
Chang, Chiang, Jiang, Keung, Kiang: 姜
Chao: 招, 趙, 曹
Chao, Chew, Chiu, Chu, Djao, Jeu,
  Jew, Jiu, Jow, Jue, Teo, Zhao: 趙
Chao, Chiu, Chu, Zhao: 招
Char, Chea, Dair, Dare, Dea, Dear,
  Der, Dere, Hsieh, Ja, Jair, Jaire,
  Jay, Jea, Jer, Shieh, Sia, Tse, Tze,
  Xie, Zia: 謝
Chau, Chiu, Chou, Chow, Jeu, Jew, Joe, Johe, Jou,
  Ju, Jue, Tcheou, Zhou: 周
Chau, Chow, Tsou, Zou: 鄒
Chay, Choy, Cui, Tsai, Tsui: 崔
Chee, Choe, Chooey, Chui, Djie, Hsu,
  Shu, Shyu, Tjhie, Tsu, Tuey, Xu,
  Zee, Zi: 徐
Chee, Chu, Dju, Gee, Jee, Jue, Kyi,
  Tsu, Zhu: 朱

Chen, Gin, Ginn, Gyn, Jan, Jean, Jein,
    Jen, Jin, Yan, Zhen: 甄

Cheng: 成, 誠, 程, 鄭

Cheng, Zheng: 鄭

Cherng: 成, 程

Chew: 趙

Chi, Chih: 遲

Chi, Ji: 吉, 紀, 季, 計, 冀, 籍

Chi, Qi: 祁, 戚, 齊

Chia, Jia, Ka: 賈

Chiang, Gong, Jiang, Kiang,
    Kong, Kung: 江

Chiang, Jeang, Jeung, Jiang, Jung: 蔣

Chiao, Qiao: 喬

Chien, Gan, Gon, Gonn, Jian, Kan: 簡

Chin: 金, 晉, 錢, 秦, 陳

Chin, Chien, Chinn, Tsien, Qian: 錢

Chin, Gam, Jin, Kam, King, Kum: 金

Chiu: 丘, 邱, 邵, 裘, 周, 招, 趙

Chiu, Chu, Heu, Hew, Hugh: 丘

Chiu, Chu, Heu, Hew, Hu,
    Khoo, Qiu: 邱

Chiu, Shao, Shaw,
    Shiu, Zau: 邵

Choy: 蔡, 崔

Chu: 丘, 邱, 朱, 竺, 招, 祝, 屈, 儲, 瞿

Chu, Qu, Wat, Watt: 屈

Chu, Zhu: 祝, 竺, 諸, 朱

Chuan, Chuen, Dzen, Quan,
    Tsuan, Zen: 全

Chuan, Chuang, Chung,
    Chwang, Trang, Zhuang: 莊

Chu Ke, Chu Ko, Zhu Ge: 諸葛

Chung: 宗, 曾, 莊, 張, 鍾

Chung, Dang, Don, Dong, Doung,
    Jang, Jing, Jung, Phang, Tsang,
    Tseng, Zane, Zeng: 曾

Chung, Tsung, Zong: 宗

Chung, Jone, Jones, Jong: 鍾

Co, Hee, Heui, Hoey, Hoo, Hoy, Hsu,
    Huey, Hui, Huie, Kho, Shu, Xu: 許

Cui, Tsai, Tsui: 崔

Dai, Taai, Tai, Tay, Tye: 戴

Dair, Dare, Dea, Dear, Der, Dere: 謝

Dang, Deng, Dong, Dunn, Ong, Tang,
    Teng, Tongg, Ung: 鄧

Dang, Don, Dong, Doung: 曾

Diao, Tiao, Tyau: 刁

Ding, Ting: 丁

Dong: 董, 曾 鄧

Dong, Dung, Tung: 董

Doo, Du, Duh, To, Tu: 杜

Duan, Dwan, Tuan: 段

Eng, Gow, Ing, Ng, Ngo, Wu: 伍

Eng, Ing, Gaw, Go, Gouw, Ng, Ngo,
    Ngaw, Ung, Woo, Wu: 吳

Eu, Ye, Yee, Yu, Yue: 余

Fan: 范, 樊

Fan, Fann, Farm, Pham: 范

Fang, Fong: 方

Feng, Fenn, Ferng, Fong, Foong, Fung,
    Funge, Phong, Phung, Voong: 馮

Fok, Ho, Hoh, Huo: 霍

Fong: 酈, 方, 馮 酈

Fong, Kuang, Kwong: 傅

Fu: 符, 金

Gam: 甘

Gam, Gan, Gom, Gum, Kam, Kan,
    Kum: 甘

Gan, Gon, Gonn, Kan: 簡

Gan, Kan: 干, 甘, 簡

Gao, Go, Goe, Gow, Kao, Kau, Ko, Koe: 高

Ge, Ke: 戈, 葛

Ge, Geh, Ger, Gott, Ke, Keh, Ko, Kuh: 葛

Gee, Jee: 朱

Gin, Ginn, Gyn, Jean, Jein, Jen, Jin: 甄

Go:	吳, 高
Gock, Gok, Guo, Keh, Kuo, Kwak, Kwee, Kwock, Kwoh, Kwok, Quach, Quo, Quock:	郭
Gong, Kung:	貢, 龔, 江
Gong, Kong, Kung:	江
Gong, Goong, Kung:	龔
Goo, Gu, Koo, Ku:	古, 顧
Goon, Guen, Juan, Nguyen, Ruan, Yuan, Yuen:	阮
Guo, Kuo, Kwoh:	郭
Gow:	伍, 高
Guan, Kuan, Kwon, Kwan, Quan, Quon:	關
Ha, Hsia, Sya, Xia:	夏
Hahn, Han, Hann, Hon:	韓
Hall, Haw, He, Ho, Hoo, Hoh, Hor:	何
Ham, Harm, Hom, Hum, Taam, Tain, Tam, Tan, Tann, Tarm, Thom, Tom:	譚
Hao:	郝
He, Ho:	賀, 赫, 何
Hee, Heui, Hoey, Hoo, Hoy, Huey, Huie:	許
Heu, Hew, Hugh:	丘, 邱
Ho:	何, 賀, 霍, 赫, 黃
Hoang:	王,
Hoang, Huang, Huynh, Hwang, Ng, Oei, Wong:	黃
Hoang, Wang, Wong, Vuong:	王
Hong:	孔, 洪, 唐, 康, 湯
Hong, Hung, Kong, Kung:	孔
Hong, Kang:	康
Hong, Tang, Tong:	唐, 湯
Hou, How, Howe:	侯, 候
Hsiao, Shaw, Shew, Siaw, Sieu, Siu, Su, Sue, Syau, Tieu, Xiao:	蕭
Hsieh, Shieh, Xie:	謝
Hsiung, Hung, Shiung, Xiong:	熊

Hsu, Hsue, Shu, Xu: 許, 徐

Hsueh, Said, Seid, Seit, Sidney, Sit,
    Sywe, Xue: 薛

Hu: 胡

Hua, Hwa: 華

Huang, Hwang: 黃

Huang-fu: 皇甫

Hung: 熊, 洪, 孔

Ih, Yi, Yick, Yik: 易

Im, Ngim, Yan, Yen, Yim: 嚴

In, Inn, Yoon, Yuan, Yuen: 阮, 袁

Ip, Ipp, Yap, Yapp, Ye, Yeh, Yep, Yepp,
    Yip: 葉

Iu, Yao, Yeo, Yew, Yiu, You: 姚

Ja, Jair, Jaire, Jay, Jea, Jer: 謝

Jan: 鄭, 詹, 曾

Jan, Jang, Jann, Jeng, Jhen, Jing: 鄭

Jen, Ren, Yam, Yum, Zen: 任

Jew, Ju, Jue: 趙, 周

Joe, Johe: 周

Ju, Ru : 茹

Jung: 鍾, 鄭, 蔣, 張, 曾, 容

Kan: 簡, 甘, 干

Kang: 康

Kiang: 姜, 江

King: 金

Ko: 高, 戈

Kong, Kung: 孔

Ku, Koo: 顧, 谷, 古

Kuang: 鄺, 匡

Kuang, Kwong: 鄺

Kung: 龔, 貢, 孔

Kuo, Kwoh, Quo: 郭

Kwock, Kwok, Quock: 郭

Kyi: 紀, 朱

Laai, Lai, Lye: 賴

Lai: 賴, 厲, 黎

Lai, Le, Li, Ligh, Ly, Lye: 黎

Lam, Lamb, Lamm, Land, Lem, Lim, Limm,Lin, Linn, Ling, Lum, Lym, Lynn: 林

Lam, Lan: 藍

Lang, Leon, Leong, Leung, Liang, Liong, Lung, Luong: 梁

Lao, Loo: 勞

Lau, Leo, Lew, Liu, Lou, Low, Lowe, Lue: 劉

Law, Lewis, Lo, Loh, Lor, Luo: 羅

Lay, Laye, Lee, Leigh, Li, Ly: 李

Lee, Li: 利, 李

Lei, Louey, Loui, Louie, Louis, Lue, Luey, Lui: 雷

Leo, Lew, Lewis, Liao, Liaw, Liu, Lew: 廖

Leon, Leong, Leung: 梁

Leu, Lew, Lou, Louie, Lowie, Loy, Lu, Lue, Lui: 呂

Lew: 呂, 廖, 劉

Lewis: 劉, 廖, 羅

Li: 李, 利, 黎, 厲

Ling: 冷, 林, 凌

Liu: 柳, 劉, 廖

Lo, Lock, Locke, Loh, Lok, Luck: 駱

Lo: 盧, 樓, 羅

Loh: 樂, 陸, 駱, 羅, 盧

Loh, Loo, Lou, Low, Lowe, Louis, Lu: 盧

Long, Loong, Lung: 龍

Look, Lou, Lu, Luh, Luk, Luke: 陸

Lou: 婁, 樓, 陸, 劉, 盧

Louie, Lui: 呂, 雷

Lu: 魯, 呂, 陸, 盧

Ma, Maa, Mah, Mahr, Mar, Marr: 馬

Maak, Mac, Mai, Mak, Mark, Mock: 麥

Mac, Mark, Mo, Moh, Mock, Mok, Mor: 莫

Man, Moon, Mun, Wen: 文

Man, Moon, Van, Wan: 萬

Mang, Meng: 孟
Mao: 茅,
Mao, Mau, Mo, Mow: 毛
Mei: 梅
Mew, Miao, Miu: 繆
Miao: 繆 苗,
Miao, Mu: 苗
Ming: 明
Mo, Moe, Wu: 巫
Mo, Moh, Wu: 武
Moy, Moye: 梅
Nee, Ngai, Ngaih, Ngie, Ni, Nie: 倪
New, Niu: 牛
Ng: 黃 吳, 伍,
Ngai: 艾 倪, 魏
Ngan, Yan, Yen: 顏
Ngim: 嚴
Ngo : 敖 吳, 伍,
Ni, Nie, Nieh, Nih, Nip, Nipp, Nyi: 聶
Ning: 甯 寧,
Ong: 鄧 翁, 王,
Ong, Oong, Weng, Yung, Young: 翁
Oung, Wang, Wong: 汪
O'Yang, O'Young, Ouyang, OwYang,
   Owyoung: 歐陽
Pai, Pak: 柏 白,
Pan: 盤 潘, 班,
Pan, Phan, Pon, Poon, Pun: 潘
Pan, Pon, Pond, Pun: 盤
Pang, Peng, Penn, Phang, Pong: 彭
Pang, Pong: 龐
Pei: 貝 裴, 皮,
Po, Poe, Pu: 浦 蒲,
Pu: 濮 浦, 卜,
Qi: 齊 戚, 祁,
Quan: 關 全,
Ren: 任
Ru: 茹

188

Ruan, Yuan, Yuen:	阮
Sai, She:	佘
Said, Seid, Seit, Sit:	薛
Sam, Sheen, Shen, Shenn, Shum, Sim:	沈
Sam, Shem, Shum, Sum:	岑
Seeto, Seto, Situ, Soo Hoo, Ssu-tu, Stowe, Sze To:	司徒
Sen, Sin, Sing, Xian:	冼
Seu, Shew, Sieu, Siaw, Siu, Su, Sue, Syau:	蕭
Shao, Shaw, Zau:	邵
Shek, Shi, Shih, Shyr, Stone, Zak:	石
Sheng:	盛
Shentu:	申屠
Shi, Shih:	石, 史, 時, 施
Sia, Zia:	謝
Sin:	冼,
Sin, Soon, Soong, Suen, Sun, Ton:	孫
So, Soe, Soo, Su, Sue:	孫 蘇
Song, Soong, Sung:	宋
Sze:	史, 斯, 絲, 施
Taam, Tam, Tan, Tann, Tarm, Thom, Tom:	譚
Tan:	陳, 談, 譚,
Tang:	唐, 湯, 鄧
Tao, Tow:	陶
Tian, Tien, Tin, Tyan:	田
Tiao, Tyau:	刁
Tom:	譚
Tong:	湯
Tong, Toung, Tung:	童
Toy, Toye:	蔡
Tran, Tren:	陳
Trinh:	鄭
Tse, Tze:	謝
Tso, Zuo:	左
Tsui:	徐, 崔

Tu:	屠, 杜端木
Tuan-mu, Twanmoh:	端木
Ung:	伍, 吳
Voo, Wu:	武, 烏
Wai, Wei, Wy, Wye:	韋
Wan, Wen, Won, Wone, Woon:	溫
Wang, Wong:	王, 汪, 黃
Wei:	韋, 衛, 魏
Wen:	文, 聞, 溫
Weng, Yung:	翁
Wong:	王, 汪, 黃
Woo:	吳, 胡, 鄔
Wu:	巫, 烏, 鄔, 吳, 伍, 武, 胡
Xie:	謝
Xiong:	熊
Xu:	徐, 許
Yan:	言, 晏, 燕, 閻, 顏, 嚴
Yang, Yeang, Yeung, Yong, Young, Yung:	楊
Yao:	姚, 饒
Yap, Yapp, Yep, Yepp, Yip:	葉
Ye, Yeh:	葉
Yee:	余
Yeo, Yiu, Yo, You, Yu:	尤, 姚, 楊
Yick, Yik:	易
Yim:	嚴
Yin:	尹, 殷
Yin, Yoon, Yorn, Yuin, Yuan, Yuen:	袁
Yu, Yue:	于, 尤, 余, 俞, 喻, 游, 虞
Yuan, Yuen:	阮, 袁
Zane:	冼, 曾
Zee, Zia:	徐, 謝
Zen:	任, 慎
Zung:	程, 陳

The following list represents some of the new surnames that arose acci-
dentally for Chinese Americans. Most are patronyms taken from the personal

name of the family's progenitor who settled in this country. The Chinese character for the actual family name is included (in parentheses) only when it is known to the author.

Afong, Ahfong (Chuck — 卓), Ahana (Wong — 黃 or Chun — 陳), Ahchu, Ahee, Ah Leong (Lau — 劉), Ahloy (Kam — 甘), Ahpong (Ng — 吳), Ah Sam, Ah-Tye (Yee — 余), Ahuna (Tong — 唐), Aiina (Chee — 徐), Akina (Goo — 古 or Yuen — 袁), Akwai (Tai — 戴), Aloiau (Wong — 王), Among, Anin, Asing, and Assing.

Bing, Bo-Linn (Wong — 黃), Bow, and Bowen (Lee — 李).

Chan Dick, Chan-Lam, Chin-Bing, Chin-Bow, Chin-Lee, Chin-Park, Chong Der, Chop (Yip — 葉), Chun-Hoon (Chun — 陳), Chu Lin (Chu — 趙), and Chung-Hoon.

Den, Der-Bing (Der — 謝), Din, Dofoo (Louie — 雷), Doshim (Wu — 伍), Dun, and Dunn.

Fat (Dong — 鄧), Fatt, Fay, Foo, Fook, Foon, and Foy.

Garbern (Yee — 余), Gate (Mark — 麥), Gim, Ging, Glenchur (Chong — 張), Gong-guy (Gong — 江), Goon Dip (Goon — 阮), Goonyep, Goo-Sun (Goo — 古), Got, Gott (Low — 劉), Gow, and Guey.

Ham (Huey — 許), Hee, Heen, Heng, Him, Hing, Hipon (Wong — 黃), Hong, Howe, and Hoy.

Isee (Ren — 任).

James (Yum — 任), Jarm (Yee — 余), Jen Kin (Jen — 鄭), Jewell (Jew — 趙), Jewik (Jew — 趙), Jig (Wong — 黃), Jone (Yee — 余), and Jower (Wan — 溫).

Kai, Kaikee (Ching — 程), Kay, Kee, Kim, Kimm, Kimlau (Lau — 劉), and King.

Lai Mye (Lai — 黎), Lai Sun, Lau Kee, Lee-Fong, Lee Sing, Leewong, Leong Ming (Leong — 梁), Leong Way (Leong — 梁), Lett, Lew Kay (Lew — 劉), Lew Wing (Lew — 劉), Loo Kay (Loo — 盧), Louis (Wong — 黃), Louis Kay (Louis — 盧), Loy, and Lumho (Lum — 林).

Mafong (Ma — 馬), Mammon (Ma — 馬), Man-Son-Hing, Marfoe (Mar — 馬), Mar Hing (Mar — 馬), Mar Jip (Mar — 馬), Ming, Monwai (Won — 溫), Mook, Moon (Wong — 黃), and Mooncai (Wong — 黃).

Nahme (Lee — 李).

On, Ott.

Park, Park Li, and Poy.

Quan Foy (Quan — 關), Quey, Quil, and Quin.

Saiget (Kong—江), Sam, Schoon (Gee—朱), See, Sheng (Tom—譚), Shoong (Joe—周), Sing, and Suey.

Tankhim (Tan—譚), Ten (Lew—劉), Tim, Timm, Tinloy (Kan—簡), Tsoming (Wong—黃), and Typond (Lee—李).

Unguez.

Wah, Watson, Wing, Wingshee, Wongham, Wongwai, Woo-Sam, and Woon.

Yaplee (Sung—宋), Yee Quil, Yook, and Yuke.

GLOSSARY

Ah (亞 or 阿): a syllable usually heard as a prefix to names and kinship terms (a central and southern Chinese custom). Seen in some Chinese American patronyms, as in *Ahsing*.

Bai Jia Xing or *Bo Jia Xing* (百 家 姓): the title of a well-known compilation of nearly 500 Chinese family names.

Cantonese: the people and language, including subdialects, of Guangdong province in southern China. Standard Cantonese is lingua franca of this province and Hong Kong. It has been an important language in Chinese American communities since Chinese immigration began. Cantonese includes the subdialects important to the early Chinese immigrants called *Chungshan, Sam Yup* or Three Districts dialect, and *Sze Yup* or Four Districts dialect.

Character: refers to a Chinese word or ideograph. "Surname character" refers to the ideograph for a family name.

Chinese Exclusion period: In America, from 1882 to 1943, Chinese Exclusion Acts restricted Chinese immigration. Chinese laborers were banned, but certain Chinese persons were permitted entry, such as merchants, merchants' wives and children, students, and children of native-born citizens.

Chinese national language: commonly called Mandarin. Based on the Northern Mandarin dialect spoken in Beijing. Adopted in 1919 and revised in 1932.

Clan: a group of families having the same patrilineal family name and claiming descent from a common ancestor.

Dialect: regional division of a language; patois of a locality.

Disyllabic name: a name having two syllables; a two-character Chinese name.

Dithemic name: a given name composed of two meaningful elements, as in *Robert*, an Anglo-Saxon name that means "fame, bright."

Generation name: usually one of the two characters in a Chinese given name that is repeated in the names of siblings. Brothers and sisters traditionally have different generation names.

193

Given name: a name usually given at birth. Some people give themselves a new given name. Commonly called "first name" by Americans because it comes first in an American name.

Family name: the hereditary name of a family, usually patrilineal. Also called surname. Commonly called "last name" by Americans.

Foreign-born: in this book, used to indicate birth outside of the United States.

Han Chinese: term for the vast majority of the people of China, excluding those of non–Chinese extraction such as Manchus and Mongolians.

Hao (號)*:* traditionally an additional name adopted by a Chinese man when he marries. Called "marriage name" or "adult name." Popular usage differs from literary form, which states the *zi* is the adult name.

Ideographic writing: describes the Chinese system of writing wherein a syllable or thought is represented by an ideograph or character.

Maiden name: the original surname of a married woman who has taken her spouse's surname.

Mandarin: common term for the Chinese national language.

Major Chinese dialects: the following are usually mentioned: Mandarin (Northern, Southern, and Southwest), Hsiang, Wu or Shanghai, Northern Min (Fuzhou), Southern Min (Amoy-Swatow, Hokkien, Teochiu), Cantonese, and Gan-Hakka.

Middle name: the second of the two given names which the majority of Americans possess; frequently represented by its initial, as in John J. Doe.

Ming (名)*:* the Chinese word meaning "name."

Monosyllabic name: a one syllable name; a one-character Chinese name.

Name style: the way a name is written or stated, as in Jane Doe.

Native-born: in this book, used to indicate birth in the United States of America.

"Paper name": name used by an illegal immigrant who came to America during the Chinese Exclusion period and took his name from a falsified identification certificate.

"Paper surname": "paper name" inherited by children of the illegal immigrant using the name.

Patronym: a surname adopted from a grandfather's or father's name.

Personal name: refers to the given name and family name, as in John Lee.

Pinyin: the standard system of writing Chinese in the Roman (or Latin) alphabet. Adopted in 1958 by the People's Republic of China and officially promulgated abroad in 1979. Literally means "spelling the sound."

Romanization: the transcription of Chinese sounds into the Roman alphabet.

Shi (氏)*:* Chinese word meaning clan, clan name, and a married woman's maiden name or her original family name. Commonly spelled "Shee" in the names of the early immigrants who came as wives.

Transcribe: to write down in phonetic notation the sounds of speech; for example, to spell the sounds of Chinese using Roman letters.

Transliterate: to spell the words of one language using the letters of another alphabet; for example, to write Greek words by substituting a Roman letter for each Greek letter.

Wade-Giles system: devised by two British scholars and diplomats for romanizing Mandarin. The system was begun in 1859 by Sir Thomas Francis Wade and modified by Herbert Allen Giles in 1912. It was widely used in the English-speaking world until replaced by Pinyin in 1979.

Xing (hsing — 姓)*:* family name or surname. Denotes lineage.

Xing-shi (姓-氏)*:* compound word meaning "family name."

Zi (tzu — 字)*:* a courtesy name or style, but its literary meaning is "adult name" or "marriage name." Popular usage reversed the meanings for *zi* and *hao*.

NOTES

Chapter 1: History, Myths and Family Names

p. 16 "Not even after a hundred generations": James Legge, trans., *Li Chi: Book of Rites*, ed. Ch'u Chai and Winberg Chai (1885; reprint, New Hyde Park NY: University Books, 1967), 2: 63.

pp. 20-1 **Lingering Traditions:** Marriage laws and punishments to violators are discussed in Maurice Freedman, *Lineage Organization in Southeastern China*, Monographs on Social Anthropology, no. 18 (London: Univ. of London, Althone Press, 1958), 4; and Maurice Freedman, *The Study of Chinese Society: Essays by Maurice Freedman*, ed. G.W. Skinner (Stanford: Stanford Univ. Press, 1979), 111–12.

p. 21 "It is most improbable": C.P. Fitzgerald, *The Horizon History of China*, ed. Norman Kotker (New York: American Heritage Publishing, 1969), 99.

Chapter 2: Sources of Family Names

p. 23 "genealogical purity": Chi Li, *The Formation of the Chinese People: An Anthropological Study* (Cambridge: Harvard Univ. Press, 1928), 142–43.

The sinologist Herbert A. Giles: Giles's work is the source for many of the surname stories in this chapter. Herbert A. Giles, "The Family Names," *Journal of the China Branch of the Royal Asiatic Society*, n.s., 21 (1886–87): 255–88.

p. 29 "Occupations ... looked up to": Elsdon C. Smith, *New Dictionary of American Family Names* (New York: Harper & Row, 1973), xviii.

Chapter 3: Some Characteristics of Family Names

p. 33 Chinese almanac: Martin Palmer, ed. and trans., *T'ung Shu: The Ancient Chinese Almanac* (Boston: Shambhala, 1986), 9.

p. 34 the pre–1905 classical education: This included memorizing the Three Character Classic, the Thousand Character Essay, and the Classic of Filial Piety. Kenneth Scott Latourette, *The Chinese: Their History and Culture*, 4th ed. rev. in 1 vol. (New York: Macmillan, 1964), 662.

10,000 family names: Du Ruofu, letter to author, 28 December 1988; and Yuan Yida and Du Ruofu, *Zhonghua Xing Shi Da Zidian* (Beijing, 1996).

p. 35 Korean and Vietnamese ... surnames: Eui-Hang Shin and Eui-Young Yu, "Use of Surnames in Ethnic Research: The Case of Kims in the Korean American Population, "*P/AAMHRC Research Review* 3 (1984): 12; and Phuoc Huu Nguyen and Tuyet-nga T. Nguyen, "Differences in Value Orientations Between American and Vietnamese" (mimeographed paper, 1970s?).

Japan ... surnames: Mrs. Yamamoto, author of *Kamon Japanese Family Crest*, conversation with author, August 1989.

p. 35   a mere 19 *surnames*: *Chung Pao* [*Chinese Daily News*] 4 May 1987, p. 3. (In Chinese.)

Most Popular Surnames: The surname Li was discussed by Du Ruofu, letter to author, 2 July 1987. Zhang (Chang) is cited as the most common surname in several books and articles, including Christopher P. Anderson, *The Name Game* (New York: Simon & Schuster, 1977), 52; and Geoffrey W. Royall, "What Is in a Name in China?" *The Missionary Review of the World* 61 (1938): 122.

p. 38   10 great surnames of Taiwan: *Chung Pao*, 25 February 1988.

"Even if the character happens to be": Dr. Yuen Ren Chao, letter to author, 19 February 1977.

p. 39   "the meaning of the word": Smith, *New Dictionary*, xxvii–xxviii.

p. 40   mother's surname as a given name: Lu Zhongti and Celia Millward, "Chinese Given Names Since the Cultural Revolution," *Names* 37 (1989): 277.

"Massive name changing": Chen Shao-hsing and Morton Fried, *The Distribution of Family Names in Taiwan* (Taipei, Taiwan: National Taiwan University, 1968), 1: vi.

p. 41   report on names and human rights: Bjorn H. Jernudd, "Personal names and human rights," in *Linguistic Human Rights: Overcoming Linguistic Discrimination*, ed. Tove Skutnabb-Kangas (New York: Mounton de Gruyter, 1994), 121–23.

Chapter 4: On Chinese Given Names

p. 42   "balanced, symmetrical and hierarchical view": Wm. Theodore de Bary, Wing-tsit Chan, and Burton Watson, comps., *Sources of Chinese Traditions*, vol. 1 (New York: Columbia Univ. Press, 1960), 114.

p. 45   *William* is a dithemic name: Smith, *New Dictionary*, xix.

"If names are not correct": James Legge, trans., *The Chinese Classics*, vol. 1, *The Confucian Analects*, 2nd ed. rev. (Oxford: Clarendon, 1893), 263–64.

comment extends to personal names: Dr. Wu Tehyao, letter to author, 29 July 1990.

"If a name is on a list": Tyler Marshall, "Old Fears Await the Coming of One Germany," *Los Angeles Times*, 2 October 1990.

p. 46   the late Bruce Lee: *Asianweek*, 30 April 1993, p. 20.

The terms *hao* and *zi*: Wolfgang Bauer, *Der Chinesische Personenname* [Chinese Personal Names], *Asiatische Forschungen* (Wiesbaden: Otto Harrassowitz, 1959): 14; and Yuen Ren Chao, *Aspects of Chinese Sociolinguistics: Essays by Yuen Ren Chao*, ed. Anwar S. Dil (Stanford: Stanford Univ. Press, 1976), 317.

pp. 46-7   Teachers could bestow the *da ming*: Cornelius Osgood, *Village Life in Old China: A Community Study of Kao Yao, Yunnan* (New York: Ronal, 1963), 266–67.

p. 47   Famous writers usually had several: Pao-liang Chu, *Twentieth Century Chinese Writers and Their Pen Names* (Boston: G.K. Hall, 1977), ix, 122.

bie hao of Sun Yat-sen: Him Mark Lai, "Roots and Lineages: A Journey Through the Pearl River Delta, Pt. 4: Zhongshan," *East/West*, 7 January 1981, p. 3.

pp. 47–8   **One-Character vis-à-vis Two-Character Given Names**: Bauer, *Chinesische Personenname*, 66–73.

p. 48   The vocative *"Ah"*: James Legge, trans., *The Chinese Classics*, vol. 3, *The Shoo King* (n.d.; reprint, Hong Kong: Hong Kong Univ. Press, 1970), 199–200.

p. 50   "honorific": H.L. Mencken, *The American Language: An Inquiry into the Development of English in the United States*, 4th ed. (New York: Alfred A. Knopf, 1937), 443.

"Mr.": Fitzgerald, *Horizon History of China*, 34.

the Hokkien place *Ah* after the name: Samuel Wells Williams, *The Middle Kingdom* (New York: John Wiley, 1879), 2: 66.

neither the family name ... should be stated by itself: Chao, *Aspects of Chinese Sociolinguistics*, 314–15.

Chapter 5: The Generation Name

p. 51   Hungarians and Rumanians follow this name order: Mencken, *American Language*, 440.

p. 52   *Pai-hang* : Bauer, *Chinesische Personenname*, 147–222.

early German immigrants: George R. Stewart, *American Given Names* (New York: Oxford Univ. Press, 1979), 20–21, 29.

p. 53   Liu clan ... name poem: Bauer, *Chinesische Personenname*, 211.

p. 54   **Women and the Pai-hang**: *ibid.*, 363–65.

p. 55   generation name was no longer required for male cousins: *ibid.*, 220.

p. 56   "reactionary thought of bourgeois society": Hsiang-lin Lo, "The Preservation of Genealogical Records in China," in *Studies in Asian Genealogy*, ed. Spencer J. Palmer (Provo UT: Brigham Young Univ. Press, 1972), 50–51.

charting a family tree: Ch'eng Ch'ing-I, *Chung-kuo Tsu-Pu Pien Tsuan Chien Shuo* [A Concise Compilation for Chinese Genealogy] (Taipei, Taiwan: Lien-ho Pao ... Hsien Kuan, 1987.)

famous Soong sisters: Elmer T. Clark, *The Chiangs of China* (New York: Abingdon-Cokesbury, 1943), 41–42.

Chapter 6: Who Are Chinese Americans?

p. 61   "All family names": Elsdon C. Smith, *American Surnames* (Philadelphia: Chilton, 1969), 5.

"Asians in the U.S.": John Kuo Wei Tchen, "'Race' & Cultural Democracy: Historical Challenges & Future Possibilities" (Keynote Address delivered at the Martin Luther King, Jr., Holiday Celebration held at NMNH, Smithsonian Institution, 16 January 1989), 2–3.

"find it hard to believe": "Dear Abby," *Los Angeles Times*, 28 April 1986.

p. 62   "*Asian American*": Michael Omi, "Out of the Melting Pot and into the Fire: Race Relations Policy." *The State of Asian Pacific America: A Public Policy Report* (Los Angeles: LEAP and UCLA Asian American Studies Center, 1993): 199–214.

"ethnic-consciousness": William Wei, *The Asian American Movement* (Philadelphia: Temple Univ. Press, 1993), 1.

p. 63   "exotic, mysterious": Ronald Takaki, *Strangers from a Different Shore: A History of Asian Americans* (Boston: Little, Brown, 1989), 487.

"Eurocentric": William Safire, *What's the Good Word?* (New York: New York Times, 1982), 115–18.

"And Chinese-American": Maxine Hong Kingston, *Tripmaster Monkey* (New York: Vintage, 1989), 327.

"political status": "Chinese Americans: Who Defines Us?" *Amerasia Journal* 14 (1988): vii–ix.

p. 64   "Those who still retain": *ibid.*, viii.

"common ancestry": Tu Wei-ming, "Cultural China: The Periphery as the Center," *Daedalus* 120 (Spring 1991): 22.

p. 65   *foreign stock* and *native stock*: Marjorie P.K. Weiser, ed., *Ethnic America*, The Reference Shelf Series, vol. 50 (New York: H.W. Wilson, 1978), 11.

cohesiveness of an ethnic group: Tamotsu Shibutani and Kian M. Kwan, *Ethnic Stratification: A Comparative Approach* (Toronto, Canada: Macmillan, 1969), 217–18.

"Conflict is implicit": Laurence Yep, "A Cord to the Past," *CMLEA Journal* 15 (Fall 1991): 8.

p. 66   "accommodation strategy": L. Ling-chi Wang, "Roots and Changing Identity of the Chinese in the United States," *Daedalus* 120 (Spring 1991): 200, 205.

"Many people from Taiwan": *Asianweek*, 1 April 1994, 19.

"not really Chinese": Maureen Fan, "All the Wrong Assumptions," *Chinese American Forum* 6, (October 1990): 15.

ABC: Karen W. Chan, "Climbing Out of the 'Black Hole' of ABCs," *Asianweek*, 20 August 1993, pp. 2, 19.

"Many do not speak the Chinese language": Victoria S. Lim, "Myths of ABCs and American Education," *Chinese American Forum* 4 (1988): 18.

p. 67   "I grew up in Northern China": *Asianweek*, 14 April 1995, p. 14.

"neither merchants nor the descendants of coolies": Wang Gungwu, "Among Non-Chinese," *Daedalus* 120 (Spring 1991): 197.

filled with self-hatred: Lynn Pan, *Sons of the Yellow Emperor: The Story of the Overseas Chinese* (London: Octopus/Mandarin, 1991), 276, 286–88.

moving out of the Chinatowns: L. Ling-chi Wang, "Roots and Changing Identity," 188, 196–97.

"adventurous": Wolfram Eberhard, "Chinese Genealogies as a Source for the Study of Chinese Society," in *Studies in Asian Genealogy*, ed. Spencer J. Palmer (Provo UT: Brigham Young Univ. Press, 1972), 37.

"By allowing merchants to have their wives": Sucheng Chan, "The Exclusion of Chinese Women, 1870–1943," in *Entry Denied: Exclusion and the Chinese Community in America, 1882–1943*, ed. Sucheng Chan (Philadelphia: Temple Univ. Press, 1991), 139.

p. 68   "predominant form of family life": Betty Lee Sung, *The Story of the Chinese in America* (New York: Macmillan Collier, 1967), 154–56.

A recent genealogical report: David Hom, "My Family in the United States," *Gum Saan Journal* 12 (June 1989): 17–23.

1.5 generation: May Lam, "Who Really Belongs to the 1.5 Generation?" *Asianweek*, 22 July 1994, pp. 1, 23.

p. 69   "culturally much easier": Myron L. Cohen, "Being Chinese: The Peripheralization of Traditional Identity," *Daedalus* 120 (Spring 1991): 133.

"origin from somewhere in China": *ibid.*, 121.

Chapter 7: A Great Variety in Dialect Sound and Surname Spelling

p. 70   nine ways to spell Jones: Ethel W. Williams, *Know Your Ancestors* (Rutland VT: Charles E. Tuttle, 1960), 23–24.

p. 71   system of writing symbolizes thought: Mario Pei, *The Story of Language*, rev. ed. (Philadelphia: J.B. Lippincott, 1965), 90.

p. 72   main Chinese dialect groups: Yuen Ren Chao, *Cantonese Primer* (New York: Greenwood, 1947), 4.

p. 73   "It is a pity": J. Dyer Ball, *Things Chinese*, 5th ed. rev. by E. Chalmers Werner (Shanghai: Kelly & Walsh, 1925), 177–78.

"at least seventy-five percent": John de Francis, *Nationalism and Language Reform in China* (Princeton NJ: Princeton Univ. Press, 1950), 193.

"no intrinsic difference": Pei, *Story of Language*, 47.

p. 76   Han Pinyin system: *Christian Science Monitor*, 23 January 1989, p. 4.

p. 80   Boxer Rebellion indemnity payments: Foster Rhea Dulles, *China and America: The Story of Their Relations Since 1784* (Princeton NJ: Princeton Univ. Press, 1946), 182.

p. 81   "most intimately concerned": Smith, *American Surnames*, 39.

Chapter 8: A Choice of Name Styles

p. 82   In very ancient times: Legge, trans. *Li Chi: Book of Rites*, 1: 144.

All the infants mentioned: *Asianweek*, 2 February 1990, p. 24.

Names of parents and grandparents: *Asianweek*, 27 March 1992, p. 16.

p. 83   Seven distinct American name styles: Elsdon C. Smith, *Treasury of Name Lore* (New York: Harper & Row, 1967), 134–36.

p. 84   "Eleanor's full name": Louise Leung Larsen, *Sweet Bamboo: A Saga of a Chinese-American Family* (Los Angeles: Chinese Historical Society of Southern California, 1989), 124–25.

p. 86   "Until very recently": Arthur E. Bostwick, "Modern Chinese Personal Names," *Library Journal* 57 (1932): 868.

fictitious business names: *Asianweek*, 1 May 1992, p. 26; and *Asianweek*, 23 June 1995, p. 26.

p. 87   "Certainly the use of initials": T'ang Leang-li, ed., *China Facts and Fancies*, China Today, Series 7 (Shanghai: China United, 1936), 117.

"For more than anything else" and "obtain uniformity": *ibid.*

p. 88   hyphenated name ... attributed to Giles: Arthur W. Hummel, "Transcription of Chinese Names," *Library Journal* 57, 1 (1932): 1006–1007.

Wu went by the name *Ng Choy*: Herbert A. Giles, *A Chinese Biographical Dictionary* (Shanghai: Kelly & Walsh, 1898), 594–95.

"more logical and in accordance": T'ang, *China Facts and Fancies*, 119.

pp. 88-9   equivalent to the American "middle name": Kiang Kang-Hu, *On Chinese Studies* (1934; reprint ed., Westport CT: Hyperion, 1977), 138, 154; and Thomas W. Chinn, "Genealogical Sources of Chinese Immigrants to the United States," *Studies in Asian Genealogy*, ed. Spencer J. Palmer (Provo UT: Brigham Young Univ. Press, 1972), 224.

p. 89   "dithemic" name: Mary V. Seeman, "Name and Identity," *Canadian Journal of Psychiatry* 25 (1980): 130.

"The mystification over Chinese names": Lin Yutang, *My Country and My People* (New York: Halcyon House, 1938), 366.

p. 91   *Yi Ling Chen-Josephson*: *Los Angeles Times*, 9 May 1986, p. 1. Credit under photo of freed Soviet prisoner Anatoly Shcharansky.

p. 91   Billy Ho Lung: 10th U.S. Census, 1880, California, Sacramento County, E.D. 76, p. 20; and Wells Fargo & Co., *Express Directory of Chinese Business Houses of San Francisco, Sacramento, Stockton, Marysville, San Jose, Portland & Virginia City, Nev.* (1878), 50.

Chapter 9: Chinese Names in Early Official Records

p. 95   *Weaverville Joss Temple State Park*: Moon L. Lee, "Weaverville," *Cathay in Eldorado: The Chinese in California*, Book Club of California, 1972, Keepsake Series, no. 1 (San Francisco: Cranium Press, 1972).

Bok Kai Temple: Reuben Ibanez, ed., *Historical Bok Kai Temple in Old Marysville, California* (Marysville: Marysville Chinese Community, 1967), 2; and Clark Buschmann, ed., *Third City* (Yuba Sutter Arts Council, 1991), 9.

p. 96   passenger lists for San Francisco: Louis J. Rasmussen, *San Francisco Ship Passenger Lists*, Ship 'n' Rail Series (Colma CA: San Francisco Historic Record and Genealogy Bulletin, 1965), 2: vii, xiii–xvi; and Louis J. Rasmussen, *San Francisco Ship Passenger Lists*, Ship 'n' Rail Series, November 7, 1851, to June 17, 1852 (Chicago: Adams, 1967), 3: 81, 101, 247.

p. 97   S.S. *Victoria*: *Inbound Passenger Manifests (Chinese Arrivals)*, USINS, U56-1, Reel 2, 1882–1916.

p. 98   "I found about 80 Chinese": Alan P. Bowman, comp., *Index to the 1850 Census of the State of California* (Baltimore: Genealogical, 1972), xix.

p. 99   Random samplings of censuses: *8th U.S. Census*, 1860, California, San Francisco County, 4th District, p. 269; *8th U.S. Census*, 1860, California, Plumas County, p. 22; *9th U.S. Census*, 1870, Idaho, Boise County, Beaver Creek, p. 2; Buena Vista, pp. 14, 22; *8th U.S. Census*, 1860, Oregon, Jackson County, pp. 16–17; *8th U.S. Census*, 1860, California, Yuba County, p. 9, 74; Ronald Vern Jackson, ed., *Washington* 1870 *Territorial Census Index* (Salt Lake City, Accelerated Indexing System, 1979), 6; and *9th U.S. Census*, 1870, Oregon, Multnomah County, Portland, pp. 64, 205.

China Mary: Judy Young, *Chinese Women in America: A Pictorial History* (Seattle: Univ. of Washington Press, 1986), 28.

Wa Chung: *9th U.S. Census*, 1870, Washington Territorial Census, King County, p. 47.

Quan Wo and *Poy Kee*: *10th U.S. Census*, 1880, San Francisco County, Ward 1, E.D. 22, pp. 15–16; and Wells Fargo & Co., *Express Directory* (1878), 23.

Ah Jack: *Chinese Exclusion Acts Case Files, 1895–1943*, Record Group 85, Box 1, PTO #97, re: pre-investigation status of *Wing Sing*, merchant, Port Townsend, Washington. National Archives–Pacific Northwest Region in Seattle.

p. 101   name of a store: Augustus Loomis, "Chinese in California: Their Sign-board Literature," *Overland Monthly* 1 (August 1868): 152–156.

Man Jan Company and Peking Bazaar: *Chinese Partnership Case Files, 1894–1944*, Record Group 85, #13502/528 and #13502/625B. National Archives — Pacific Sierra Region in San Bruno, California.

a matter of convenience: Huie Kin, *Reminiscences* (Peiping: San Yu, 1932), 6.

p. 104   A sampling of the 1900 federal census: *12th U.S. Census*, 1900, California, San Francisco County, E.D. 277, p. 4; E.D. 272, p. 2; E.D. 274, p. 2; and E.D. 271, p. 6.

Jee Gam: Wesley Woo, "Chinese Protestants in the San Francisco Bay Area," in *Entry Denied: Exclusion and the Chinese Community in America, 1882–1943* ed. Sucheng Chan (Philadelphia: Temple Univ. Press, 1991), 222–23.

the word "mon": *12th U.S. Census*, 1900, California, San Francisco County, E.D. 272, p. 1; and E.D. 279, p. 4.

Chapter 10: Stabilizing Surnames

p. 109   proposed registration for all aliens: U.S. Department of Labor, *Tenth Annual Report of the Secretary of Labor* (Washington DC: GPO, 1922), 111. The first alien voluntary registration law of 1929 is mentioned in U.S. Department of Labor, *Annual Report of the Commissioner-General of Immigration* 1931/32 (Washington DC: GPO, 1932), p. 36. The Nationality Act of 1940 re: compulsory alien registration is cited in *USINS Annual Report* 1941/42, p. 4. Alien registration was repealed by Public Law 97–116, section 11, 8 U.S.C., 1305, United States Code, 97th Cong., 1st Sess., vol. 1.

reregister every Chinese: "Report of Commission-General of Immigration" in *Report of Department of Commerce and Labor*, 59th Congress, 2nd Sess., 1906–1907, House Docs., vol. 22 (Washington DC: GPO, 1907), 563–65; and Mary Robert Coolidge, *Chinese Immigration* (1909; reprint ed., Arno Press and *The New York Times*, 1969), 311–12.

p. 111   certificates of residence: "Segregated Chinese Files," Record Group 85, National Archives of the United States, Washington DC (random sampling obtained April 1976.)

sampling of return certificates: Certificates of Departure 1895–1900, 1903–1910; Certificates for Chinese Merchants 1903–1907, Wing Luke Museum, Seattle, Washington.

Chinese Habeas Corpus Cases: *Index to Chinese Habeas Corpus Cases in Admiralty*, 1882– , Book 2, June 1887–1888; Book 3, August 1888 to April 1894, cases #8748, #8922, #8979, and #8985. National Archives–Pacific Sierra Region in San Bruno, San Francisco.

Chapter 11: It's Only a "Paper" Name

p. 114   price of a certificate: H. Mark Lai and Philip P. Choy, *Outlines: History of the Chinese in America* (San Francisco: privately printed, 1971), 96.

Chinese appreciated the opportunity: "Report of Commissioner General of Immigration, 1913" in *Reports of the Department of Labor* (Washington DC: GPO, 1914), 318.

"to trap or trick": Sung, *Story of the Chinese in America* , 101.

p. 115   Burlingame, California: Erwin G. Gudde, *1,000 California Place Names* (Berkeley: Univ. of California Press, 1947), 10.

Chapter 12: Attempts to Standardize Chinese Name Spelling

p. 117   In American law: Elsdon C. Smith, *The Story of Our Names* (New York: Harper, 1950), 200.

names were respelled: *Chinese Habeas Corpus Indexes*, vols. 1–5, 1882–1904, Record Group 21 (Admiralty Court) #2915 and #2840. National Archives–Pacific Sierra Region in San Bruno, California.

p. 118   John Gardner: Wesley S. Woo, "Presbyterian Mission: Christianizing and Civilizing the Chinese in Nineteenth Century California," *American Presbyterians* 68 (Fall 1990): 175.

p. 120   "It is practically impossible": *Treaty, Laws, and Rules Governing the Admission of Chinese* (Washington DC: GPO, 1917).

p. 121   **Telegraphic Code:** *Chinese Telegraphic Code with Mandarin, Cantonese and Toyshan Transliterations* (Cantonese Dialect Alphabetized) (n.p., n.d.); and Chu Chia-hua, *China's Postal and Other Communications Services* (London: K. Paul, Trench, Trubner, 1937), 6, 148–154.

p. 122   similar to the Welsh *Ll* sound: A. Don, "The Llin-nen Variation of Cantonese," *China Review* 11 (June, July 1882–1883): 23, 242–43.

Chapter 13: Americanization of Names

p. 123   "to alter an unfamiliar name": Smith, *New Dictionary*, p. xxii.

p. 125   surname Jew: Robert M. Rennick, "What's in a "Jewish" Name: Don't Jump to Conclusions," *Bulletin of the Illinois Names Society* 2 (Fall 1984): 14.

p. 126   Lieaou Ah-See: Thomas W. Chinn, H. Mark Lai, Philip P. Choy, eds., *A History of the Chinese in California: A Syllabus* (San Francisco: Chinese Historical Society of America, 1969), 7–8.

Charles Jamison: Alexander McLeod, *Pigtails and Gold Dust* (Caldwell ID: Claxton, 1947), 265.

Yo Hing: Patricia Lin, "Perspectives on the Chinese in Nineteenth-Century Orange County," *Journal of Orange County Studies* (Fall 1989/Spring 1990): 30.

records of the Chinese Women's Home: *Register of Inmates of Chinese Women's Home, 1874–1909* (San Francisco: Chinese First Presbyterian Church).

Chinese in Idaho: Fern Cobb Trull, "The History of the Chinese in Idaho from 1864 to 1910" (M.A. thesis, University of Oregon, 1946), 67–68.

"American surnames": Rev. Edwar Lee, conversation with author, November 1976.

p. 127   Jee Man Sing and Yee Kai Man: Warner M. Van Worden, *Who's Who of the Chinese in New York* (New York: n.p., 1918), 33.

Dean Lung: Chiang Yee, *The Silent Traveller in San Francisco* (New York: W.W. Norton, 1964), 225–29.

Kay Jum Ng: Eileen Hubbell MacDonald, "A Study of Chinese Migrants in Certain Idaho Settlements and of Selected families in Transition" (M.S. thesis, University of Idaho, 1966), 67.

Tom Wang Yuet: Mike Culbertson, "The Chinese Involvement in the Development of the Flower Industry in Santa Clara County," in *Chinese Argonauts*, ed. Gloria Sun Hom (Los Altos Hills CA: Foothill Community College, 1971), 56.

p. 128   Dr. Mary Stone: Margaret E. Burton, *Notable Women of Modern China* (New York: Fleming H. Revell, 1912), 161–62.

p. 130   There is no "r" sound: Robert Ferguson, *Surnames as a Science* (New York: Heraldic, 1967), 109–110.

Chapter 14: Transferring Name Traditions

p. 132   Dragon Tin Loong Siu: *East/West*, 12 March 1987, p. 11.
p. 133   "flight from old social customs": George R. Stewart, *American Given Names* (New York: Oxford Univ. Press, 1979), 42.
"stronger cultural identities": Leonard R.N. Ashley, *What's in a Name? ...Everything You Wanted to Know* (Baltimore: Genealogical, 1989), 10, 13.
Robert Tai: Smith, *Treasury of Name Lore*, 173; and *28th Annual Narcissus Festival Souvenir Program* (Honolulu: Chinese Chamber of Commerce of Hawaii, 1977): 42.
p. 134   Jefferson Shannon Kitt: S. Michael Opper and Lillie L. Lew, "A History of the Chinese in Fresno, California," in *The Life, Influence and the Role of the Chinese in the United States, 1776–1960* (Proceedings/Papers of the National Conference held at the University of San Francisco, July 10–12, 1975): 50–51.
Jee Gam: "20th Annual Report, 1894–1895" for Central San Francisco, California Chinese Mission, in *Chinese in America 1853–1933*, vol. 3: 6–7.
p. 135   "somewhat bizarre combinations" and "more pretentious names": Mencken, *American Language*, 513.
pattern of gradual adoption: Smith, *Treasury of Name Lore*, 15.
p. 136   Ahhanga and Ahhung: Sister M. Alfreda Elsensohn, *Idaho Chinese Lore* (Cottonwood ID: Idaho Corporation of Benedictine Sisters, 1979), 31.
p. 137   change-of-name notice: *Asianweek*, 14 October 1988, 30.
Juniors: Smith, *American Surnames*, 279–280.
p. 138   Hom family: *Los Angeles Times*, 2 November 1984, Pt. 2: 1, 6.

Chapter 15: New Patronyms and Other New Names

p. 140   patronym *Ah-Tye*: Howard Ah-Tye, "My Understanding of How the Tongs Began," *East/West*, 5 December 1979, p. 7.
p. 141   Ah-Fong family: Christopher Muench, "One Hundred Years of Medicine: The Ah-Fong Physicians of Idaho," *Chinese Medicine on the Golden Mountain: An Interpretive Guide*, ed. Henry G. Schwarz (1984), 52–53.
Ah Luis ... original spelling: W. Young Louis, the eldest son, conversation with author, 21 June 1980; and A.R. Dunbar's *Chinese Directory of Principal Chinese Business Houses of the United States, British Columbia, Canada and Honolulu, T.H.* (Portland OR: A.R. Dunbar, 1892), 130.
Tom Quin: "Ah Quin: Founder of Family and Fortune," *San Diego Union*, 4 November 1962.
early Chinese families in Hawaii: Wai-Jane Char, "Three Chinese Stores in Early Honolulu," *Hawaiian Journal of History* 8 (1974): 35–36; and Tin-Yuke Char, comp. and ed., *The Sandalwood Mountains* (Honolulu: Univ. Press of Hawaii, 1975), 333–34.
p. 142   Jew Dip: Paul Justi, "SF's Oldest Public School Celebrates 130th Anniversary," *East/West*, 13 April 1983, p. 3.
Richard Wing: Joseph E. Doctor, "Hanford's China Alley," in *Cathay in Eldorado: The Chinese in California*, Book Club of California, 1972 Keepsake Series, no. 9 (San Francisco: Cranium Press, 1972).
Han surnames ... adopted by Koreans: John K. Fairbank, Edwin O.

Resichauer, Albert M. Craig, *East Asia: Transition and Transformation* (Boston: Houghton Mifflin, 1973), 290–91.

p. 146 James Wong Howe: "The Best in the Business," *Jade* 1 (Spring 1975): 7–9, 42–43; and from information in James Wong Howe photo exhibit, sponsored by Friends of the Chinese American History Museum, Los Angeles, 1992.

Victor Sen Yung: Conversation with author, November 1978.

p. 148 Moon Lim Lee: H.K. Wong, *Gum Sahn Yun: Gold Mountain Men* (n.p., 1987), 242.

Chapter 16: Surname Clumping and Family Associations

p. 149 *Wong ... ranked 457: Report of Distribution of Surnames in the Social Security Number File,* September 1, 1984 ([Baltimore:] Department of Health and Human Services, Social Security Administration, 1985).

p. 150 "blue eyes": Gerald E. Rudolph, "The Chinese in Colorado, 1869–1911" (M.A. thesis, University of Denver, 1964), 24, 29.

clustering has also been traced: K. Chu, *History of the Chinese People in America* (New York: China Times, 1975), 48. (In Chinese.)

p. 151 Ning Yung Association: Liu Pai-chi, *Mei-kuo Hua-ch'iao Shih* (Taipei: Li Ming ... Shih-yeh, 1981), 198. (In Chinese.)

p. 154 name of the ancient territory: *Chung Pao [Chinese Daily News]*, 25 February 1988. (In Chinese.)

The *jun* ... was a forerunner: Dirk Bodde, *China's First Unifier: A Study of the Ch'in Dynasty as Seen in the Life of Li Ssu* (Hong Kong: Hong Kong Univ. Press, 1967), 134.

One hundred *jun ming*: Herbert A. Giles, *Chinese-English Dictionary* (1892), 1363.

Lung Kong: Asianweek, 24 September 1981, p. 10.

p. 155 Way Ben Association: Garding Lui, *Inside Los Angeles Chinatown* (n.p., 1948), 141.

"some blood or other ... relationship": Ching Chao Wu, "Chinatown, A Study of Symbiosis and Assimilation" (Ph.D. diss., University of Chicago, 1928), 239.

Soo Yuen Association: *Soo Yuen Journal*, 9th Issue (San Francisco: Fong Brothers Printing, 1976), 2–3.

Gee How Oak Tin Association: Tien-sou Chan, "History of Our Clan," *Gee How Oak Tin Journal* (San Francisco: Gee How Oak Tin Association of America, 1964), 8–10.

p. 157 "he is as good as my brother": Lo Kuan-chung, *Three Kingdoms: China's Epic Drama*, ed. and trans. Moss Roberts (New York: Random House/ Pantheon, 1976), 227.

Changing Role: *Asianweek*, 25 November 1982, pp. 12–13; "S.F. 'convention center' for family associations," *Asianweek*, 15 July 1982, pp. 1, 10; "Wong Family meets in S.F.," *Asianweek*, 19 August 1982, p. 8; "All men are brothers: The Lung Kong Tien Yee Association holds its 11th Quadrennial Convention," *Asianweek*, 26 August 1982, pp. 12–13; and "Dennis Wong Looks at Family Assoc. Convention, Changing Role," *East/West*, 11 August 1982, p. 7.

a few new family associations: Aileen O.L. Lee, "The Surname Tongs in Hawaii" (B.A. thesis, University of Hawaii, 1966), 19–55.

Cheng Association: "Cheng Family Assoc. Holds First Gathering," *East/West*, 31 March 1982, p. 6.

Gee How Oak Tin Association: Dolores Ziegler, "Legal Battles Sear San Francisco's Chinese Family Associations," *Asianweek*, 21 August 1992, pp. 1, 9.

"too early to consign": Stanford M. Lyman, *Chinese Americans* (New York: Random House, 1974), 31–32.

p. 158   surnames can become extinct: L.L. Cavalli-Sforza, "Importance of the Study of Migration and the Use of Surnames" (Paper delivered at the Conference on Chinese Population Movements, sponsored by the Center for International Human Population Studies, California State University, Long Beach CA, 2 March 1985).

Chapter 17: Parsing the Character

p. 163   describing the surname character aloud: Giles, *Chinese-English Dictionary*, 1356.

p. 167   "most intimate possession": Williams, *Know Your Ancestors*, 24.

Chapter 18: Preserving the Surname Character

p. 168   "work only one way": Yuen Ren Chao, *Language and Symbolic Systems* (New York: Cambridge Univ. Press, 1968), 47.

p. 170   "One's family tree should begin": Hsiang-lin Lo, "The History and Arrangement of Chinese Genealogies," in *Studies in Asian Genealogy*, ed. Spencer J. Palmer (Provo UT: Brigham Young Univ. Press, 1972), 14.

p. 173   Many case files contain documents: Waverly B. Lowell, comp., "Historical Resources for Chinese Americans at the National Archives, Regional Archives System," *Gum Saan Journal* 18 (1995): 3–26.

SELECTED BIBLIOGRAPHY

To guide the reader to sources relevant to his or her particular area of interest, this bibliography is organized into the following categories:

I. Books and Articles About Chinese Names

Bauer, Wolfgang. "Der Chinesische Personenname" [Chinese Personal Names]. *Asiatische Forschungen* 4 (1959): 1–407.

Chang, Z.P. *Chinese Surnames Romanized.* Shanghai: Chung Hwa, 1936.

Chen Shao-hsing and Morton Fried. *The Distribution of Family Names in Taiwan.* 2 vols. Taipei: National Taiwan University, 1968.

Chen Tse-ming. *Pai Chia Hsing* [The Family Names]. Taiwan: Shih-chi Shu-chu, 1983.

Chi Pin-hsiung. *Pai Chia Hsing.* Taipei: Hua-I Shu-chu, 1985.

Chinese Personal Names. Washington DC: U.S. Central Intelligence Agency, 1961.

Chu, Pao-liang. *Twentieth-Century Chinese Writers and Their Pen Names.* Boston: G.K. Hall, 1977.

Chung Pao [Chinese Daily News]. 4 May 1987.

Chung Pao [Chinese Daily News]. 25 February 1988.

Du Ruofu. "Surnames in China." *Journal of Chinese Linguistics* 14 (1986): 315–327.

Gardner, Jno Endicott, comp. *List of Chinese Family Names.* U.S. Department of Commerce and Labor, Bureau of Immigration and Naturalization. Washington DC: GPO, 1909.

Giles, Herbert A. "The Family Names." *Journal of the China Branch of the Royal Asiatic Society,* n.s., 21 (1886–87): 255–288.

Hsu, Francis L.K. "Observations on Cross-cousin Marriage in China." *American Anthropologist,* n.s., 47 (1945): 83–103.

Hsu Chun-yuan et al., eds. *Chung-kuo Jen te Hsing-shih* [Surnames of the Chinese People]. Hong Kong: South China, 1988.

Jamieson, G. "Translations from the Lu-Li, or General Code of Laws." *China Review* 10 (September and October 1881): 89–93.

Jones, Russell. *Chinese Names: Notes on the Use of Surnames and Personal Names by the Chinese in Malaysia and Singapore.* N.d. Reprint, Selangor, Malaysia: Pelanduk, 1984.

Kiang Kang-hu. *On Chinese Studies.* 1934. Reprint, Westport CT: Hyperion, 1977.

Legge, James, trans. *The Confucian Analects.* Vol. 1 of *The Chinese Classics.* Oxford: Clarendon, 1893.

_____, trans. *Li Chi: Book of Rites.* Vol. 2, edited by Ch'u Chai and Winberg Chai. 1885. Reprint, New Hyde Park NY: University, 1967.

Lin Shan. *What's in a Chinese Name.* 3d ed. N.d. Reprint, Singapore: Federal, 1986.

Lu Zhongti and Celia Millward. "Chinese Given Names Since the Cultural Revolution." *Names* 37 (1989): 265–280.

Mu Liu-sen. *Pai Chia Hsing Tsu-tien* [Dictionary of Chinese Family Names]. Hong Kong: I-wen Yin Shu-kuan, 1977[?].

Parker, Edward Harper. "Comparative Chinese Family Law." *China Review* 8 (1879): 70–103.

Sung, Margaret M.Y. "Chinese Personal Naming." *Journal of the Chinese Teachers Association* 16 (1981): 67–90.

Tan, Thomas Tsu-wee. *Your Chinese Roots: The Overseas Chinese Story.* Union City CA: Heian International, 1987.

Teng Hsien-ching. *Chung-kuo Hsing-shih Chi Mu Tzu* [Surnames of China]. Taipei: Kufen Yu Hsien, 1971.

Waltner, Ann. *Getting an Heir: Adoption and the Construction of Kinship in Late Imperial China.* Honolulu: Univ. of Hawaii Press, 1990.

Yuan Yida and Du Ruofu. *Zhonghua Xing Shi Da Zidian*. Beijing: Jiaoyu Ke Xue, 1996.
Zhu Bin and Celia Millward. "Personal Names in Chinese." *Names* 35 (1987): 8–21.

II. Books and Articles about Euro-American Names

Adamic, Louis. *What's Your Name?* New York: Harper, 1942.
Anderson, Christopher P. *The Name Game*. New York: Simon & Schuster, 1977.
Arthur, William. *An Etymological Dictionary of Family and Christian Names*. New York: Sheldon, Blakeman, 1857.
Ashley, Leonard R.N. *What's in a Name? ...Everything You Wanted to Know*. Baltimore: Genealogical, 1989.
Barker, Howard F. "How the American Changes His Name." *The American Mercury* 36 (September 1935): 101–103.
_____. "Surnames in the United States." *The American Mercury* 26 (June 1932): 223–230.
Brown, Samuel L, comp. *Surnames Are the Fossils of Speech*. N.p., 1965.
Cottle, Basil. *The Penguin Dictionary of Surnames*. Baltimore: Penguin, 1967.
Dunkling, Leslie, and William Gosling. *The New American Dictionary of Baby Names*. New York: Penguin/Signet, 1985.
Dunkling, Leslie Alan. *First Names First*. New York: Universe, 1977.
_____. *Our Secret Names: What Names Reveal and Conceal*. Englewood Cliffs NJ: Prentice-Hall, 1981.
Ewen, C. L'Estrange. *A History of Surnames of the British Isles*. London: Kegan Paul, Trench, Trubner, 1931.
Ferguson, Robert. *Surnames as a Science*. New York: Heraldic, 1967.
Hazen, Barbara Shook. *Last, First, Middle and Nick: All About Names*. Englewood Cliffs NJ: Prentice-Hall, 1979.
Hook, J.N. *Family Names*. New York: Macmillan/Collier, 1982.
Jones, George F. *German-American Names*. Baltimore: Genealogical, 1990.
Kaplan, Justin, and Anne Bernays. *The Language of Names*. New York: Simon & Schuster, 1997.
Lawson, Edwin D., comp. *Personal Names and Naming: An Annotated Bibliography*. New York: Greenwood, 1987.
_____, comp. *More Names and Naming: An Annotated Bibliography*. New York: Greenwood, 1995.
Lebell, Sharon. *Naming Ourselves, Naming Our Children: Resolving the Last Name Dilemma*. Freedom CA: Crossing, 1988.
Lee, Mary Price, and Lee, Richard S. *Last Names First...And Some First Names Too*. Philadelphia: Westminster, 1985.
Mencken, H.L. *The American Language*. Supplement 2. New York: Alfred A. Knopf, 1962.
_____. *The American Language: An Inquiry into the Development of English in the United States*. 4th ed. New York: Alfred A. Knopf, 1937.
Report of Distribution of Surnames in the Social Security Number File, September 1, 1984. [Baltimore] 1985.
Rossi, Alice S. "Naming Children in Middle-Class Families." *American Sociological Review* 30 (1965): 499–513.
Smith, Elsdon C. *American Surnames*. Philadelphia: Chilton, 1969.
_____. *New Dictionary of American Family Names*. New York: Harper & Row, 1973.

_____. *The Story of Our Names*. New York: Harper, 1950.

_____. *Treasury of Name Lore*. New York: Harper & Row, 1967.

Stewart, George R. *American Given Names: Their Origin and History in the Context of the English Language*. New York: Oxford Univ. Press, 1979.

III. Books and Articles About Other Surnames

Bennett, Linda A. *Personal Choice in Ethnic Identity Maintenance: Serbs, Croats, and Slovenes in Washington, D.C.* Palo Alto CA: Ragusan, 1978.

Cavalli-Sforza, L.L. "Importance of the Study of Migration and the Use of Surnames." Paper delivered at the Conference on Chinese Population Movements, California State University, Long Beach, 2 March 1985.

Jernudd, Bjorn H. "Personal names and human rights." In *Linguistic Human Rights: Overcoming Linguistic Discrimination*, edited by Tove Skutnabb-Kangas, 121–32. New York: Mounton de Gruyter, 1994.

Kamon: Japanese Family Crest: A Basic Guidebook for Japanese Americans. Gardena CA: N.p., 1989.

Korean Personal Names. Washington DC: Central Intelligence Agency, 1962.

Lasker, Gabriel Ward. *Surnames and Genetic Structure*. Cambridge: Cambridge Univ. Press, 1985.

Loseff, Eunice Devera. "A Comparative Study of Names and Naming Patterns in Selected Cultures." Master's thesis, University of Southern California, 1952.

Nguyen, Phuoc Huu, and Tuyetnga T. Nguyen. "Differences in Value Orientations Between American and Vietnamese." Mimeographed, 1970s[?].

Reinecke, John E. "Personal Names in Hawaii." *American Speech* 15 (1940): 345–352.

Seeman, Mary V. "Name and Identity." *Canadian Journal of Psychiatry* 25 (1980): 129–137.

Shin, Eui-Hang, and Eui-Young Yu. "Use of Surnames in Ethnic Research: The Case of Kims in the Korean American Population." *P/AAMHRC Research Review* 3 (July/October 1984): 11–13.

Smith, Elsdon C. *Personal Names: A Bibliography*. New York: New York Public Library, 1952.

IV. Books About Chinese History

Bodde, Derk. *China's First Unifier: A Study of the Ch'in Dynasty as Seen in the Life of Li Ssu*. 1938. Reprint, Hong Kong: Hong Kong Univ. Press, 1967.

Chang, K.C. "Sandai Archaeology and the Formation of States in Ancient China: Processual Aspects of the Origins of Chinese Civilization." In *The Origins of Chinese Civilization*, edited by David Keightley, 495–521. Berkeley: Univ. of California Press, 1983.

Chow Tse-Tsung. *The May Fourth Movement: Intellectual Revolution in Modern China*. Cambridge MA: Harvard Univ. Press, 1960.

Fairbank, John King. *China: A New History*. Cambridge MA: Harvard Univ. Press, Belknap, 1992.

_____, Edwin O. Resichauer, and Albert M. Craig. *East Asia: Transition and Transformation*. Boston: Houghton Mifflin, 1973.

Fitzgerald, C.P. *China: A Short Cultural History*. New York: Frederick A. Praeger, 1961.

_____. *The Horizon History of China,* Edited by Norman Kotker. New York: American Heritage, 1969.

Gernet, Jacques. *Ancient China: From the Beginning of Empire.* Berkeley: Univ. of California Press, 1968.

Hsu, Immanuel C.Y. *The Rise of Modern China.* New York: Oxford Univ. Press, 1970.

Hucker, Charles O. *China's Imperial Past: An Introduction to Chinese History and Culture.* Stanford CA: Stanford Univ. Press, 1975.

Keightley, David, ed. *The Origins of Chinese Civilization.* Berkeley: Univ. of California Press, 1983.

Latourette, Kenneth Scott. *The Chinese: Their History and Culture.* 4th ed. New York: Macmillan, 1964.

_____. *A History of Christian Missions in China.* New York: Macmillan, 1929.

Legge, James, trans. *The Shoo King.* Vol. 3 of *The Chinese Classics.* 1893[?]. Reprint, Hong Kong: Hong Kong Univ. Press, 1960.

_____, trans. *The Ch'un Ts'ew with the Tso Chuen.* Vol. 5 of *The Chinese Classics.* 2nd ed. 1895[?] Reprint, Hong Kong: Hong Kong Univ. Press, 1970.

Li, Chi. *The Formation of the Chinese People: An Anthropological Study.* Cambridge MA: Harvard Univ. Press, 1928.

Lo Kuan-chung. *Three Kingdoms: China's Epic Drama.* Edited and translated by Moss Roberts. New York: Random House/Pantheon, 1976.

T'ang Leang-li. *The New Social Order in China.* "China Today" Series, no. 6. Shanghai: China United, 1936.

_____, ed. *China Facts and Fancies.* "China Today" Series, no. 7. Shanghai: China United, 1936.

Twitchett, Denis, ed. *Sui and T'ang China, 589–906.* Vol. 3 of *The Cambridge History of China.* Edited by Denis Twitchett and John K. Fairbank. Cambridge: Cambridge Univ. Press, 1979.

_____, and Michael Loewe, eds. *The Ch'in and Han Empires, 221 B.C.–A.D. 220.* Vol. 1 of *The Cambridge History of China.* Cambridge: Cambridge Univ. Press, 1986.

Wright, Arthur E. *The Sui Dynasty: The Unification of China, A.D. 581–617.* New York: Alfred A. Knopf, 1978.

V. Books and Articles About Chinese Society and Customs

Ball, J. Dyer. *Things Chinese.* 5th ed. Shanghai: N.p., 1925.

Ch'eng Ch'ing-I. *Chung-kuo Tsu-Pu Pien Tsuan Chien Shuo* [A Concise Compilation for Chinese Genealogy]. Taipei: Lien Ho Pao..., 1987.

Ching, Frank. *Ancestors: 900 Years in the Life of a Chinese Family.* New York: Ballantine/Fawcett Columbine, 1988.

Chu Chia-Hua. *China's Postal and Other Communications Services.* London: Kegan Paul, Trench, Trubner, 1937.

Cohen, Myron L. "Being Chinese: The Peripheralization of Traditional Identity." *Daedalus* 120 (Spring 1991): 113–134.

Couling, Samuel. *Encyclopedia Sinica.* 1917. Reprint, Taipei: Literature House, 1964.

Daedalus (Journal of the American Academy of Arts and Sciences) 120 (Spring 1991) and *Daedalus* 122 (Spring 1993).

de Bary, Wm. Theodore, Wing-Tsit Chan, and Burton Watson, comps. *Sources of Chinese Tradition.* Vol. 1. New York: Columbia Univ. Press, 1960.

Eberhard, Wolfram. "Chinese Genealogies as a Source for the Study of Chinese Society." In *Studies in Asian Genealogy*, edited by Spencer J. Palmer, 27–37. Provo UT: Brigham Young Univ. Press, 1972.

Feng, Han-yi. *The Chinese Kinship System*. Cambridge MA: Harvard Univ. Press, 1967.

Freedman, Maurice. *Lineage Organization in Southeastern China*. Monographs on Social Anthropology, no. 18. London: Univ. of London/Athlone, 1958.

_____. *The Study of Chinese Society: Essays by Maurice Freedman*. Edited by G.W. Skinner. Stanford CA: Stanford Univ. Press, 1979.

Giles, Herbert A. *A Chinese Biographical Dictionary*. 1898. Reprint, Taipei: Literature House, 1962.

_____. *A Glossary of Reference on Subjects Connected with the Far East*. 3d ed. Shanghai: Kelly & Walsh, 1900.

Lin Yutang. *My Country and My People*. New York: Halcyon House, 1938.

Liu, Hui-chen Wang. *The Traditional Chinese Clan Rules*. Locust Valley NY: J.T. Augustin, 1959.

Liu T'sun-yan. "The Chinese Psyche and the Chinese Mind." Paper delivered at the China and Confucianism Conference in Los Angeles, 1990.

Lo, Hsiang-lin. "The History and Arrangement of Chinese Genealogies." In *Studies in Asian Genealogy*, edited by Spencer J. Palmer, 13–26. Provo UT: Brigham Young Univ. Press, 1972.

_____. "The Preservation of Genealogical Records in China." In *Studies in Asian Genealogy*, edited by Spencer J. Palmer, 38–55. Provo UT: Brigham Young Univ. Press, 1972.

Mayers, William Frederick. *The Chinese Readers Manual*. 1874[?]. Reprint, Shanghai: Presbyterian Mission Press, 1924.

Osgood, Cornelius. *Village Life in Old China: A Community Study of Kao Yao, Yunnan*. New York: Ronal, 1963.

Waley, Arthur, trans. *The Analects of Confucius*. New York: Random House/Vintage, 1938.

Williams, Samuel Wells. *The Middle Kingdom*. 2 vols. New York: John Wiley, 1879.

Wu, Ching-Chao. "The Chinese Family: Organization, Names, and Kinship Terms." *American Anthropologist*, n.s. 29 (1927): 316–325.

VI. Books and Articles About Chinese Americans

Amerasia Journal 14, no. 2 (1988).

Barth, Gunther. *Bitter Strength: A History of the Chinese in the United States, 1850–1870*. Cambridge MA: Harvard Univ. Press, 1964.

Bear, Dorothy, and David Houghton. "The Chinese of the Mendocino Coast." *Mendocino Historical Review* 15 (Winter/Spring 1990–91): 1–34.

Beck, Louis J. *New York's Chinatown: An Historical Presentation of Its People and Places*. New York: Bohemia, 1898.

Cathay in Eldorado: The Chinese in California. Book Club of California 1972 Keepsake Series. San Francisco: Cranium Press, 1972.

Chan, Sucheng, ed. *Entry Denied: Exclusion and the Chinese Community in America, 1882–1943*. Philadelphia: Temple Univ. Press, 1991.

Char, Tin-Yuke, comp. and ed. *The Sandalwood Mountains: Readings and Stories of the Early Chinese in Hawaii*. Honolulu: Univ. Press of Hawaii, 1975.

Char, Wai-Jane. "Three Chinese Stores in Early Honolulu." *Hawaiian Journal of History* 8 (1974): 11–38.

Chen, Kwong Min. *The Chinese in America*. New York: Overseas Chinese Culture, 1950.

Chin, Doug, and Art Chin. *Uphill: The Settlement and Diffusion of the Chinese in Seattle, Washington*. Seattle: Shorey Original, 1973.

Chinese of Hawaii. Vol. 2. Honolulu: Overseas Penman Club, 1936.

Chinese of Hawaii: Who's Who 1956–1957. Honolulu: United Chinese Penman Club, 1957.

Chinese American Experience: Papers from the Second National Conference on Chinese American Studies (1980). Edited by Ginny Lim. San Francisco: Chinese Historical Society of America, 1981.

Chinn, Thomas W. *Bridging the Pacific: San Francisco Chinatown and Its People*. San Francisco: Chinese Historical Society of America, 1989.

_____. "Genealogical Sources of Chinese Immigrants to the United States." In *Studies in Asian Genealogy*, edited by Spencer J. Palmer, 221–28. Provo UT: Brigham Young Univ. Press, 1972.

_____, H. Mark Lai, and Philip P. Choy, eds. *A History of the Chinese in California: A Syllabus*. San Francisco: Chinese Historical Society of America, 1969.

Chu, Y.K. *History of the Chinese People in America*. New York: China Times, 1975.

Condit, Ira. *The Chinaman as We See Him*. Chicago: Fleming H. Revell, 1900.

Coolidge, Mary Roberts. *Chinese Immigration*. 1909. Reprint, Arno Press and the *New York Times*, 1969.

Culbertson, Mike. "The Chinese Involvement in the Development of the Flower Industry in Santa Clara County." In *Chinese Argonauts*, edited by Gloria Sun Hom. Los Altos Hills CA: Foothill Community College, 1971.

Doctor, Joseph E. "Hanford's China Alley." In *Cathay in Eldorado: the Chinese in California*. Book Club of California 1972 Keepsake Series, no. 9. San Francisco: Cranium Press, 1972.

Elsensohn, Sister M. Alfreda. *Idaho Chinese Lore*. Cottonwood, Idaho: Idaho Corporation of Benedictine Sisters, 1979.

Fan, Ting-chiu. "Chinese Residents in Chicago." Master's thesis, University of Chicago, 1926.

Farrar, Nancy. *The Chinese in El Paso*. Southwestern Studies Monograph, no. 33. El Paso: Texas Western Press, 1972.

Hawaiian Journal of History 8 (1974).

Haynes, Norman S., and Charles N. Reynolds. "Chinese Family Life in America." *American Sociological Review* 2 (1937): 630–637.

Hoexter, Corinne K. *From Canton to California: The Epic of Chinese Immigration*. New York: Four Winds, 1976.

Hom, Gloria Sun, ed. *Chinese Argonauts*. Los Altos Hills CA: Foothill Community College, 1971.

Hoobler, Dorothy, and Thomas Hoobler. *The Chinese American Family Album*. New York: Oxford Univ. Press, 1994.

Hoy, William. *The Chinese Six Companies*. San Francisco: Chinese Consolidated Benevolent Association, 1942.

Huie Kin. *Reminiscences*. Peiping: San Yu, 1932.

Jones, David D. *The Surnames of the Chinese in America*. San Francisco: Chinese Name Spelling, 1904.

Journal of Arizona History 21 (Autumn 1980).

Kung, S.W. *Chinese in American Life: Some Aspects of Their History, Status, Problems, and Contributions*. Seattle: Univ. of Washington Press, 1962.

Lai, H.M[ark]. "Roots and Linkages: A Journey Through the Pearl River Delta." *East/West*. Part I: "Guangzhou," 26 March 1980; Part II: "Foshan and Nanhai," 9 April 1980; Part III: "Kaiping," 16 April 1980; Part IV: "Taishan," 25 June 1980; Part IV: "Xinhui," 10 September 1980; Part VI: "Doumen," 10 December 1980; Part VII: "Zhongshan," 7 January 1981; and Part VIII: "Zhuhai," 4 February 1981.

_____, and Philip P. Choy. *Outlines: History of the Chinese in America*. San Francisco: N.p., 1971.

Larsen, Louise Leung. *Sweet Bamboo: A Saga of a Chinese-American Family*. Los Angeles: Chinese Historical Society of Southern California, 1989.

Lee, Aileen O.L. "The Surname Tongs in Hawaii." B.A. thesis, University of Hawaii, 1966.

Lee, Calvin. *Chinatown U.S.A.* New York: Doubleday, 1965.

Lee, Douglas W. "The Early Chinese Community in Washington, D. C., 1880– 1930." In *The Annals of the Chinese Historical Society of the Pacific Northwest*, 86–120. 1983.

Lee, Moon L. "Weaverville." In *Cathay in Eldorado: The Chinese in California*. Book Club of California 1972 Keepsake Series, no. 1. San Francisco: Cranium Press, 1972.

Lee, Rose Hum. *The Chinese in the United States of America*. Hong Kong: Hong Kong Univ. Press, 1960.

_____. "The Decline of Chinatowns in the United States." *American Journal of Sociology* 54 (1949): 422–432.

Leong Gor Yun. *Chinatown Inside Out*. New York: Barrows Munsey, 1936.

Lew, Ling. *The Chinese in North America*. Los Angeles: East-West Culture, 1949.

The Life, Influence and the Role of the Chinese in the United States, 1776–1960. Proceedings/ Papers of the National Conference Held at the University of San Francisco, July 10–12, 1975.

Lin, Patricia. "Perspectives on the Chinese in Nineteenth-Century Orange County." *Journal of Orange County Studies* (Fall 1989/Spring 1990): 28–36.

Liu Pai-chi. *Mei-kuo Hua-ch'iao Shih* [History of the Chinese in America]. Taipei: Li Ming Wen-hua Shih-yeh, 1981.

Loewen, James W. *The Mississippi Chinese: Between Black and White*. Cambridge MA: Harvard Univ. Press, 1971.

Loomis, Augustus. "Chinese in California: Their Sign-board Literature." *Overland Monthly* 1 (August 1868).

Louie, Emma Woo. "Chinese American Name Styles and Their Significance." In *Origins & Destinations: 41 Essays on Chinese America*, 407–416. Los Angeles: Chinese Historical Society of Southern California, 1994.

_____. "History and Sources of Chinese American Family Names." *Gum Saan Journal* 10 (1987): 1–12.

_____. "History and Sources of Chinese American Family Names." *Publications of the North Central Name Society* 2 (1987): 83–98.

_____. "Name Styles and Structure of Chinese American Personal Names." *Names* 39 (September 1991): 225–237.

_____. "A New Perspective on Surnames Among Chinese Americans." *Amerasia Journal* 12 (1985–1986): 1–22.

_____. "Surnames as Clues to Family History." *Chinese America: History and Perspectives 1991*. San Francisco: Chinese Historical Society of America, 1991: 101–108.

Lowe, Pardee. *Father and Glorious Descendant*. Boston: Little, Brown, 1943.

Lowell, Waverly B., comp. "Historical Resources for Chinese Americans at the National Archives, Regional Archives System." *Gum Saan Journal* 18 (June 1995): 3–27.

Lui, Garding. *Inside Los Angeles Chinatown*. N.p., 1948.

SELECTED BIBLIOGRAPHY

Lydon, Sandy. *Chinese Gold: The Chinese in the Monterey Bay Region*. Capitola CA: Capitola, 1985.

Lyman, Stanford M. *Chinese Americans*. New York: Random House, 1974.

_____. "Marriage and the Family Among Chinese Immigrants to America, 1850–1960." *Phylon* 29 (Winter 1968): 321–330.

McCunn, Ruthanne Lum. *Chinese American Portraits: Personal Histories 1828–1988*. San Francisco: Chronicle, 1988.

MacDonald, Eileen Hubbell. "A Study of Chinese Migrants in Certain Idaho Settlements and of Selected Families in Transition." Master's thesis, University of Idaho, 1966.

McLeod, Alexander. *Pigtails and Gold Dust*. Caldwell ID: Claxton, 1947.

Mark, Diane Mei Lin, and Ginger Chih. *A Place Called Chinese America*. Dubuque: Kendall/Hunt, 1982.

Minnick, Sylvia Sun. *SAMFOW: The San Joaquin Chinese Legacy*. Fresno CA: Panorama West, 1988.

Muench, Christopher. "One Hundred Years of Medicine: The Ah-Fong Physicians of Idaho." In *Chinese Medicine on the Golden Mountain: An Interpretive Guide*, edited by Henry G. Schwarz, 51–80. 1984.

Ohnuki, Emiko. "The Detroit Chinese: A Study of Socio-cultural Changes in the Detroit Chinese Community from 1872 through 1963." Master's thesis, University of Wisconsin, 1964.

Opper, S. Michael, and Lillie L. Lew. "A History of the Chinese in Fresno, California." In *The Life, Influence and the Role of the Chinese in the United States, 1776–1960*, 47–55. Proceedings/Papers of the National Conference, University of San Francisco, July 10–12, 1975.

Origins and Destinations: 41 Essays on Chinese America. Los Angeles: Chinese Historical Society of Southern California, 1994.

Rudolph, Gerald E. "The Chinese in Colorado, 1869–1911." Master's thesis, University of Denver, 1964.

Saxton, Alexander. *The Indispensible Enemy*. Berkeley: Univ. of California Press, 1971.

Sung, Betty Lee. "Chinese American Intermarriage." *Journal of Comparative Family Studies* 21 (Autumn 1990): 337–352.

_____. *The Story of the Chinese in America*. New York: Macmillan/Collier, 1967.

Trull, Fern Cobb. "The History of the Chinese in Idaho from 1864–1910." Master's thesis, University of Oregon, 1946.

"20th Annual Report, 1894–1895." Central San Francisco California Chinese Mission. In Vol. 3, *Chinese in America, 1853–1933*.

Van Worden, Warner M. *Who's Who of the Chinese in New York*. New York: N.p., 1918.

Wang, L. Ling-chi. "Roots and Changing Identity of the Chinese in the United States." *Daedalus* 120 (Spring 1991): 181–206.

Wells, Mariann Kaye. "Chinese Temples in California." Master's thesis, University of California–Berkeley, 1962.

Wong, H.K. *Gum Sahn Yun: Gold Mountain Men*. N.p., 1987.

Woo, Wesley S. "Chinese Protestants in the San Francisco Bay Area." In *Entry Denied: Exclusion and the Chinese Community in America, 1882–1943*, edited by Sucheng Chan, 213–245. Philadelphia: Temple Univ. Press, 1991.

_____. "Presbyterian Mission: Christianizing and Civilizing the Chinese in Nineteenth Century California." *American Presbyterians* 68 (Fall 1990): 167–180.

Wu, Ching Chao. "Chinatown, A Study of Symbiosis and Assimilation." Ph.D. dissertation, University of Chicago, 1928.

Yung, Judy. *Chinese Women of America: A Pictorial History.* Seattle: Univ. of Washington Press, 1986

VII. Books and Articles About Language

Ball, J. Dyer. *Hong Shan or Macao Dialect.* Hong Kong: 'China Mail' Office, 1897.
_____. *The Shun-Tak Dialect.* Hong Kong: 'China Mail' Office, 1901.
Boyle, Elizabeth Lattimore. *Cantonese Basic Course.* Vol. 1. Washington DC: Department of State, 1970.
Campbell, W. *A Dictionary of the Amoy Vernacular.* Yokohama: Fukuin Printing, 1923.
Chan, Shau Wing. *Chinese Reader for Beginners.* Stanford CA: Stanford Univ. Press, 1942.
Chao, Yuen Ren. *Aspects of Chinese Sociolinguistics : Essays by Yuen Ren Chao.* Edited by Anwar S. Dil. Stanford CA: Stanford Univ. Press, 1976.
_____. *Cantonese Primer.* New York: Greenwood, 1947.
_____. *A Grammar of Spoken Chinese.* Berkeley: Univ. of California Press, 1968.
_____. *Language and Symbolic Systems.* Cambridge: Cambridge Univ. Press, 1968.
_____, and Lien Sheng Yang. *Concise Dictionary of Spoken Chinese.* Cambridge MA: Harvard Univ. Press, 1966.
Chinese Telegraphic Code with Mandarin, Cantonese and Toyshan Transliterations (Cantonese Dialect Alphabetized). N.p., n.d.
Coulmas, Florian. *The Writing Systems of the World.* New York: Basil Blackwell, 1989.
Davis, D.H. *Shanghai Vernacular Chinese-English Dictionary.* Shanghai: American Presbyterian Mission Press, 1900.
de Francis, John. *Nationalism and Language Reform in China.* Princeton: Princeton Univ. Press, 1950.
Dictionary of Spoken Chinese. New Haven: Yale Univ. Press, 1966.
Don, A. "The Llin-nen Variation of Cantonese" *China Review* 11 (1883): 236–247.
Dunn, Robert, comp. *Chinese-English and English-Chinese Dictionaries in the Library of Congress.* Washington DC: Library of Congress, 1977.
Fenn, Henry C., ed. *Chinese Characters Easily Confused.* New Haven: Yale Univ. Press, 1953.
Giles, Herbert A. *A Chinese-English Dictionary,* London: Bernard Quaritch, 1892.
_____. *A Chinese-English Dictionary.* 2d ed., rev. and enl. Shanghai: Kelly & Walsh, 1912.
Key to Wade-Giles Romanization of Chinese Characters. Washington DC: War Dept., U.S. Army Map Service, 1944.
Legeza, Ireneus Laszlo. *Guide to Transliterated Chinese in the Modern Peking Dialect.* Vol. 1. Leiden: E.J. Brill, 1968.
_____. *Guide to Transliterated Chinese in the Modern Peking Dialect.* Vol. 2. Leiden: E.J. Brill, 1969.
Li, Fang-Kuei. "Languages and Dialects of China." *Journal of Chinese Linguistics* 1 (1973): 1–12.
Maclay, R.S., and C.C. Baldwin. *An Alphabetic Dictionary of the Chinese Language in the Foochow Dialect.* Foochow: Methodist Episcopal Mission Press, 1870.
MacKenzie, M.C. *A Chinese-English Dictionary, Hakka Dialect.* 2d ed. Shanghai: Presbyterian Mission Press, 1926.

Morrison, R. *A Dictionary of the Chinese Language*. 2 vols. 1815. Reprint, Shanghae: London Mission Press, 1865.

Pei, Mario. *The Story of Language*. Rev. ed. Philadelphia: J.B. Lippincott, 1965.

Reform of the Chinese Written Language. Peking: Foreign Languages Press, 1958.

Reinecke, John E. *Language and Dialect in Hawaii: A Sociolinguistic History to 1935*. Edited by Stanley M. Tsuzaki. Honolulu: Univ. of Hawaii Press, 1969.

Wieger, L. *Chinese Characters*. Translated by L. Dvrout. 2d rev. ed. New York: Paragon/Dover, 1965.

Williams, S. Wells. *A Tonic Dictionary of the Chinese Language in the Canton Dialect*. Canton: Office of the Chinese Repository, 1856.

VIII. Books and Articles About Identity and Ethnicity

Allport, Gordon W. *Pattern and Growth in Personality*. New York: Holt, Rinehart and Winston, 1961.

Baumeister, Roy F. *Identity, Cultural Change and the Struggle for Self*. New York: Oxford Univ. Press, 1986.

Che, Kenneth J. "To Be or Not to Be: Insights into Defining the 'Chinese' in Chinese American." *Chinese American Forum* 7 (April 1992): 7–8.

Chun-Hoon, Lowell. "Jade Snow Wong and the Fate of Chinese-American Identity." *Amerasia Journal* 2 (1971): 52–63.

Dion, Kenneth L. "Names, Identity, and Self." *Names* 31 (1983): 245–57.

Harvard Encyclopedia of American Ethnic Groups. Edited by Stephan Thernstrom. Cambridge MA: Harvard Univ. Press, 1980.

Hotz, Robert Lee. "Is Concept of Race a Relic?" *Los Angeles Times* 15 April 1995: 1, 14.

Morgan, Ted. *On Becoming an American: A Celebration of What It Means and How It Feels*. Boston: Houghton Mifflin, 1978.

Petersen, William, Michael Novak, and Philip Gleason. *Concepts of Ethnicity*. Cambridge MA: Harvard Univ. Press/Belknap, 1982.

Shibutani, Tamotsu, and Kian M. Kwan. *Ethnic Stratification: A Comparative Approach*. Toronto: Macmillan, 1969.

Weiser, Marjorie P. K., ed. *Ethnic America*. The Reference Shelf Series. Vol. 50. New York: H.W. Wilson, 1978.

IX. Books and Articles about Immigration

Auerbach, Frank L. *The Immigration and Nationality Act: A Summary of the Principal Provisions*. New York: Common Council for American Unity, 1952.

Eckerson, Helen F. "Immigration and National Origins." *The Annals of the American Academy of Political and Social Science*. Vol. 367 (September 1966).

Gardner, Robert W., Bryant Robey, and Peter C. Smith. "Asian Americans: Growth, Change, and Diversity." *Population Bulletin* 40 (October 1985).

Molloy, Timothy J. "A Century of Chinese Immigration: A Brief Review." *USINA Monthly Review* 5/6 (June–July 1947–1949): 69–75.

Tucker, Robert W., Charles B. Keely, and Linda Wrigley, eds. *Immigration and U.S. Foreign Policy*. Boulder CO: Westview, 1990.

X. Other Books and Articles of Interest

Campbell, Joseph, with Bill Moyers. *The Power of Myth.* New York: Doubleday, 1988.

Chung, Kun Ai. *My 79 Years in Hawaii.* Hong Kong: Cosmorama Pictorial, 1960.

Counterpoint: Perspectives on Asian Americans. Edited by Emma Gee. Los Angeles: Asian American Studies Center, 1976.

Kitano, Harry H.L., et. al. "Asian-American Interracial Marriage." *Journal of Marriage and the Family* 46 (1984): 179–190.

Lee, Joann Faung Jean. *Asian American Experiences in the United States.* Jefferson NC: McFarland, 1991.

Palmer, Albert W. *Orientals in American Life.* New York: Friendship, 1943.

Pan, Lynn. *Sons of the Yellow Emperor: The Story of the Overseas Chinese.* London: Octopus/Mandarin, 1991.

Register of Inmates of Chinese Women's Home, 1874–1909. San Francisco: Chinese First Presbyterian Church.

Smith, William Carlson. *Americans in Process: A Study of Our Citizens of Oriental Ancestry.* 1937. Reprint, New York: Arno Press and the *New York Times,* 1970.

State of Asian Pacific America: A Public Policy Report, Policy Issues to the Year 2020. Los Angeles: LEAP, Asian Pacific American Public Policy Institute and UCLA Asian American Studies Center, 1993.

Takaki, Ronald. *Strangers from a Different Shore: A History of Asian Americans.* Boston: Little, Brown, 1989.

Uchida, Naosaku. *The Overseas Chinese.* Stanford CA: Hoover Institute, 1960.

Wang, Yi Chi. *Chinese Intellectuals and the West, 1872–1949.* Chapel Hill: Univ. of North Carolina Press, 1966.

Wei, William. *The Asian American Movement.* Philadelphia: Temple Univ. Press, 1993.

Who's Who Among Asian Americans, 1994/95. Edited by Amy L. Unterburger. Detroit: Gale Research, 1994.

Williams, Ethel W. *Know Your Ancestors.* Rutland VT: Charles E. Tuttle, 1960.

Williams, Lea E. *Overseas Chinese Nationalism: The Genesis of the Pan Chinese Movement in Indonesia 1900–1916.* Glencoe IL: Free Press, 1960.

XI. Chinese Business Directories

American Chinese Business Directory. Edited by N.C. Cham. Tucson: American Chinese Report, 1976.

Asian Yellow Pages Serving San Francisco North Bay Area. 1991–92.

Business Guide for Chinese Community/New York & Eastern U.S.A. 1986.

Business Guide for Chinese Community/Southern California. 1986.

Chinese American Restaurant Association of Greater New York, Inc. 24th Anniversary. 1957.

Chinese Business in America. Ed. Beto Young. 1985.

Chinese Directory of Los Angeles and Bakersfield. 1950.

Chinese Directory of New York, New Jersey, and New England. 1930.

Chinese Directory of Seattle and Vicinity. 1949.

Chinese Merchants Business Directory. Honolulu: United Chinese Penman Club, 1938–39.

Dunbar's Chinese Directory of Principal Chinese Business Houses of the United States, British Columbia, Canada and Honolulu, T.H. Portland OR: A.R. Dunbar, 1892.

Handbook of Chinese in America. Compiled by Chan Nay-choy. New York: People's Foreign Relations Ass'n of China, 1946.

Los Angeles Chinese Business Directory. 1975–1976.
San Francisco and Oakland Chinese Telephone Directory. February 1949.
Southern California Chinese Consumer Yellow Pages. 1995.
Washington, D.C. Chinese Directory. 1950–1951.
Washington State Chinese Community Directory. 1971.
Wells Fargo & Co. *Express Directory of Chinese Business Houses of San Francisco, Oakland, Sacramento, San Jose, Stockton, Marysville, Los Angeles, Portland, Virginia City, Nevada, Victoria, B.C. and Denver, Colorado.* 1882.
_____. *Express Directory of Chinese Business Houses of San Francisco, Sacramento, Stockton, Marysville, San Jose, Portland and Virginia City, Nevada.* 1878.

XII. Chinese Student Directories

Directory of Chinese Students and Alumni in Greater New York. Compiled and edited by Hsien Lu. New York: Chinese Student Association of New York, 1962.
Directory of Chinese Students in America, 1938–1939. New York: Chinese Students' Christian Association in North America, 1939.
Directory of Chinese University Graduates & Students in America. New York: China Institute in America, 1943.
Directory of Chinese University Graduates & Students in America. New York: China Institute in America, 1945.
Dragon Student. Chinese Students' Alliance of America, 1905.
Handbook Chinese Student League of Greater New York, 1938–1939. New York: Chinese Student League, 1939.

XIII. U.S. Documents

"Abstracts of Reports to the Immigration Commission." In *U.S. Immigration Commission Reports.* U.S. 61st Cong., 3d Sess., Sen. Doc. no. 747. Washington DC: GPO, 1911.
Bowman, Alan P., comp. *Index to the 1850 Census of the State of California.* Baltimore: Genealogical, 1972.
Bureau of the Census. *8th U.S. Census*, 1860; *9th U.S. Census*, 1870; *10th U.S. Census*, 1880; and *12th U.S. Census*, 1900.
_____. 1990 census information on Asian Americans. Mimeographed. Courtesy of Jerry Wong, Information Services Specialist with the Los Angeles Regional Office of the Bureau of the Census, U.S. Department of Commerce.
Chinese Exclusion Acts Case Files, 1895–1943. Record Group 85. National Archives–Pacific Northwest Region. Seattle, Washington.
Chinese Habeas Corpus Indexes. Vols. 1–5, 1882–1904. (Admiralty Court). Record Group 21. National Archives–Pacific Sierra Region, San Bruno, California.
Chinese Partnership Case Files, 1894–1944. Record Group 85. National Archives–Pacific Sierra Region. San Bruno, California.
Directory of Chinese Personal Names in Bangkok. U.S. Department of State, 1952.
Directory of Chinese Personal Names in Indonesia. U.S. Department of State, 1953.
Directory of Chinese Personal Names in the Philippines. U.S. Department of State, 1953.
Directory of Chinese Personal Names in Singapore. U.S. Department of State, 1953.

SELECTED BIBLIOGRAPHY

Inbound Passenger Manifests (Chinese Arrivals). USINS, U56-1, Reel 2. Seattle (Port Townsend), 1882–1916.

Index of Clan Names by Villages for Chungshan District. Compiled by American Consulate General, Hong Kong, 1966. Photocopy. Oakton VA: Center for Chinese Research Materials, 1973.

Index of Clan Names by Villages for Hoiping District. Compiled by American Consulate General, Hong Kong. 1965. Photocopy. Oakton VA: Center for Chinese Research Materials, 1973.

Index of Clan Names by Villages for Sunwui District. Compiled by American Consulate General, Hong Kong, 1965. Photocopy. Oakton VA: Center for Chinese Research Materials, 1973.

Index of Clan Names by Villages for Toishan District. Compiled by American Consulate General, Hong Kong, 1963. Photocopy. Oakton VA: Center for Chinese Research Materials, 1973.

"Report of Commission-General of Immigration." In *Report of Department of Commerce and Labor.* 59th Congress, 2d Session, House Documents, vol. 22. Washington DC: GPO, 1907.

"Report of Commissioner General of Immigration, 1913." In *Reports of the Department of Labor.* Washington DC: GPO, 1914.

Report of the Joint Special Committee to Investigate Chinese Immigration. U.S. 44th Congress, 2d Sess. Sen. Rpt. No. 689. Washington DC: GPO, 1877.

Segregated Chinese Files. Record Group 85. National Archives of the United States. Washington, D.C.

A Study of Selected Socio-economic Characteristics of Ethnic Minorities Based on the 1970 Census. Vol. 2, "Asian American." Department of Health, Education, and Welfare.

Synopses of Rulings and Decisions Since Act of October 1, 1888. Washington DC: GPO, 1896.

Treaty, Laws, and Rules Governing the Admission of Chinese. Washington DC: GPO, 1917.

Treaty, Laws, and Rules Governing the Admission of Chinese. Washington DC: GPO, 1926.

U.S. Department of Commerce. *Reference Aid: Handbook for Pinyin Romanization of Chinese Proper Names, First Edition.* Arlington VA: Joint Publications Research Service, December 1978.

U.S. Immigration Law and Policy: 1952–1979. U.S. 96th Cong., lst sess. Washington DC: GPO, 1979.

"U.S. Population by Race and Hispanic Origin." Table in *Chinese American Forum* 7 (July 1991): 26.

Washington Territorial Census Index, 1870. Edited by Ronald Vern Jackson. Salt Lake City: Accelerated Indexing System, 1979.

INDEX

ABC 66; *see also* group names, derogatory
accidental surnames: "paper" surname 113, 115–16; patronyms, new 139–47; various sources 147–148
Adamic, Louis 124
adoption of sons 17
"Ah" vocative in names 50, 96, 98–99, 111, 126, 136, 140–41
American, perceived as white person only 63–64
American citizenship 64, 69, 80, 114, 115
American name traditions: changes in name practices 132–33; custom of middle name 52, 82, 83–84; diacritic marks, omission of 78–79; dithemic names 44–45; family names, number of 35; most popular surnames 38; mother's maiden name as child's middle name 40; name fashions 44; name styles, seven distinct ones 83; repetition of given names 44; stabilization of surnames, reasons for 106; surname clumping 149
Americanization of names: adopting "American" surnames 126–27; adopting employer's name 126; Euro-American surnames among Chinese Americans 124–25; influence of original name 127; letter "r" in surnames 130; methods of 127–30; personal whim 123; reasons for 123–24, 128; risk of ostracism 126
Amoy-Swatow dialect 72, 73, 74, 77, 79
ancestor worship 17, 20
ancient consonant ending 74–75
anglicized names 123, 130; *see also* Americanization of names
Ashley, Leonard, R.N. 133

Asian Americans 61–62
Asian American Movement 62–63

Bai Jia Xing 23, 26–27, 33–34
bai xing 34; *see also lao bai xing*
Ball, John Dyer 73, 119
Barker, Howard F. 106, 124, 127
Bauer, Wolfgang 42, 43, 46, 47, 51–52, 53, 54–55
Beck, Louis 105
Bok Kai Temple, Marysville, California 95–96
Bostwick, Arthur 86

Cavalli-Sforza, L.L. 158
Cantonese: antagonism toward 67; Chungshan dialect 120, 176; "Canton," origin of the word 73; predominant dialect for Chinese Americans 80; preservation of ancient consonant endings 74–75; S.W. Williams romanization of 77; Sam Yup or Three Districts dialect 118–19; spelling spillovers 79, 167; Sze Yup or Four Districts dialect 118–20; ten "great" family names of 38; Toishan dialect 121–22; 175–76; *Zhuji Xiang* 176; *see also* Chinese Americans; dialects
census, Chinese names in early records: "Ah" in names 98, 99, 140–41; American given names recorded 98–99; Chinese-looking Euro-American surnames 98; Chinese name traditions revealed 101–4; Chinese store names 99, 101; 1850 census baseline 97–98; generic names 98–99; interracial marriages 105; monosyllabic given names,

prevalence of 98, 101; same generation name for brothers and sisters 104; Soundex listing 86, 99; Spanish names recorded 98; usual Chinese name, gradual increase of 101, 111–12
certificates of identity 106–10
Chan, Sucheng 67
change of name notices 132, 137
changes in names: by Chinese Americans 126–27, 147–48; by Chinese in other countries 41; in ancient China 26, 30–31; in Taiwan 40–41
Chao, Yuen Ren 38, 46, 50, 72, 74, 86–87, 168
Charley, as popular name for early immigrants 99; see also John
Chen, Shao-hsing 40
Chen Tse-ming 25, 34
China Mary see generic names
Chinese: founding ancestors or progenitors of 15; interpretation of word 66; perception of being 63–66, 69
Chinese American name practices: adding middle American given name 84; "Ah" vocative in names 96, 97, 98, 111; American given names, creative 132–33; American given names, selection of 82, 84–85, 135–38; Americanization, acquiescence to 124–25; bestowing Chinese given names 82, 136–37; change-of-name notices 132, 137; generation name 51–52, 104; initialing Chinese given name 87; initialing the surname 143; matching sounds of American and Chinese names 135–37; name styles, ten distinct ones 92; omitting hao 54; phoneticizing Western given name into Chinese 111, 136–37; Sr. and Jr. to Chinese name, addition of 137; "Shee" in married woman's name 18, 85–86, 104, 171, 173; surname first, observance of 86; surname in middle 91–92; synthesis of, American and Chinese name traditions 133–35, 137; teachers bestowing American given name 136; transferring Chinese naming traditions 133–35; transferring Pai–hang naming system 137–38; usual Chinese name of three

words 85, 101, 111; see also "Ah" vocative in names; Americanization of names; name styles; patronyms, new
Chinese Americans: American citizenship 64, 69, 80; being American, perception of 61–62, 64, 65; being Chinese, perception of 64–65; conflict in identity 65–66; counting by generation in America 67–69; criticism of descendants of early immigrants 66–67; descendants of early merchants 67; family history in America 170; fan guei, lo fan, use of 63–64; genealogy research resources 170–76; group names 62–63; history and dialect representation 80–81; hyphen, removal of 63; interracial marriages, early families 105, 126; most popular surnames 149; native-born vs. foreign-born, ratio of 62, 80; surname clumping, early patterns of 149–50; Wong, most popular surname 149, 158–60; see also family or clan associations; surname clumping
Chinese given name: da ming or school name 46–47, 53, 54; disyllabic or two-character name, predominance of, historically 47–48; as a dithemic name 44–45, 89; equating with American given name 88–89; generation name 51–56; hao and zi, reversal in original meaning 46; "I-want-a-son name" 46, 104; manufactured names 43–44; meaning of 44; monosyllabic name is stated with family name or another word 50; monosyllabic or one-character name, increased use in mainland China 56; mother's maiden name as child's given name, increased use of 40; same generation name for brothers and sister 56, 104; structure of, in Chinese American name styles 83, 85–92; superstititions expressed 46; transcribing name backwards 89; see also census; name styles; patronyms, new; Pai–hang naming system; taboos; women, traditional names of
Chinese-looking surnames 98, 123
Chinese name traditions: adoption by